The Middle Way

The Middle Way

*Puritanism and Ideology
in American
Romantic Fiction*

Michael T. Gilmore

RUTGERS UNIVERSITY PRESS
New Brunswick, New Jersey

Publication of This Book Was Supported by a Grant
from Brandeis University

Library of Congress Cataloging in Publication Data

Gilmore, Michael T.
  The middle way.

  Includes bibliographical references.
  1. American fiction — 19th century — History and criticism. I. Title.
PS377.G5   813'.4'09   76–54254
ISBN 0–8135–0837–1

For my parents

Contents

Preface

This study seeks to trace some of the connections between the Puritan mind of the colonial era and the great flowering of American literature in the nineteenth century. It presents the thesis that the Puritan ideal of inner-worldly sainthood—the ideal of the middle way—decisively influenced the formal and thematic concerns of the prose romance. Concentrating on works by Hawthorne and Melville, and glancing briefly at James, I portray the romancers as social and political critics who carry on the Puritan spirit and who call attention to the gap between the promise of America and its actual achievement. It is not my intention to offer a comprehensive reinterpretation of nineteenth-century American fiction, but to suggest new lines of inquiry into the ideological and cultural continuity of American letters.

I develop my argument through close readings of particular texts, and I have been highly selective in accordance with my interests. Since I am concerned with the assimilation of Puritan habits of thought into American romanticism, I devote most of my chapter on Hawthorne to *The Scarlet Letter*, the action of which takes place in the seventeenth century. I treat only *The House of the Seven Gables* among the later romances for much the same reason: because that work opens with an account of the Salem witchcraft and explores the persistence of Puritan themes into the present. In the case of Melville, the problem of selection proved particularly difficult. I have included just two works from the middle fifties: *Israel Potter* because Benjamin Franklin, who is crucial to my argument, appears as a character in that book; and "Benito Cereno" because I read the story as an attack not only on the institution of slavery, but also on the legalistic mentality which justifies its existence and violates the spirit of the middle way.

One further word of explanation is in order with regard to my chapter on James. The purpose of this section is merely to outline how my argument might be applied to a major American writer other than Hawthorne and Melville. While a full treatment of James is beyond the scope of this study, I believe that certain of the ideas central to my reading of *The Golden Bowl* can also be shown to figure importantly in works like *Roderick Hudson*, *The Portrait of a Lady*, and "The Jolly Corner."

———•———

This book originated as a doctoral dissertation at Harvard University under the direction of Professors Alan Heimert and Joel Porte; I am grateful to both of them for their advice and suggestions. A number of my colleagues at Brandeis took the trouble to read the manuscript at various stages of composition, and I would like to thank Allen Grossman, Milton Hindus, Peter Swiggart, and Philip Fisher for their helpful criticisms. I owe a special debt of gratitude to Daniel Aaron of Harvard for his sympathetic reading of the completed version. Friends who helped to improve the manuscript and encouraged its author include Stephen Botein, Lewis Wurgaft, Alexander Keyssar, Richard Strier, Ronald Sanders, Martin Jay, and particularly Paul Weissman. Other readers have given their views, commented on mine, and saved me from numerous errors. I hope that they will accept a general expression of thanks for their assistance.

Part of Chapter V originally appeared in a somewhat different version as "Melville's Apocalypse: American Millennialism and Moby-Dick," *ESQ: A Journal of the American Renaissance* 21 (1975): 154–61. Two paragraphs from this essay are included in *Twentieth Century Interpretations of Moby-Dick*, ed. Michael T. Gilmore (Englewood Cliffs, N.J.: Prentice-Hall, 1977).

I

Introduction

The great works of the American Renaissance were still to be written when Alexis de Tocqueville visited the United States in 1831. Although he readily admitted that America had produced no literature to speak of, Tocqueville confidently pictured the democratic art of the future. In a democracy, he observed, where there exists no shared body of inherited institutions and attitudes,

> each citizen is habitually engaged in the contemplation of a very puny object: namely, himself. If he ever raises his looks higher, he perceives only the immense form of society at large or the still more imposing aspect of mankind. His ideas are all extremely minute and clear or extremely general and vague; what lies between is a void.

This dualistic habit of thought, according to Tocqueville, was also fostered by America's Puritan heritage. Calvinism set the individual believer in direct relation to the Deity and diminished the role of ecclesiastical authority. Hence the subject of democratic literature would be "man himself, taken aloof from his country and his age and standing in the presence of Nature and of God." Such literature, Tocqueville predicted, "will be forever losing itself in the clouds and . . . will range at last to purely imaginary regions."[1]

1. Alexis de Tocqueville, *Democracy in America*, ed. Phillips Bradley, 2 vols. (1835, 1840; New York: Alfred A. Knopf, 1945), 2: 82–83.

1

Tocqueville was a better observer than prophet, and it is unfortunate that his pronouncements on religion and literature remain the commonplaces of American criticism. His prediction about democratic art gives an inaccurate picture of the dominant genre in American fiction, the prose romance. It is based on a misunderstanding of Calvinist theology, and it obscures rather than clarifies the unique characteristics of our imaginative literature. A closer look at the religious background of American culture challenges the notion that the romance is polarized, extreme, and "forever losing itself in the clouds."[2]

———————•—•———————

Following Tocqueville's lead, many students of American literature have argued that Calvinism weakens or even destroys concern

2. Perhaps the most influential statement of the thesis that American fiction is romantic, that its concerns are idealistic rather than social, and that it is marked by a penchant for melodrama, abstraction, and contradiction, was advanced by Richard Chase in *The American Novel and Its Tradition* (Garden City, N.Y.: Doubleday and Co., Anchor Books, 1957). Chase's argument was anticipated by Lionel Trilling in his essay, "Manners, Morals, and the Novel," which appeared in his *The Liberal Imagination: Essays on Literature and Society* (New York: Viking Press, 1950), pp. 199–215. Similar arguments have been made by Marius Bewley in *The Eccentric Design: Form in the Classic American Novel* (New York: Columbia University Press, 1959); Daniel Hoffman in *Form and Fable in American Fiction* (New York: Oxford University Press, 1965); Leslie A. Fiedler in *Love and Death in the American Novel*, rev. ed. (New York: Dell Publishing Co., 1966); and Joel Porte in *The Romance in America: Studies in Cooper, Poe, Hawthorne, Melville, and James* (Middletown, Conn.: Wesleyan University Press, 1969). Although I am indebted to all these critics, I believe that they have overstated the distinction between the American romance and the English novel. I believe that the distinction itself has validity, and I find unpersuasive the attempts to discredit it by critics like Martin Green (*Re-Appraisals: Some Commonsense Readings in American Literature* [New York: W. W. Norton and Co. 1965]) and Nicolaus Mills (*American and English Fiction in the Nineteenth Century: An Antigenre Critique and Comparison* [Bloomington: Indiana University Press, 1973]). At the same time, I feel that such "antigenre" criticism provides a useful corrective to Chase's claim that the American imagination has been absorbed by the aesthetic possibilities of alienation, polarity, and radical disorder. For an excellent treatment of American fiction as a mixed medium which combines both novelistic and romantic elements, see Richard H. Brodhead's *Hawthorne, Melville, and the Novel* (Chicago: University of Chicago Press, 1976), particularly pp. 9–25.

for society and encourages a kind of spiritual individualism.³ In fact, however, as it developed in England and America, Calvinism followed a middle way between enthusiasm or antinomianism on the one hand, and Arminianism or a worldly faith on the other. Orthodox Calvinists regarded direct revelation as heresy, and few indeed ever dispensed with the principle of ecclesiastical mediation. Grace came through the word, but the word was preached by duly ordained ministers of the gospel. And because of their historical ties to the Anglican Church, American Calvinists in particular evolved a carefully defined middle position between the left- and right-wing denominations of English Protestantism: between those who self-righteously separated from the world for the sake of their souls, and those who embraced the world in its entirety. Responding to Roger Williams's attack on the Massachusetts churches, John Cotton described the New England Way as follows:

> wee conceive the Lord hath guided us to walke with an even foote betweene two extreames; so that we neither defile ourselves with the remnant of pollutions in other Churches, nor do wee for the remnant of pollutions renounce the Churches themselves, nor the holy ordinances of God amongst them, which ourselves have found powerful to our salvation.⁴

Perhaps the most compelling formulation of Calvinist doctrine in America came from the pen of Jonathan Edwards, whose treatises on the nature of true religion highlight the continuity between the Great Migration and the Great Awakening and mirror the stand taken a century earlier by John Cotton. In works like *Religious Affections* (1746) and its widely read companion piece,

3. For example, Chase, *American Novel and Its Tradition*, p. 8; John F. Lynen, *The Design of the Present: Essays on Time and Form in American Literature* (New Haven: Yale University Press, 1969), pp. 1–86; Larzer Ziff, *Puritanism in America: New Culture in a New World* (New York: Viking Press, 1973), pp. 305–6. An important recent exception is Sacvan Bercovitch, *The Puritan Origins of the American Self* (New Haven: Yale University Press, 1975), pp. 136–86, passim.
4. John Cotton, "A Letter of Mr. John Cotton . . . to Mr. Williams," in *Publications of the Narragansett Club*, 6 vols. (Providence, R.I., 1866), 1: 308. Cotton's letter was first published in London in 1643.

Life and Diary of David Brainerd (1739), Edwards championed
"the right path in the middle" between the legalism of the established clergy and the otherworldliness and spiritual pride of the
Separate zealots. Against the Arminians, Edwards argued that God
required "a fervent, vigorous engagedness of the heart." But this
did not imply, as enthusiasts believed, that "the saints are made
partakers of [His] essence." The principal sign of a gracious disposition, Edwards asserted, is Christian practice on earth in the service
of God and for the good of the brethren. The elect had an obligation to the community at large. It was better, he reasoned, to bring
the unregenerate under the guidance of the saints than to expel or
forsake them and abandon the world to their care.[5]

The Calvinist middle way, as articulated by Cotton and Edwards,
must not be confused with the Anglican conception of the *via
media*. Divines like Richard Hooker and Archbishop Laud who
framed the compromise of Anglican polity insisted upon the
authority of tradition as well as Scripture and stopped short of
the reformation desired by the Puritans. Adopting elements of both
Catholicism and Protestantism, they created a "half-way house"
between Rome and Geneva. Anglicanism, especially as it developed
in the period after the Restoration, can be seen as a temperate
and liberal religion committed above all to the welfare of the visible
church. It frowns on a spiritual zeal which infuses earthly activity
with the fervor of sainthood, and it casts a wide net in its preoccupation with the structure and workings of society. Keyed to the
actual, it is often critical of specific abuses without aspiring to
regenerate the world.

The differences between Anglicanism and Puritanism help to
account for the dissimilar paths taken by English and American
fiction. The English novel in its representative form excludes
supernatural elements and aspires to render an authentic portrayal
of life. Although it makes use of myth and symbolism, its province
is emphatically the realm of the actual, and its concerns are moral

5. Jonathan Edwards, *A Treatise Concerning Religious Affections*, ed.
John E. Smith (1746; New Haven: Yale University Press, 1959), pp. 88, 99,
203, 383–461. See also Alan Heimert, *Religion and the American Mind: From
the Great Awakening to the Revolution* (Cambridge: Harvard University
Press, 1966), p. 124.

and social rather than metaphysical. The American romance incorporates a spiritual dimension and assumes a much greater latitude in the presentation of human experience. It neither escapes into the purely imaginary nor limits its range to the actual. As a literary genre, it corresponds to the middle way of Calvinist theology, which shuns otherworldliness but does not accommodate itself to things as they are.

Even in England the Calvinist tradition had important literary consequences. Nonconformity managed to survive and even to prosper as a vital force in the religious life of the English nation. The survival of Puritanism ensured the presence in England of two traditions of prose fiction: the broadly novelistic mainstream which tends to reflect the orientation of the Established Church; and the minor romantic or Gothic genre which flourished during the second half of the eighteenth century and the first decades of the nineteenth and which takes its form and tone from the Puritan mind. Many, though by no means all, of the writers who worked within this lesser mode were of Calvinist background or persuasion—one immediately thinks of William Godwin, Mary Shelley, and James Hogg—and the literature they produced possesses in common with the American romance an aura of "spiritual reality."[6] Seen in relation to the main development of English fiction, *Wuthering Heights* constitutes, as F. R. Leavis has said, "a kind of sport." But Richard Chase is exactly right when he adds that, if *Wuthering Heights* had been written by a novelist "of New England Calvinist or Southern Presbyterian background," it would not be a sport at all. Instead it would be a representative work of the American imagination.[7]

American writers themselves regularly spoke of their art in terms of a metaphorical middle way or "neutral territory" where antithesis is resolved at the point of interpenetration. To construe their pronouncements as a reformulation of Calvinist doctrine is not to imply that the writers in question were "Puritans" in any literal

6. The phrase "spiritual reality" is used by Walter Allen in reference to *Wuthering Heights* in his *The English Novel: A Short Critical History* (New York: E. P. Dutton and Co. 1954), p. 226.
7. Chase, *American Novel and Its Tradition*, pp. 3–4, 21.

sense. Rather, it is to suggest that they appropriated Calvinism's
grammar of thought for their own imaginative purposes. Consider,
for example, Cooper's preface to *The Leather-Stocking Tales*. As
an author of romance, he claims the privilege to portray his characters in the "*beau-ideal*." Yet "in order to preserve the *vraisemblable*,"
he has depicted Natty from a realistic as well as "a poetical view,"
thereby averting the spectacle of "a 'monster of goodness.'" Poe,
in his "Marginalia," similarly locates the source of his inspiration
in a "border-ground" where "the confines of the waking world
blend with those of the world of dreams." He strongly implies
that his visions and fancies, affording as they do "a glimpse of
the spirit's outer world," meet at the juncture of time and eternity.
Poe's interest in exploring such states is closely analogous to
Hawthorne's well-known concern with a poetic precinct or "avail-
able foothold between fiction and reality," a "Faery Land, so
like the real world, that . . . one cannot well tell the difference."
In the imaginary setting where romance takes place, adds Hawthorne, everything is "essentially a day-dream, and yet a fact."[8]

Hawthorne is our foremost theorist on the subject of romance,
and he was at particular pains to distinguish his art from the
effusions of the Transcendentalists on the one hand and the "great
body of pen-and-ink men" on the other. Whereas the Transcendentalists were altogether too metaphysical and abstract, the popular
writers appealed solely to the multitude and excluded all but the
factual and concrete. Hawthorne seemed to himself "to occupy an
unfortunate position" in the middle: his tales and romances, for all

8. Citations are from *Cooper's Novels*, 32 vols., Darley edition (New York,
1861), 6: v–x; *The Complete Works of Edgar Allan Poe*, ed. James A. Harrison, 17 vols., Virginia edition (New York: Thomas Y. Crowell, 1902), 16:
88–90; and Hawthorne's preface to *The Blithedale Romance* in *The Works
of Nathaniel Hawthorne*, Centenary Edition, ed. William Charvat et al.
(Columbus: Ohio State University Press, 1962–), vol. 3, *The Blithedale Romance and Fanshawe* (1964), pp. 1–3. The idea of the "middle way," as
enunciated by the American romancers, is akin to Coleridge's notion of the
poetic image as a link between spirit and matter. Similar definitions of the
romance can also be found in the prefaces and essays of Clara Reeve, Horace
Walpole, and Sir Walter Scott. I do not mean to slight the importance of
these theories, but rather to suggest other sources of influence indigenous to
America.

their fantastic imagery, nevertheless produce the impression that we are still "within the limits of our native earth."[9]

Hawthorne's remarks suggest an important corollary to the aesthetic program of the American romancers: namely, that the form of their art frequently reflects its theme. The neutral territory of romance provides an imaginative context in which inner-worldly sainthood can be repossessed as a secularized ideal. Melville, in *Moby-Dick*, has Ishmael say to the reader:

Oh, man! admire and model thyself after the whale! Do thou, too, remain warm among ice. Do thou, too, live in this world without being of it. Be cool at the equator; keep thy blood fluid at the Pole. Like the great dome of St. Peter's, and like the great whale, retain, O man! in all seasons a temperature of thine own.[10]

The adjurement to live in the world without being of it, analogous to the Puritan state of election, can be realized only in a literary framework where the material and the spiritual are combined. The ideal it expresses can take many forms, among them the tragic acceptance of a Hester Prynne, the inner-worldly renunciation of an Isabel Archer, and the sober hopefulness of Ishmael himself. It can also take the form, as it does with Natty Bumppo, of dwelling on the outskirts of civilization, in a "border" region where the hero "keeps the center of his . . . consciousness steady and unperturbed."[11] To heed Ishmael's advice—to live, in the lexicon of

9. See Hawthorne's preface to "Rappaccini's Daughter," in *The Works of Nathaniel Hawthorne*, Centenary Edition, ed. William Charvat et al. (Columbus: Ohio State University Press, 1962–), vol. 10, *Mosses from an Old Manse* (1974), pp. 91–93. According to Barbara Novak, a similar commitment to "the preservation of the fact" can be observed in the work of the major American painters of the nineteenth century. "Only a very small number of American artists," she writes, "have ever been willing to give themselves over to the vague world of the irrational and impalpable, with no hold on reality." See *American Painting of the Nineteenth Century: Realism, Idealism, and the American Experience* (New York: Praeger Publishers, 1969), p. 59.

10. Herman Melville, *Moby-Dick*, Norton Critical Edition, ed. Harrison Hayford and Hershel Parker (New York: W. W. Norton and Co., 1967), p. 261.

11. D. H. Lawrence, *Studies in Classic American Literature* (1923; New York: Viking Press, 1964), p. 60.

Puritanism, with weaned affections—is neither to withdraw from
the world nor to accept it on its terms. It is to make a conscious
choice to "follow the middle way."

Even Henry James, who liked to think of himself as a novelist
of manners, exhibits this characteristically American attitude. A
book like *The American*, avowedly a romance according to its
preface, reveals unmistakably that he remained, as he once observed
of Charles Eliot Norton, "a son of the Puritans." The representative
Jamesian novel, it is often said, ends on a note of defeat, despair,
or unresolved contradiction; but what James sought in his art was
a "sublime consensus," an encompassing of the richness and complexity of Europe and the idealism of America.[12] This was his
version of the creed of his Calvinist forebears, his alternative to the
medieval dichotomy between society and sainthood. There is a
profound difference, after all, between Christopher Newman's resig-
nation *in* the world and Claire de Cintré's renunciation *of* the world
for the habit of a nun.

————————•—•·————————

The existential dilemmas which seem to confront so many
American characters are independent of economic, social, and
political issues. And yet these issues have a crucial importance in
our imaginative literature. American writers have been deeply engaged by a conflict of values which stems from the dominance in
this country—or so our writers have often felt—of an ideology
that threatens the survival of art. It is an ideology that enthrones
material progress at the expense of spiritual aspirations, and for
many American authors it is symbolized, if only obliquely, by the
person of Benjamin Franklin. Like countless other students of our
history, they saw Franklin as a landmark in the secularization and

12. Henry James, "An American Art-Scholar: Charles Eliot Norton," in
The American Essays of Henry James, ed. Leon Edel (New York: Alfred A.
Knopf, Vintage Books, 1956), p. 127; the phrase "sublime consensus" appears
in the preface to "Lady Barbarina," in idem, *The Art of the Novel: Critical
Prefaces by Henry James*, ed. R. P. Blackmur (1934; New York: Charles
Scribner's Sons, 1962), p. 203.

corruption of the Puritan mind, a leading exponent of the "bourgeois heresy" that worldly success is the means or sign of redemption. They were critical of him and others like him for substituting prudence, moderation and the competitive ethic for religious imperatives and beliefs.[13]

One brief illustration, drawn from the turbulent decade before the Civil War, may give some idea of the literary response to the values associated with Franklin. It may also serve as an introduction to the concerns that will command our attention in the following pages. The example is Melville's "Lightning-Rod Man," which originally appeared in *Harper's* in 1854.[14] It has often been noticed that Melville's story shows the influence of the *Magnalia Christi Americana*, reprinted the year before, and the indebtedness yields a clue to its underlying theme: the nostrum peddled by the title character in the name of religion perverts the faith of a Puritan like Mather. It is quite to the point that the stranger deals in mechanical safety devices to protect men from the "supernal bolt." Melville surely expects the reader to remember that Franklin invented the lightning rod.

The salesman is Melville's reminder that Franklin's ideas are a fundamental component of American thought. He preaches a doctrine of salvation by prudence, imploring the narrator—a mountaineer and "lover of the majestic"—to quit his hearth and stand in "the exact middle of the cottage." We learn in the course of the

13. A word of caution is in order in generalizing about what Americans thought or believed. We have learned, for example, a good deal about the social and economic views of the Puritan leaders. But our information is only fragmentary when it comes to their followers, the ordinary inhabitants of the New England colonies. We are almost as ignorant about the sentiments of the average citizen of the nineteenth century, who is quite inarticulate from the standpoint of history. When I speak of an American ideology, I am referring to the beliefs of specific individuals such as Franklin, and I do not wish to make the claim that the convictions or impressions of a few necessarily reflect the attitudes of the populace at large. What can be said with some certainty is that our greatest writers have voiced their opposition to a system of values whose prevalence in America has been remarked on by critics and advocates alike. They have challenged those values from a world view rooted in essentially Calvinist premises.

14. The story is reprinted in Herman Melville, *The Complete Stories of Herman Melville*, ed. Jay Leyda (New York: Random House, 1949), pp. 213–21.

story, however, that the stranger's rods and precautions are inimical
to the spirit of authentic religion and jeopardize its very existence.
The steeple of a nearby church, equipped with one of his devices,
has only the week before been destroyed by lightning, and he
himself takes particular care never to touch iron in the midst of
a thunder storm, not excluding bells in belfries. He says that he
makes it his business to shun crowds and especially tall men, at
which the horrified narrator blurts out, "Do I dream? Man avoid
man? and in danger-time, too?" Exclaiming *"Mine* is the only
true rod," he thrice commands the narrator, "Come hither to
me!"—to the safety of the middle of the room. But the mountaineer,
drawing himself up as erect as he can, refuses to budge from
his hearthstone. Thus does Melville, who trusts that "the Deity
will not, of purpose, make war on man's earth," hurl his denial
at the satanic temptors of his day, an act of resistance which
provokes the frustrated salesman to denounce him as an "impious
wretch."

Melville and writers like him were indeed irreverent in their
hostility toward an ideology which they feared was becoming a
national faith. The pun on "rod," in the salesman's exclamation,
and the final disclosure that the stranger still dwells in the land,
driving "a brave trade with the fears of man," vividly convey
Melville's deep disquiet over the state of America as the Civil War
neared. The rod of an angry God was poised to descend upon a
people who had forsaken their principles by countenancing slavery
and deserting Protestantism for the Protestant ethic. It is not by
chance that *The Confidence-Man,* published three years later, ends
with an apocalyptic vision in which an old man, presumably Uncle
Sam, is escorted into the metaphorical darkness of hell. The hopes
that sped the *Arbella* in 1630 perished for Melville aboard the
Fidèle.

II

The Puritans

The Puritans who came to America in the first half of the seventeenth century did not think in terms of simple polarities. Although Calvin's doctrine of predestination was always susceptible to the abuse of intolerable self-righteousness, the Puritans actively discouraged the notion that ordinary men could determine who were the elect and who were damned. The power of discernment in these matters rested with God alone and to pretend otherwise was presumptuous and heretical. It was arduous enough for a man to achieve an incomplete assurance about the state of his own soul, and utterly impossible to pass judgment with certainty on the condition of his fellows.

The fanatics who usurped such power by claiming to be "Christed with Christ" were known as antinomians because they usually denied that they were bound by the obligations of the Old Testament law. As John Cotton explained it, the antinomian heresy was based on a misapprehension of the covenant of grace and the nature of justification. Under the new dispensation brought by Christ, Cotton argued, the saints were freed from the covenant of works, the covenant by which God had bound Adam to a strict fulfillment of the law and which Adam had abrogated when he disobeyed God's instructions. The saints were dead to the *covenant* of the law, but antinomianism went wrong when it supposed that they were therefore dead to the *commandment* of the law, which continued in effect and enjoined them to live a moral life insofar

11

as this was humanly possible. Men were redeemed by Christ, Cotton affirmed, but redemption did not exempt them from ethical duties.[1] While antinomianism represented one extreme which the Puritans endeavored to suppress, Arminianism represented another. After the Synod of Dort upheld the five major tenets of Calvinism in 1619, the Anglican Church under the leadership of Archbishop Laud began to move gradually away from the mild predestinarianism of the "Thirty-Nine Articles," and Puritans became persuaded that the errors of Jacobus Arminius were gaining a foothold with the hierarchy. Arminianism was as dangerous a departure from the faith as antinomianism, albeit in an opposite direction. Instead of discarding the law, the Arminians swung over to the contrary extreme of asserting that man was active in the process of regeneration and could choose or refuse election. The implication of this teaching readily disclosed itself to Puritan critics, although the Arminians hesitated to proclaim it: man could use his natural capabilities to win salvation and so dispense with the necessity of experiencing grace. In reply the Puritans argued that obedience to the law was impossible without the assistance of Christ—given mankind's fallen nature—and that even for the justified saint perfect

1. John Cotton, *The Way of Life* (London, 1641), pp. 236-40. The scholarship on American Puritanism is voluminous and impressive, and I have tried to acknowledge specific debts in the footnotes that follow. It may be proper, however, to offer a more general explanation about my approach. The past decade has witnessed a growing interest in the place of typology and millennialism in Puritan thought. I have in mind the work of scholars such as Sacvan Bercovitch, Ursula Brumm, and Jesper Rosenmeier; an annotated bibliography can be found in Bercovitch, ed., *Typology and Early American Literature* (Amherst: University of Massachusetts Press, 1972). There also now exists an extensive literature on the social history of colonial America, typified by the demographic and family studies of scholars like John Demos, Philip J. Greven, Jr., Kenneth A. Lockridge, and Michael Zuckerman. A convenient survey of research in this area is Richard S. Dunn's "The Social History of Early New England," *American Quarterly* 24 (1972): 661-79. Although I have tried, where possible, to make use of both developments in current scholarship, my chief concern has been to explore the implications for imaginative literature of Perry Miller's more traditional approach. My greatest debt, accordingly, is to the framework developed by Miller in his two magisterial volumes, *The New England Mind: The Sixteenth Century* (1939; Cambridge: Harvard University Press, 1954) and *The New England Mind: From Colony to Province* (Cambridge: Harvard University Press, 1953).

obedience was out of the question. Antinomians would sacrifice the world to what they deemed the promptings of the Holy Spirit, but the crux of the Arminian fallacy was that it utterly excluded the Deity from the life of man, and without the Deity damnation was assured. The truth, according to the Puritans, was found between the two extremes.

The Puritans had a name for the truth: they called it the "middle way." In praising Thomas Shepard, for example, Jonathan Mitchell wrote that "God taught him and helped him to teach others the true middle way of the gospel between the Legalist, on the one hand, and the Antinomian, or loose gospeler, on the other."[2] Mitchell's formulation was a commonplace and was echoed by every Puritan who sought to tread the narrow path between extremist half-truths. Salvation came through grace, such Puritans said in effect, but the gracious saint exerted himself to do the bidding of the law.

The feeling for balance thus evinced was reinforced by the Puritan attitude toward vocation and sainthood. The Puritans regarded themselves as strongly practical men whose theology was intended to assist and guide them in their daily affairs, and whose conception of sainthood opened what was a special and limited category in Roman Catholicism to all regenerate Christians. The Catholics erred, said Puritan theologians, because they segregated the saint from the rest of humanity and attributed to him a purity beyond the reach of ordinary men, whereas every believer who possessed grace and lived a fully sanctified life on earth was as much a saint as God empowered any man to be. God placed man in the world, and the effort to flee it flouted His will; rather the world was the arena within which the believer was to work for a destiny beyond the world. And hence the importance of the doctrine of vocation in Puritan faith; for the calling, as William Perkins explained, was nothing less than "the order and manner of living in this world."[3]

2. Jonathan Mitchell, preface to Thomas Shepard, *The Parable of the Ten Virgins Unfolded* (1659), in *The Works of Thomas Shepard*, ed. John Albro, 3 vols. (Boston, 1853), 2: 9.
3. William Perkins, *The Work of William Perkins*, ed. Ian Breward (Berkshire, England: Sutton Courtenay Press, 1970), p. 447.

Ministers like Perkins who addressed themselves to the issue
of vocation were reacting against the excesses of worldly self-
indulgence and otherworldly asceticism which they associated with
medieval Catholicism. They wished to heal the breach between
the world and the spirit which derived from what has been called
the Catholic double standard of morality, a standard which, on
the one hand, glorified those who spurned the world and took
monastic orders and, on the other, tolerated in the laity—especially
the ruling classes—an unprincipled pursuit of wealth and pleasure.[4]
Monks in particular were subjected to a torrent of Puritan abuse,
since they often seemed to embody what was most reprehensible
in the Catholic division, the extremes meeting in unresolved contradiction. As William Ames complained, they were pious hypo-
crites who professed humility and poverty, "but in deed are
most rich, possessing large mannours, great incomes, and mighty
wealth."[5]

The doctrine of the calling was the spearhead of the Puritan
assault on the medieval double standard of morality. Puritan
divines strove to impress upon their auditors the urgency of walking
in two sorts of callings, the general or Christian and the particular
or personal. "The general calling is the calling of Christianity which
is common to all that live in the church of God. The particular
is that special calling which belongs to some particular men: Such
as the calling of a magistrate or the calling of a minister."[6] Addressed to everyone, the insistence on the twofold calling struck
down the Catholic categories at their source, for in theory at least
it ensured that religious experience was to be unified with the
ordinary business of life. William Perkins spoke for all Puritans

4. Charles H. and Katherine George, *The Protestant Mind of the English Reformation, 1570–1640* (Princeton: Princeton University Press, 1961), pp. 83–87. The English Protestant view of the Roman Church, as summarized by the Georges, slights the complexity of Catholicism, underestimating the importance of the doctrine of good works. Cf. Christopher Hill, *Change and Continuity in Seventeenth-Century England* (Cambridge: Harvard University Press, 1975), pp. 82–85.

5. William Ames, *Conscience with the Power and Cases thereof, Divided into five Bookes*, in *The Workes of the Reverend and Faithfull Minister of Christ William Ames* (London, 1643), p. 224.

6. Perkins, *Work*, p. 451.

when he warned that the two callings "must be joined as body and soul are joined in a living man." Dutiful actions in one's particular calling, according to Perkins, were "damnable sins in the doer" unless they were performed in a pious frame of mind.[7]

John Cotton was no less insistent than Perkins on the indivisibility of the two vocations. In a passage from *The Way of Life*, he likened the saints to the beasts in the Bible that were accounted clean because they walked with a divided hoof. In the same way, Cotton said, "It is onely a cleane person, that walkes with a divided hoofe, that sets one foote in his generall, and the other in his particular calling; he strikes with both, he serves both God and man." In order to walk with a "cloven hoofe," the Puritan endeavored to wrench his heart from the love of creature comforts and possessions; he kept heaven always before him, fixing his mind on God even as he toiled at his craft or plowed his fields.[8] As Cotton put it elsewhere, "When he lives a most busie life in this world, yet he lives not a worldly life."[9] For such a Christian, there could be no surcease from the taxing demands of his faith, no partitioning of earthly and spiritual obligations. The Puritan who heard the word from ministers like John Cotton strove in his own life to bring the world and the spirit into a state of almost perfect union. He yoked the two spheres together; he reintegrated the polarities of the medieval double standard in a successful synthesis. Since he was neither wholly in the world, nor wholly out of it, he could also be said to resolve the Catholic dichotomy by taking a middle way between the extremes. To the Puritan himself,

---

7. Ibid., pp. 457, 464. I am aware, of course, that Anglicans also advocated the calling, and that there were many similarities between the Puritan and Anglican attitudes toward vocation. On this point see C. H. and Katherine George, *Protestant Mind of the English Reformation*, pp. 126–43; and Timothy H. Breen, "The Non-Existent Controversy: Puritan and Anglican Attitudes on Work and Wealth, 1600–1640," *Church History* 35 (1966): 273–87. I believe, however, that the two callings interpenetrated for the Puritan to a degree that was alien to the Anglican sensibility. The most persuasive case for the differences between Puritanism and Anglicanism has been made by John S. Coolidge, *The Pauline Renaissance in England: Puritanism and the Bible* (Oxford: Clarendon Press, 1970), pp. 1–54.

8. Cotton, *Way of Life*, pp. 438, 442, 449.

9. Ibid., p. 270.

the condition that he hopefully achieved was known as "weaned-ness," a term for which John Norton, Cotton's biographer and successor at the First Church in Boston, furnished an admirable gloss when he said of the saints that they "lived in heaven, while they lived on earth."[10]

Norton's aphoristic rendering of the Puritan balance or tension, the state of weanedness, must not be misunderstood. Like Cotton's image of the "cloven hoofe," it can be forced to yield a meaning contrary to its true intent if it is interpreted to indicate a lack of concern for society. Such indifference would actually come closer to the spirit of Catholic mysticism than to Puritanism, positing as it does an unmediated relationship between the individual worshipper and the Deity. No Puritan—unless he drifted into outright anti-nomianism—thought of himself as standing in isolation and receiving counsel directly from God. Because God worked through means like the sermon and the covenant, the Puritan belonged to a church where he was instructed by a minister and guided by the brethren; because the world needed reformation, he remained a member of society and served God in the serving of his fellows. A calling was not "warrantable," Cotton told his listeners, if it relieved a man from the duty of seeking his brother's welfare or failed to promote the "publique good."[11] Weanedness was a state of mind, an internal condition; it did not preclude—indeed it demanded—a willingness to exert oneself on behalf of one's fellow creatures, since it was precisely through such action that the Christian demonstrated that he was not exclusively preoccupied with his own narrow interests.

But what if the churches were filled with pollutions and the land so overspread with sins that no amount of action seemed to accomplish any good? What was the proper stance for the godly English Puritan to adopt toward his backsliding native country and its wayward national church?

It was to this question in particular that the American emigrants

10. John Norton, *Memoir of John Cotton*, ed. Enoch Pond (New York, 1842), p. 13. Norton's biography of Cotton was originally published in 1658 under the title *Abel being dead, yet speaketh*.
11. Cotton, *Way of Life*, p. 439.

directed their attention, and in answering it they succeeded in restating the Puritan tension on the level of ecclesiastical polity. Before the removal to Massachusetts, they wrestled with the problem of whether to stay in England and try to reform her, or to reject her in entirety, casting off the good along with the bad. The latter position was that of the Brownists, or separatists, who advocated "reformation without tarrying for any"—the title of Robert Browne's tract of 1582—and betook themselves apart in order to form independent congregations of true believers which repudiated the Church of England and denied it was the true catholic church. The men who fashioned American thinking agreed that this alternative was unacceptable—smacking of a self-righteous, monastical withdrawal—and for a time they leaned toward the hope that England could be salvaged at home. Thus John Cotton, improving the text *"And the land shall mourne,"* bewailed the "sinnes of the times" but held out the hope that godly Christians, who were precious to the Lord and stood in his sight for the nation as a whole, could forestall a judgment on their countrymen by sincere repentance. Although Cotton cautioned his hearers against contamination, he did not advise them to draw apart in censorious judgment and wash their hands of England. Rather he urged them to "reforme what is amisse in our selves and ours" so that their mourning would be counted good for all the land.[12]

Yet Cotton did not foreclose the possibility of removal, a possibility he recognized by acknowledging that the Almighty might blast the land regardless of the efforts of a saving remnant. The land would surely perish, he said, if there was no "Intercessor" to plead for it, if the godly were hounded into silence and forbidden to mourn.[13] It was largely for this reason that Cotton himself left England, and while other motives undoubtedly played a part in the decision of most American Puritans, few of them construed physical departure as a rejection of the homeland or a selfish flight to safety. They had come to believe that England could not be saved in England, but they clung to the hope that by

12. Ibid., pp. 70–84. Quotations are from pp. 76, 81.
13. Ibid., pp. 77–79.

establishing a Christian commonwealth in exile they could somehow
rescue England from herself. John Winthrop, responding to the
objection that the emigrants by their departure were laying England
open to the dreaded judgment, offered the defense that by their
going they might rouse "such as remaine to turne from there evill
waies, that they may praevent it, or to take some other course that
they may escape it." And if England still resisted reformation?
Even then, the Americans could render service, since Christ's
Church was universal "without distinction of Countries," and the
good done in one place benefited the Church wherever it existed.[14]
The implication of Winthrop's second defense was that the saving
remnant could fulfill its function abroad as well as at home. The
exiles could keep faith with their countrymen so long as they
respected their ties to England and remained within its national
church.

What the New Englanders managed to frame, in short, was a
third alternative to compromise or desertion, and the name they
gave it was "that very *middle way*."[15] By the middle way they
meant the system of nonseparating Congregationalism which com-
prised a third option between Presbyterianism and Brownism. As
the name suggests, they differed from the Presbyterians in asserting
the autonomy of the local congregation, yet they did not follow the
Brownists in withdrawing from the Church of England.[16] The men

14. John Winthrop, "Reasons to be Considered, and Objections with Answers," in *Winthrop Papers*, 5 vols. (Boston: Massachusetts Historical Society,
1931), 2: 141–42.
15. The phrase is used by Thomas Goodwin and Philip Nye in their introduction, "To the Reader," to John Cotton's *The Keys of the Kingdom of
Heaven*, in *John Cotton on the Churches of New England*, ed. Larzer Ziff
(Cambridge: Harvard University Press, 1968), p. 77.
16. On the evolution of the Bay polity see Perry Miller, *Orthodoxy in Massachusetts 1630–1650* (Cambridge: Harvard University Press, 1933). Parts of
Miller's thesis about nonseparating Congregationalism have been modified by
subsequent research. See, for example, Darrett B. Rutman, *Winthrop's Boston:
A Portrait of a Puritan Town, 1630–1649* (Chapel Hill: University of North
Carolina Press, 1965); and David D. Hall, *The Faithful Shepherd: A History
of the New England Ministry in the Seventeenth Century* (Chapel Hill:
University of North Carolina Press, 1972). Cf. Larzer Ziff, *The Career of
John Cotton: Puritanism and the American Experience* (Princeton: Princeton
University Press, 1962). Ziff believes that the profession of the exiles differed
from their practice.

who devised the middle way frankly stated their intentions even before embarking for the New World, and while they may not have fully worked out the details of their program, they were determined to eschew separation from the first. When John Cotton traveled to Southampton in 1630 to deliver the farewell sermon to the Winthrop expedition, he assured the emigrants that their removal was warrantable and holy and spelled out the guiding principle that was to govern them. England being the *"Jerusalem at home,"* they were to be ever mindful of the true church from which they sprang. "Forget not the wombe that bare you," Cotton pleaded, "and the brest that gave you sucke."[17] Cotton's plea was repeated in roughly the same terms by John Winthrop and the other leaders of the migration. In "The Humble Request" they invoked the national church as "our deare Mother" and entreated the brethren at home to pray for "a Church springing out of your owne bowels."[18] If Cotton and Winthrop were weak on specifics, they were nevertheless firm in denying that Massachusetts Bay Colony harbored schismatical intentions. By the time the Westminster Assembly convened in 1643, the Bay apologists were ready with more elaborate descriptions, but the general outline of their polity was constant and unchanged. John Norton was simply restating in 1648 what they had professed from the outset when he declared that schism from a true church was unlawful, and identified the New England way as lying "between compromise on the left hand and separation on the right."[19]

Thus the church polity of American Puritanism reinforced the tension embodied in Cotton's image of the "cloven hoofe." The Puritan saint despised the sins of the world but not the world itself, and strove to live a godly life on earth; the saints who followed John Winthrop to Massachusetts withdrew from the corruptions of the English Church but not the church itself, and aspired to implement the pure ordinances of God. To Winthrop, separatists were "those that dreame of perfection in this world," but he knew

17. John Cotton, *Gods Promise to His Plantations* (London, 1630), in *Old South Leaflets* 3, no. 53 (1874–76): 14.
18. Printed in *Winthrop Papers*, 2: 232.
19. John Norton, *The Answer*, trans. Douglas Horton (1648; Cambridge: Harvard University Press, 1958), pp. 178, 182.

that such perfection was unattainable for the godly Christian who
dwelt among fallible men, and having suppressed the separatist
impulse in himself, he worked to restrain its outbreak in New
England.[20] His life-long attempt to adhere to the middle way, in
politics as well as in religion, has been aptly characterized as the
dilemma of how "to live in the world without being of it."[21]

There was a second respect in which the middle way of nonseparating Congregationalism replicated the Puritan tension. While
preserving a tie to England, and by inference the world, the
Americans also sought a distinctive relationship with the Deity, a
relationship which appeared in the requirement they established for
admission to their churches.[22] When they charged that the Anglican
Church was corrupt, what they meant in part was that unrepentant
sinners were admitted to full membership and entitled to the
sacraments of baptism and the Supper. On this point the New
Englanders had company: all Puritans desired to bring the visible
and invisible churches into closer conformity. The exiles, however,
went to greater lengths than their English allies to put into practice
the ideal of a church of visible saints. Within a decade of the first
settlement, they had enacted into law a test for church membership
requiring a confession of saving grace—what came to be known as
a "declaring of Gods manner of working upon the soul."[23] The
Bay colonists never believed that they could weed every hypocrite
out of their churches, or that their visible gatherings were anything
more than rough approximations of God's invisible elect. They did

20. The quotation is from Winthrop's "The Humble Request," in *Winthrop
Papers*, 2:232.
21. Edmund S. Morgan, *The Puritan Dilemma: The Story of John Winthrop*
(Boston: Little, Brown and Co., 1958), pp. 31–33, passim. Morgan tends to iden-
tify the Puritan balance or tension with moderation and a willingness to compromise. It would be more accurate to say that the tension could take that
form without necessarily being the same thing, a distinction that will be
established in the remainder of the chapter.
22. The standard for church admission developed by the Americans is the
subject of Edmund S. Morgan's *Visible Saints: The History of a Puritan Idea*
(New York: New York University Press, 1963). My emphasis differs from
Morgan's.
23. The phrase is from *The Cambridge Platform* (1648) and may be found
in Williston Walker's *The Creeds and Platforms of Congregationalism*
(Philadelphia: Pilgrim Press, 1960), p. 223.

believe in making every effort consistent with human frailty to
ensure that certified saints had been touched by the eternal even
though they lived and worked in time. As John Cotton put it: "A
faithful soul knowing the Scriptures, and Christ in them, receiveth
Christ, and entereth through Him into the kingdom of heaven, both
here and hereafter."[24]

In effect the test for grace represented an attempt to legislate
the Puritan tension, to guarantee that everyone who enjoyed the
sacraments lived on the blade edge between the world and the
spirit. But more than the composition of the churches was at stake
for those who wrote into law the public confession. Since in Massachusetts Bay the franchise was restricted to church members, the
law also meant that power in the society reposed in men who had
felt the breathings of the Lord, and whose policies would be guided
by both godly and practical considerations.

From this conception of the body politic it followed almost inevitably that devout New Englanders thought of themselves as the
new chosen people. Their belief was rooted in the branch of her-
meneutics known as typology, a method of reading the Scriptures
whereby events and personages in the Old Testament were interpreted as foreshadowing aspects of the story of Christ. Jonah's
three days in the whale, for example, prefigured Christ's harrowing
of hell, while the ancient Hebrews were a type of the true catholic
church. Typology also lent itself to a millenarian theory of history
in which Old Testament figures were related not only to the Incarnation, but to the Second Coming as well. To Protestant thinkers,
steeped in the books of Daniel and Revelation, history was a universal theodicy which consisted of five, or more often seven,
temporal stages, and they were persuaded, as they studied such
signs of the times as the decline of the Papacy, that the work of
redemption was hastening towards its consummation. The colonial
venture, when seen in this context, became an anticipation of the
New Jerusalem itself. Indeed, it became more than an anticipation,
for the emigrants hoped that the American strand would be the
actual site of Christ's kingdom on earth. The colonists, accordingly,

24. Cotton, *Keys of the Kingdom of Heaven*, p. 95.

were the remnant designated by God to usher in the last stage of history and inaugurate the millennium.[25]

Such expectations were not confined to the ministry, moreover. They molded the outlook of a lay leader like Edward Johnson, for whom all history converged upon the climactic founding of Massachusetts Bay. In *Wonder-Working Providence* (1654), his account of the commonwealth's infancy, Johnson composed a typological drama which featured the American Puritans as an Israel *redivivus* and boldly announced of New England that "this is the place where the Lord will create a new Heaven, and a new Earth." The emigrants, he wrote, were the righteous and militant vanguard destined to complete the Reformation by dealing a deathblow to Satan. They had been summoned to the wilderness "to proclaime to all Nations, the neere approach of the most wonderfull workes that ever the Sonnes of men saw." Concluding his history on a note of triumphant expectancy, Johnson virtually duplicated the language of Revelation to convey a final vision of the apocalyptic marriage of Christ to his church, an event, he was sure, which would begin in America. Yet Johnson was not a separatist, and he was careful to state of the colonists that "for Englands sake they are going from England to pray without ceasing for England." There was nothing in his millennial fervor that violated the spirit of the middle way; like most of his fellow emigrants, he scorned the otherworldliness of medieval mysticism and exhorted the saints to do battle in the world.[26]

More than a set of dry theological doctrines, the middle way

25. On American millennialism and its background see Sacvan Bercovitch, "Horologicals to Chronometricals: The Rhetoric of the Jeremiad," in *Literary Monographs*, ed. Eric Rothstein (Madison: University of Wisconsin Press, 1970), 3: 3–124; J. F. Maclear, "New England and the Fifth Monarchy: The Quest for the Millennium in Early American Puritanism," *William and Mary Quarterly* 32 (1975): 223–60; Charles L. Sanford, *The Quest for Paradise: Europe and the American Moral Imagination* (Urbana: University of Illinois Press, 1961); and Ernest Lee Tuveson, *Redeemer Nation: The Idea of America's Millennial Role* (Chicago: University of Chicago Press, 1968).

26. Edward Johnson, *Johnson's Wonder-Working Providence*, ed. J. Franklin Jameson (1654; New York: Barnes and Noble, 1959), pp. 24–25, 61, 271–72, 53. On Johnson's use of typology see in particular Sacvan Bercovitch's "The Historiography of Johnson's *Wonder-Working Providence*," *Essex Institute Historical Collections* 104 (1968): 138–61.

of American Puritanism was an outlook, an attitude, a manner
of living and acting in the world. Rejecting antinomianism and
Arminianism, it was nourished by the doctrine of the calling,
quickened by millennial longings, and strengthened by the complex
of beliefs that made up nonseparating Congregationalism. What
distinguished it was the enormous burden it placed on the individual saint, for it offered no comforting refuge in single-minded
absolutes—although it dealt in absolutes—and openly repudiated the
extremes of absorption in this earthly life and God-intoxicated
separation from it. It has its tragical side, without being tragic,
and at its best it had affinities to the stoicism that counseled fortitude and resolution in the face of worldly misfortune. Perhaps the
finest description of what it meant appeared in the little volume
John Norton wrote to commemorate the life of his worthy predecessor at the First Church in Boston. Norton strung together a
series of images with which he tried to capture the balance at the
core of Puritan faith:

> Those things in nature which cannot suffer, cannot mixe. Timber
> that will not endure cutting, is unfit for jointing. The sword
> that is good metal will bow to the hilts, and yet come strait
> again. No metal more solid than gold, no metal more yielding
> under the hammer.[27]

Committed as they were to the middle way of Congregationalism,
the colonial leaders also gave their allegiance to a second, and far
less exacting, middle way. They were determined to narrow the
range of economic and social extremes which they had left behind
in England. The emigrants themselves, it appears, were mostly men
of the "middling sort": tradesmen and freeholders who were a class
removed from the ignorant peasantry and were not enslaved to
landlords as the tenants were.[28] The question of economic back-

27. Norton, *Memoir of John Cotton*, p. 66.
28. A detailed study of 237 migrants for the year 1637 indicates that most of
them were urban artisans who were relatively affluent. See T. H. Breen and
Stephen Foster, "Moving to the New World: The Character of Early Massachusetts Immigration," *William and Mary Quarterly* 30 (1973): 189–222. Ob-

ground, however, does not really take us to the heart of the American attitude toward the existence of classes. Indeed, whether or not a "middle class," as we use the term today, had actually come into existence by the 1630s seems unimportant. What does seem clear is that the men who shaped American thinking were as alert to the dangers of riches as they were unsympathetic to beggary and servile dependency. Their appeal was middle class in the sense that they made a virtue of neither abundance nor want; and their teachings, carried to the American strand where development in comparative isolation was assured, would be transformed by later thinkers into a dislike of all social and economic extremes whatever.

Even the men who did not emigrate to New England contributed to the formation of the American bias. William Ames, in a book which was popular in Massachusetts throughout the seventeenth century, *Conscience with the Power and Cases thereof*, admitted that "true poverty which is necessary"—as opposed to the counterfeit poverty practiced by monks—"hath no crime in it, or fault to bee ashamed of"; but it had little to commend it either in Ames's sight, since it was often sent by God as a trial or correction and was always "a miserable state." Ames was friendlier to riches, which in themselves he considered "morally neither good nor bad, but things indifferent which men may use either well or ill." For Christians concerned with the condition of their souls, however, the pitfalls of wealth appeared to outweigh its advantages: "By reason of humane corruption and infirmity, the possession of large riches is joyned with so much danger, that it containes the evill of great and desperate temptations: so that it is very difficult for a rich man to enter into the Kingdome of Heaven." Ames had special praise for "honest thrift," and he counseled "a moderation in the desire of gaine" as the correct course for the godly to follow.[29]

In the writings of John Cotton, an avowed admirer of Ames, is found one of the clearest statements of the Puritan preference for a middling station. Cotton said that every man in the course of a civil life was exposed to either adversity or prosperity—sometimes both—

viously not all the emigrants shared the ideology of the Puritan leadership. I have used the term "Puritan" to describe them largely as a convenience.

29. Ames, *Workes*, pp. 248–59.

and he canvassed the dangers attendant upon each condition. The rich man was prone to legalism, attributing his successes to his own endeavors and arrogating to himself the credit that belonged to the Deity. "We are never more apt to forget God," according to Cotton, "than when he most prospers us." Turning to adversity, Cotton argued that tribulations were of use because they stirred the Christian to search his heart for the causes of heaven's displeasure and gave a spur to reformation. But if a man's faith was not secure, misfortune could become an occasion to murmur, "to be impatient, to contest with gods providence, and to quarrell with instruments." Poverty, like riches, was a severe trial of faith, and Cotton wished that both could be shunned. It was the holy man Agur, from Proverbs 30:8, who expressed the attitude of which he approved: *"Give me neither poverty nor riches, feed me with food convenient."* Since the extremes were dangerous, "therefore this holy and good man desires but a meane."[30]

Other examples of the colonial feeling about classes appeared in the literature of dissuasion which emanated mostly from Plymouth and was intended to head off several kinds of prospective colonists. Robert Cushman's lay sermon of 1621 contained the warning that self-love and idleness if not restrained would splinter the newly formed settlement and issue in "gentry and beggary." Cushman was especially critical of "mere worldlings" who booked passage to the New World in hopes of "gathering riches" and becoming landed gentlemen. In his "Epistle Dedicatory," he invited over any who were equipped for hard labor and satisfied with "competent dwellings," while bluntly discouraging those who craved "great riches, ease, pleasures, dainties, and jollity in this world."[31]

Cushman's hope that America would be free of "gentry and beggary" alike resurfaced in more comical form in Edward Winslow's *Good Newes from New England,* a "true" relation of 1623 which derided the inflated notion that the fountains of the New

30. Cotton, *Way of Life,* pp. 451–81. Quotations are from pp. 456–57, 471.

31. Robert Cushman, "Of the State of the Colony, and the Need of Public Spirit in the Colonists," in *Chronicles of the Pilgrim Fathers,* comp. Alexander Young (Boston, 1841), pp. 256, 263–68.

World "should stream forth wine or beer, or the woods and rivers be like butchers' shops, or fishmongers' stalls." Yet Winslow professed no wish to downgrade the new country and in fact called attention to its abundance of fowl, venison, and fish. What he did wish was to steer away all those who couldn't live without luxuries or were "too desirous of gain," and he pitched his appeal exclusively to the industrious sort whose faith would sustain them in hardship and whose labor would transform the plenty around them into usable commodity. Plymouth being an enterprise where "religion and profit jump together (which is rare)," Winslow followed Cushman's lead in declaring the settlement off limits to both the "dainty tooth" and the "beggar's purse," and he implied that only those who fell within the two extremes would find a home in the New World. He got so carried away with his thesis that he even projected it into the New England climate, avowing somewhat unrealistically that while at Plymouth he had neither been exposed to "extremity of heat, nor nipped by biting cold."[32]

Even John Winthrop's "A Model of Christian Charity," although it is often interpreted otherwise, supports this assumption about the colonial bias against economic extremes. True, Winthrop prefaced his discourse with the heading that God had so ordered the condition of mankind that "in all times some must be rich some poore, some highe and eminent in power and dignitie; others meane and in subjeccion." It should be noted, however, that Winthrop mentioned neither aristocracy nor beggary, only rich and poor, suggesting that at the very outset of the migration he was already thinking in terms of a contraction of the social possibilities that existed in England. By the poor he clearly meant the working poor,

32. Edward Winslow, *Good Newes from New England*, in *Chronicles of the Pilgrim Fathers*, comp. Alexander Young (Boston, 1841), pp. 372-74. Larzer Ziff's comment on Winslow is apposite here: "The fantasy of an earthly paradise undergoes an informative change in Puritan consciousness. Natural resources that have immediate value without the intermediary of work are supplanted by those that argue some form of production: gold and rubies and diamonds are replaced by free butcher shops, fishmonger stalls, and fountains of beer and wine. Even when it runs loose and free, the Puritan imagination fantasizes in terms of the abundance of the products of labor." From *Puritanism in America: New Culture in a New World* (New York: Viking Press, 1973), p. 46.

since he shared the Puritan dislike for those "unclean beasts" who lived without a calling. He defined rich men, moreover, as "all such as are able to live comfortably by their owne meanes duely improved," a definition not too far removed from the ideal advocated by Agur but scarcely capable of accommodating the lavish holdings of the great English lords.[33]

The American colonists, in sum, were favorably disposed toward a society which was relatively uniform in comparison with England, a society where aristocracy was devalued, beggary excluded, and a middling condition regarded as less fraught with danger than riches or indigence. And these sentiments were inevitably strengthened by—and tended to strengthen in turn—the Puritan revulsion from the sins of excess, a revulsion which originated in Elizabethan England and which issued repeatedly in calls for the godly to acquire the virtues of moderation and temperance. This is not to say that the New England Puritans were uncritical advocates of the Aristotelian golden mean, or that they had anything but scorn for lukewarm Christians who were satisfied with only a moderate love of the Deity. The counsel of moderation was related to but must not be confused with the tension of living in the world without being of it, since the latter could inflame the conscientious saint to the prodigies of revolutionary zeal that carried the New Model Army to victory at Naseby and Dunbar.[34] Yet moderation was an

---

33. See *Winthrop Papers*, 2: 282–95, for the text of the sermon. Quotations are from pages 282–83. A good discussion of Winthrop's speech in particular, and the Puritan social ethic in general, appears in Stephen Foster's *Their Solitary Way: The Puritan Social Ethic in the First Century of Settlement in New England* (New Haven: Yale University Press, 1971), pp. 41–64.

34. A classic illustration of this difference as it appears in Renaissance literature may be found in books I and II of *The Faerie Queene*, which deal, respectively, with Saint George and Sir Guyon. As a type of Christ and a representative of holiness, Saint George is clearly the superior of Guyon, who embodies for Spenser the virtue of temperance or right reason. It is relevant to note in this connection that Spenser, as opposed to a Jesuit like Tasso, holds that the pleasures of the flesh are natural and healthy if enjoyed in moderation. For Tasso, writes A. Bartlett Giamatti, a man either "serves the spirit or he wallows in sensuality. There is no middle ground." See *The Earthly Paradise and the Renaissance Epic* (Princeton: Princeton University Press, 1966), p. 192.

offshoot of the tension insofar as it rested on the same assumptions about the nature of man and the universe.

God created man with passions and appetites which were neutral in themselves but vicious if indulged to excess. He intended the things of this life to be enjoyed but He strictly forbade enslavement to them. Temporal indulgences such as food, drink, and sexual relations in marriage were to be taken in moderation; for in these matters, too, the middle way was best and the extremes were to be avoided, although occasions might naturally arise when the glory of God demanded abstinence from even lawful gratification. The right attitude for the Puritan was pinpointed by William Ames when he explained that temperance involved governing or "moderating" the affections, not wholly suppressing them but taking away their "inordinatnesse." Drinking Ames permitted but drunkenness or "immoderate drinking" he condemned as sinful.[35]

Puritans like Ames regularly drew connections between the sins of "inordinatnesse" and the economic situation of the sinner. William Perkins observed that "many of the richer sort" riotously misspent their wealth in gaming and sporting, while great landlords extorted immoderate rents and enclosed grounds that had lain common for time out of mind. Perkins attributed the greed of the wealthy to "want of sobriety and temperance in diet and apparel."[36] Ames portrayed rogues and "lusty begging vagabonds" as given over to sensuality and intemperance,[37] and Hugh Peter, who returned to England after the outbreak of the Civil War, intimated that in a land without indigents the sins of excess vanished as well: "I have lived in a country," he told Parliament, "where in seven years I never saw beggar, nor heard an oath, nor looked upon a drunkard."[38] Although Peter was embellishing for rhetorical purposes, most American Puritans would have agreed that in their own less stratified society the sins of excess were held to a comparative minimum. At any rate England furnished an instructive contrast. There the rich were getting richer and

35. Ames, *Conscience with the Power and Cases thereof*, p. 249.
36. Perkins, *Work*, p. 468.
37. Ames, *Conscience with the Power and Cases thereof*, p. 249.
38. Quoted in Christopher Hill, *The Century of Revolution, 1603-1714* (New York: W. W. Norton and Co., 1966), p. 84.

the poor becoming poorer. As Robert Cushman put it, "one of a hundred" lived on sweet morsels while "the bulk, body and commonality" were reduced to snapping at crusts.[39] And England, as all good Puritans were aware, was overrun with intemperance and excess of riot: "Look up and down the kingdom; you shall see some roaring, drinking, dicing, carding, whoring, in taverns and blind alehouses."[40]

The strongest Puritan pronouncement on behalf of moderation came from Perkins, who wrote a full-length treatise on the doctrine *"Let your moderation of mind be known to all men: the Lord is at hand."* Mindful that no mean or moderation was appropriate with regard to the Almighty, Perkins restricted his advice to the manner in which men dealt with each other. He defined moderation as an "even and equal carriage of a man's self, in all his private words and deeds." Perkins instructed the Christian to check his resentment and overlook the defects of his neighbors, but he was equally disapproving of the opposite extreme of submitting without a murmur to violence or injustice. He closed his treatise on a mournful note that must have left a deep impression on the younger Puritans who carried his ideas to America. Glancing about him, Perkins beheld an England where compromise was banished and men hardened their hearts against compassion and mercy. "Moderation dwells in corners," he lamented in summing up, "but extremity is that which beareth sway over all the world."[41]

In the thinking of the American Puritans, then, there were *two* middle ways, one a set of economic, social, and temperamental preferences, and the other an existential readiness to serve God without withdrawing from the flawed community of men, to be in the world and yet not of it. And these two middle ways were fused in the minds of the first generation. For the founders, it

39. Robert Cushman, "Reasons and Considerations Touching the Lawfulness of Removing out of England into the Parts of America," in *A Journal of the Pilgrims at Plymouth: Mourt's Relation*, ed. Dwight B. Heath (1622; New York: Corinth Books, 1963), pp. 95–96.

40. Thomas Shepard, *The Sincere Convert* (1641), in *The Works of Thomas Shepard*, ed. John Albro, 3 vols. (Boston, 1853), 1: 95.

41. Perkins, *Work*, pp. 481–510. Quotations are from pp. 492, 509. The full title of Perkins' treatise is "EPIEIKEIA, or a Treatise of Christian Equity and Moderation."

was never enough to be Thomas Hooker's "civil" man: "outwardly just, temperate, chaste, carefull to follow his worldly businesse, who will not hurt so much as his neighbours dog, payes every man his owne, and lives of his owne; no drunkard, adulterer, or quarreller; [he] loves to live peaceably and quietly among his neighbours."[42] The formalist thus impaled on Hooker's oratory may have abjured the sins of excess, but he was far from being a regenerate Christian. Puritan ministers agreed in regarding a "blameless, innocent, honest, smooth life" as a sure road to hell unless accompanied by grace.[43] Yet these same ministers were usually the ones who recommended moderation, temperance, and a middling share of earthly possessions. Zeal and temperance went hand-in-hand, implied Michael Wigglesworth, speaking with the voice of God against a languishing New England, or at any rate spiritual insensibility and worldly excess descended together upon a backsliding people:

If these be they, how is it that I find
In stead of holiness Carnality,
In stead of heavenly frames an Earthly mind,
For burning zeal luke-warm Indifferency,
For flaming love, key-cold Dead-heartedness,
For temperance (in meat, and drinke, and cloaths) excess?[44]

The men and women who left England in the 1630s in order to enjoy purer ordinances in a tiny settlement at the edge of an unmapped continent created, as one of them put it, "a new world and new manners."[45] For a time they managed to translate their ideals

42. Thomas Hooker, *The Christians Two Chiefe Lessons* (London, 1640), p. 213. The same passage is quoted by Edmund S. Morgan in *The Puritan Family: Religion and Domestic Relations in Seventeenth-Century New England*, rev. ed. (New York: Harper and Row, Torchbooks, 1966), p. 1.

43. Shepard, *Sincere Convert*, p. 59.

44. Michael Wigglesworth, "God's Controversy with New England," in *The Puritans: A Sourcebook of Their Writings*, ed. Perry Miller and Thomas H. Johnson, 2 vols., rev. ed. (New York: Harper and Row, Torchbooks, 1963), 2:612–13.

45. Anne Bradstreet, "To My Dear Children," in *The Works of Anne Bradstreet*, ed. Jeannine Hensley (Cambridge: Harvard University Press, 1967), p. 241.

into practice.[46] They created a world in which the range of religious and social alternatives was drastically curtailed. The manners were comparatively uniform, bourgeois, and unfriendly to what were deemed extremes. The nonseparating Congregationalists held the reins of power in church and state from the beginning, and Anglicans like Thomas Morton, Presbyterians like Dr. Robert Child, and Separatists like Roger Williams were either banished, indicted for sedition, or shipped home. John Winthrop took bemused note of the reduction of theological options when, at the height of the antinomian crisis, he said that it had become "as common here to distinguish between men, by being under a covenant of grace or a covenant of works, as in other countries between Protestants and Papists."[47]

Yet there can be little doubt that by the middle decades of the seventeenth century the character of New England was changing. The emigrants, men and women of tried religious experience who had been sifted out of the mass of English Puritans, consolidated their creed in the Cambridge Platform of 1648. Barely fifteen years elapsed before the colonial divines assembled again in synod to address themselves to a problem posed by the second generation, the generation which grew up in America and was spared the trials and struggles of the English past. What especially troubled the ministry was the apparent decline of piety on the part of these offspring of the original settlers. Few of them, it seemed, could claim election, and their own children, in consequence, were not entitled to baptism. The solution reached by the clergy came to be known as the Halfway Covenant. Under this settlement, baptism was extended to the grandchildren of the founders even though their own parents were unregenerate. Full membership, which included the Supper, was confined to those who had actually been converted. Supporters of the synod collected testimony from the writings of Cotton, Shepard, and others to show that their position was consistent with the views of the first generation. They professed

46. Boston may have been an exception in this regard. Within a decade of its settlement, according to Darrett B. Rutman, the town had effectively abandoned Winthrop's ideals (*Winthrop's Boston*, pp. vii–ix, passim).

47. *Winthrop's Journal: "History of New England,"* ed. James Kendall Hosmer, 2 vols. (New York: Barnes and Noble, 1966), 1: 209.

to be seeking, as they stated in the preface to the *Propositions,* "the right middle way of Truth." They were the new chosen people, bound by "the same Covenant which God made with the National Church of Israel and their seed," and the descendants of the faithful, they argued, were therefore entitled to fellowship in the outward and visible church.[48]

Although much criticized by opponents as a retreat from Congregational purity, the Halfway Covenant did reaffirm the sanctity of communion, and it kept alive the notion that authentic sainthood was impossible without a work of the Spirit. Even its defenders, however, had been forced to acknowledge that the faith of the fathers was losing appeal. The old exhortation to live in the world without being of it was apparently falling on deaf ears. Michael Wigglesworth, of course, had recognized as much in his poem "God's Controversy with New-England," composed, as it happens, in 1662, the same year that the synod published its decision. But Wigglesworth was mistaken in associating the decline of religious fervor with the spread of worldly excess. For the problem was not that the children of the founders were becoming dissolute sinners; they were still middling and prudent, but they were not becoming saints.

When Thomas Hooker denounced the merely virtuous citizen, or Thomas Shepard berated the man who contented himself with an "innocent, honest, smooth life," they could not know that their words would apply to the descendants of the colonists who settled

48. Walker, *Creeds and Platforms of Congregationalism,* pp. 304, 206. The second quotation was reprinted by the synod from John Cotton's *Certain Queries Tending to Accomodation and Communion of Presbyterian and Congregational Churches* (London, 1654). The fullest treatment of this subject is Robert G. Pope's *The Half-Way Covenant: Church Membership in Puritan New England* (Princeton: Princeton University Press, 1969). Pope disputes the view that admissions to full communion dropped steadily after the deaths of the founders, arguing instead that admissions increased sharply after 1676 (see chap. 8 and appendix). As Stephen Foster points out, however, "the *absolute* increase in new admissions after 1676 is simply too small to offset the decine in the *proportion* of the adult male population in full communion, which fell steeply after 1650 because of the increase in total population." Foster concludes that the revival of 1676–90 was merely "a *partial* arrest in the gradual *relative* decline" in church membership that characterized the latter half of the seventeenth century (*Their Solitary Way,* appendix A).

Massachusetts Bay. Yet it was precisely such industrious and temperate New Englanders whose growing numbers made the Halfway
Covenant necessary. The Puritan tension, the challenge of sainthood in a fallen world, was being replaced by the system of social
values which the founders had so firmly assigned to a secondary
position. The figure who came closest to capturing the process of
diminution involved was Cotton Mather when he despaired of "a
visible *shrink* in all orders of men among us, from that *greatness*,
and that *goodness*, which was in the *first grain*, that our God
brought from *three sifted kingdoms*, into this land, when it was a
land not sown."[49]

49. Cotton Mather, *Magnalia Christi Americana*, 2 vols. (1702; Hartford,
1820), 1: 228.

III

Cotton Mather and Benjamin Franklin

Cotton Mather and Benjamin Franklin in their different ways foreshadow and illuminate the future development of American literature. Mather's entire career can be seen as an effort to breathe fresh life into the religion he inherited from his ancestors. This was the motive that impelled him to involve himself in the trials at Salem and to compose the witchcraft narratives in which he reaffirmed the essential rightness of the middle way. His heirs were the nineteenth-century romancers who undertook in their fiction to salvage the metaphysical vision of the first settlers of Massachusetts Bay. Franklin's purpose, in contrast, was not to preserve theological categories but to dispense with them, not to reclaim the temper of his ancestors but to secularize it. His heirs were instrumental in shaping the contours of American political and social thought, and he contributed to the emergence of an ideological conformity which the romancers opposed in their art.

———————

The years following the adoption of the Halfway Covenant witnessed a steady retreat from the exacting creed of Massachusetts Bay's first generation. As the number of those who experienced grace became an ever diminishing minority in the congregations, dissatisfaction with the 1662 settlement spread throughout the colony. The compromise had been framed, after all, in the expectation that it would somehow sustain a high level of communicants, and it was manifestly failing of its purpose. The grandchildren of the founders were simply not undergoing conversion in sufficient numbers to ensure the perpetuation of the churches, and critics of the Halfway Covenant—critics whose strength was concentrated in western Massachusetts and the Connecticut Valley—feared the eventual emptying of the pews. Accordingly, in 1667 the Reverend Solomon Stoddard took the decisive step of extending communion to all but the openly scandalous. Stoddard himself knew that without the operation of the Holy Spirit a man was not a saint, and he did not make the mistake, which Increase Mather charged against the rising generation, of imagining that "saving Grace and Morality were the same."[1] But open communion meant that so far as society and the churches were concerned, the distinction had lost its significance. The endeavor to bring the visible and invisible churches into some degree of conformity was being abandoned, for ministers who endorsed Stoddardism presumed to judge, as Perry Miller put it, "only of appearances, not of realities."[2] Stoddardism threw out the confession of grace and made a reasonable obedience to the moral law the sole criterion for admission to the churches. And within the churches themselves, it devalued the Supper by terminating its exclusivity—it had formerly been regarded as the seal of salvation—and by permitting the spiritually dead to partake alongside the living.[3]

It was not only the sense of grace which was fading from New

1. Quoted in Perry Miller, *The New England Mind: From Colony to Province* (Cambridge: Harvard University Press, 1953), p. 34.
2. Ibid., p. 277.
3. Edward Taylor refers to unregenerate sinners as the "dead" in *Preparatory Meditations: Second Series*, "Meditation 106," a poem which attacks the spread of Stoddardism. Taylor's lines are:
The Dead don't eate. Though Folly childish dotes
In th' Child that gives his Hobby Horses oates.
See *The Poems of Edward Taylor*, ed. Donald E. Stanford (New Haven: Yale University Press, 1960), p. 241. The fullest treatment of the debate over open communion, and of Puritan sacramentalism in general, is E. Brooks Holifield's *The Covenant Sealed: The Development of Puritan Sacramental Theology in Old and New England, 1570–1720* (New Haven: Yale University Press, 1974).

England; evidently the sense of evil was fading as well. By 1690 the churches were being invited to draw up lists of iniquities and to "pass their *votes*, that they count such things to be very *offensive evils*."[4] The ministers were thus reduced to entreating their flocks to vote themselves sinners, and their defensive posture testified to fears of incipient Arminianism. For if members who eschewed flagrant immorality refused to recognize that they were nevertheless sinful, it was merely a question of time before they began to claim moral capability and trust to their own strength instead of divine assistance in order to overcome vice. The weakening of belief in evil pointed toward the segregation of the Holy Spirit from the affairs of men as surely as did in a different way the absence of grace.

It was against this background of declining faith in the immanence of the invisible world that the witchcraft hysteria burst upon New England. To Cotton Mather, the visitation promised a revival of the creed of the founders. He began *The Wonders of the Invisible World*, which appeared shortly after the execution of the suspected witches, by rejoicing that despite declension there were still churches in the land where communicants were examined for grace before their admission to the Supper.[5] He stressed the importance to the New England polity of the confession and the Supper because they invested that polity with its spiritual authority. They were the visible signs of the favor of the invisible world. In the witchcraft outbreak, he found confirmation of the agency of the invisible spheres, and tacit support for the traditional notion that—in the words of his father, Increase—"the Grace of God is a discernible thing."[6]

Mather regularly stated that the existence of Satan validated the existence of God, and he conjectured that the devils had been

4. Cotton Mather, *Magnalia Christi Americana*, 2 vols., (1702; Hartford, 1820), 2: 287.
5. Cotton Mather, *The Wonders of the Invisible World* (1692; London, 1862), pp. 10–12.
6. Quoted in Miller, *New England Mind: From Colony to Province*, p. 261. For a detailed account of the economic and social origins of the Salem outbreak see Paul Boyer and Stephen Nissenbaum's *Salem Possessed: The Social Origins of Witchcraft* (Cambridge: Harvard University Press, 1974).

visited upon New England in order to confute atheism and Saddu-
ceeism. From the conviction that God existed, he hoped, would
flow conversions.[7] A good deal of what Mather wrote around the
time of the trials exhibits an almost obsessive preoccupation with
the failure of his people to experience the Deity. Tremendous
pressure, it appears, was being brought on the children to have
such experiences, since the continuation of true churches depended
on the addition of visible saints.[8] Plainly the children were failing
their community. The youngsters Mather singled out in his witchcraft narratives were under particular pressure, some of it coming
from the minister himself. Margaret Rule, born of "sober and
honest parents," was said to be on the point of becoming a "new
creature" when she had her seizure.[9] Mercy Short, like the Rule girl
placed under Mather's care, expressed anxious yearnings for heaven
and twice experienced attacks of the demons in the midst of church
services, customarily occasions for redoubled exhortations to grace.
Mercy interpreted her afflictions as proof of God's special favor,
and Mather recorded in his diary that he eventually had the satisfac-
tion of admitting her to his church.[10] In April of 1692, according to
the diary, Mather petitioned God to awaken New England, and in
both the Short and Rule documents he indicated that his prayers
had been answered. "Many of the children of God in the Neighbor-
hood were helped by Him to an extraordinary exercise of Grace,"

7. Cotton Mather, *Memorable Providences* (1689), in *Narratives of the
Witchcraft Cases*, ed. George Lincoln Burr (New York: Barnes and Noble,
1952), pp. 96–98; Mather, *Magnalia*, 2: 387; idem, "Another Brand Pluckt Out
of the Burning," in *Salem Witchcraft*, ed. Samuel P. Fowler (Salem, Mass.,
1861), p. 44. "Another Brand Pluckt Out of the Burning," which Mather
circulated in manuscript, was originally published in 1700 by Robert Calef in
More Wonders of the Invisible World.
8. Mather, *Wonders of the Invisible World*, p. 102; idem, *A Companion for
Communicants* (Boston, 1690), pp. 79–80; idem. *Addresses to Old Men, and
Young Men, and Little Children* (Boston, 1690), pp. 90–91, 118; idem, *A
Midnight Cry* (Boston, 1692), p. 49. Cf. Emory Elliott, *Power and the Pulpit
in Puritan New England* (Princeton: Princeton University Press, 1975), pp.
69–74.
9. Mather, "Another Brand Pluckt Out of the Burning," pp. 28–29.
10. Cotton Mather, *A Brand Pluckt Out of the Burning* (1693), in *Narratives of the Witchcraft Cases*, pp. 261, 269, 271, 278; Mather, *Diary of
Cotton Mather: 1681–1708*, in Massachusetts Historical Society, *Collections*,
7th ser., 7 (1911): 161.

he wrote in the first, and he gave thanks in the second that "Christ got subjects" and the churches additions from among the younger generation.[11]

The fervent interest aroused by the witchcraft confessions now takes on its special significance. Robert Calef, who bitterly assailed the whole proceeding in his sarcastically titled *More Wonders of the Invisible World* (1700), protested that the ministers took turns haranguing the accused, urging them to confess for hours at a time.[12] To the modern reader of Calef's account, the ministers' conduct calls to mind the protracted camp meetings of the eighteenth and nineteenth centuries. And the confessions played a role much like that of the personal testimonies which characterized these later revivals. They brought onlookers to God by making them "more Familiarized *with the World of Spirits*" and by furnishing proof of the operation of unseen presences upon the souls of men.[13] In what struck unsympathetic observers as one of the darker ironies of the whole affair, the confessions benefited the witches as well, since only those who admitted complicity with Satan were spared execution. If they confessed, in other words, they were "saved." In this respect, the sentences meted out at Salem marked a departure from New England precedent. There had been a flurry of prosecutions between 1647 and 1662, and in almost every case confession had been followed by execution. Only at Salem were defendants who pleaded their innocence hanged, while those who acknowledged dealings with the supernatural

11. Mather, *A Brand Pluckt Out of the Burning*, p. 277; idem, "Another Brand Pluckt Out of the Burning," pp. 49–50. As John Demos and others have observed, most of the accusers were adolescent girls. Demos, noting that the witches were predominately married or widowed older women, argues that the accusers were displacing their aggression toward their own mothers ("Underlying Themes in the Witchcraft of the Seventeenth-Century New England," *American Historical Review* 75 [1970]: 1311–26). Another possibility is that the accusers were suffering from anorexia nervosa. Nine times out of ten this disease strikes teen-aged girls. Victims are unable to eat, experience acute hunger pains, and are subject to fits of vomiting. In extreme cases they may actually starve themselves to death. As we shall see, many of the Salem bewitched exhibited the identical symptoms.
12. Robert Calef, *More Wonders of the Invisible World* (1700) in *Salem Witchcraft*, ed. Samuel P. Fowler (Salem, Mass., 1861), pp. 273–74.
13. Mather, *Wonders of the Invisible World*, p. 62. See also pp. 15–16, 27–28,

escaped with their lives.[14] In the earlier period, the apostasy from
orthodox Calvinism had not been so threatening.

The confession was a mainstay of Puritan faith, for in confessing
the believer testified to his entrance into the covenant of grace.
This was only one of several correspondences between Congregational polity and the witchcraft, correspondences which aided
Mather in his effort to make use of the episode in order to
strengthen the middle way. The Devil, he exclaimed, affected "an
Impious and Impudent *imitation* of Divine Things." Satan was
said to entice his followers into a covenant with hell, and the
witches, according to their own testimony, formed themselves after
the manner of New England churches. They even observed the
sacraments of baptism and the Supper.[15]

It is perhaps no wonder, therefore, that the most pervasive
pattern of the witchcraft was its orality. "The mouth," as John
Demos was the first to point out, "seems to have been charged
with a special kind of importance for victims of witchcraft."[16]
Although such oral concerns obviously took an unusual form at
Salem, they were by no means uncommon during periods of intense
religious excitement. Orality seems to have had a special importance for American revivalism in general. During the Northampton
awakening of 1735, according to Jonathan Edwards, church at-
tendance rose dramatically, with "every hearer eager to drink in
the words of the minister as they came from his mouth." One of
the hearers was nineteen-year-old Abigail Hutchinson, who had long
suffered from physical weakness, and whose condition inexplicably
worsened after her conversion. She eventually expired from "famine
and thirst." Edwards explained:

14. See Frederick C. Drake, "Witchcraft in the American Colonies,"
American Quarterly 20 (Winter 1968): 694–725.

15. Mather, *Wonders of the Invisible World*, pp. 159–61.

16. Demos, "Underlying Themes in the Witchcraft of Seventeenth-Century
New England," p. 1324. Demos reads this as evidence for his thesis of genera-
tional conflict in Puritan culture, and he postulates harsh and traumatic
methods of weaning as a possible cause for the oral concerns. Several victims
complained of witch bites and testified that they saw the accused suckling
animal "familiars," but Demos's provocative guess about weaning habits, as he
himself admits, will have to wait on additional research for corroboration.

Her illness, in the latter part of it, was seated much in her throat; and swelling inward filled up the pipe, so that she could swallow nothing but what was perfectly liquid, and but very little of that, and with great and long strugglings and stranglings, that which she took in flying out at her nostrils till she at last could swallow nothing at all.

Elsewhere Edwards lamented the incidence of drunkenness: too many souls were lost at the taverns for a cup of the wrong kind of beverage. All this had changed, however, as a result of the revival: "The place of resort was now altered; it was no longer the tavern, but the minister's house, that was thronged far more than ever the tavern had been wont to be." Hundreds of new converts, Edwards reported, flocked to the church to recount their religious experiences and present themselves at communion.[17]

It seems probable, in view of the similar phenomenon at Northampton, that the Salem orality was related to the current controversy over standards for admission to the Supper. Mather's involvement with the controversy prompted his publication in 1690 of *A Companion for Communicants*, a volume which he hoped to supply to every believer admitted to the Lord's Table. There he crossed swords with the effrontery of Stoddardism. He declared his passionate scorn for those unnamed pastors who held that a mere profession of historical faith together with submission to the government of the visible church entitled a man to the sacraments. This was to batter, Mather protested, at the foundation of Congregational discipline. "None but *Believers* are to Enjoy the *Supper* of the Lord." Yet Mather was admittedly distressed that so few were coming forth to eat and drink. Since the children in particular were guilty of neglect—and by implication, contempt—of the

---

17. Jonathan Edwards, *A Faithful Narrative of the Surprising Work of God* (1737), in Edwards, *The Great Awakening*, ed. C. C. Goen (New Haven: Yale University Press, 1972), pp. 151, 197–98, 161, 157. It seems probable that Hutchinson died of anorexia. Edwards was eventually forced to resign his pulpit because of his insistence on a testimony of conversion. His views are spelled out in *An Humble Inquiry Concerning the Qualifications Requisite to a Complete Standing and Full Communion in the Visible Christian Church* (1749).

Supper, he called for increased efforts to qualify them for communion.[18]

The results of such efforts can be traced once again in the Rule and Short narratives. The two girls suffered eating and drinking disturbances and underwent a series of prolonged fasts. Mercy Short had a fifteen-day fast imposed on her by the devils. She had hot irons thrust down her throat, and her tormentors brought her a small cup of whitish poison which they compelled her to drink against her will, causing her to swell prodigiously. Here was a probable analogue to the wine. At one point Mercy turned upon the spectres and referred directly to the Supper: "And pray, how durst you, after You had given yourself to the Divel, come to the Table of the Lord: I profess I wonder the Divel did not come and fetch you away alive!"[19]

In the Margaret Rule narrative, the sufferer also experienced involuntary fasts, during which time she was only permitted to swallow an occasional spoonful of rum. At other times her jaws were forced open and "something invisible would be poured down her throat"; witnesses saw traces of liquid on her neck and "she cried out of it, as of scalding brimstone poured into her." Like Mercy's comparable struggles, Margaret's resistance suggests a displaced protest against relentless pressure to partake of the Lord's Table, and also reveals anxiety that her unworthiness would damn her if she did comply. Unworthy communicants were frequently said, much like the witches who participated in the diabolical sacrament, to eat and drink their damnation. Eventually Margaret's resistance took a form which implicated Mather himself in the witchcraft. He noted in his diary that she began to complain that "Divels in *my Shape*" threatened and molested her, and he added with considerable relief that she was delivered from her fits before the story got abroad.[20]

18. Mather, *Companion for Communicants*, pp. 29–31, 40, 42, 44, 55, 79–80. The quotation is from p. 29. See also idem, *Work Upon the Ark: Meditations upon the Ark as a Type of the Church* (Boston, 1689), pp. 7–8; and idem, *Things to be Look'd for* (Cambridge, 1691), pp. 63–64.

19. Mather, *A Brand Pluck'd Out of the Burning*, pp. 265–71. The reference to the Lord's Supper appears on p. 270.

20. Mather, "Another Brand Pluckt Out of the Burning," pp. 33–35; idem,

In the Congregational polity of New England, the Supper was the ritual whereby visible saints publicly affirmed their membership in the invisible church. It was the seal of the bond between the world and the spirit. Mather, in his book for communicants, defined its value in these terms:

> The Blessed God, who has made *Sacraments* to be such very necessary and agreeable Engines for a maintaining of a Communion between the *Visible* and *Invisible World*, has in both *Testaments* appointed several such means of our fellowship with Himself.[21]

There were men in Massachusetts, neither atheists nor Sadducees, who denied that any action in time could reliably answer the purpose that Mather here attributed to the Lord's Table. In essence, they gave up any claim—however tentative—to the power of discerning a work of the invisible world. Traditionally, when a believer presented himself for communion, it signified that he had experienced the supernatural. If Stoddardism prevailed, the taking of the Eucharist would mean only that the communicant was a member of the visible church. The Supper as an "engine" for the "maintaining of a Communion between the *Visible* and *Invisible World*" would be lost. But if the visible and invisible spheres were in constant communion and flux, and this could be demonstrated, then the historic status of the Supper would be strengthened and hopefully restored.

And the occurrences at Salem did seem to bear out the view that the two worlds interpenetrated to an extraordinary degree. Effects which transcended the ordinary course of nature and baffled the ordinary senses of mankind, effects produced by unseen and supernatural agents, were shown to be real and were verified by

---

Diary, p. 178. The Rule and Short narratives support the suggestion that the Salem bewitched had anorexia. Clinical studies appear to indicate that most adolescents who suffer from the disorder are in effect trying not to grow up. In seventeenth-century New England, the conversion experience usually occurred during adolescence, and converts were treated as adults both in the churches and the larger community. The Salem outbreak originated with the female relations of the Reverend Samuel Parris, who was of orthodox Calvinist persuasion.

21. Mather, *Companion for Communicants*, pp. 1–2.

scores of witnesses. Such unimpeachable evidence of nonmaterial presence would, Mather thought, disarm even skeptics who credited nothing but what they could see and feel. The impressions made by the devils, he said, were "as *real* and as *furious*, as if the *Invisible World* were becoming Incarnate." And the reverse was true as well, for just as the unseen became material, so the visible became invisible. The devils, according to Mather, could "cover the most *Corporeal* Things in the World with a *Fascinating Mist of Invisibility*." The witches were able to appear to their victims as spectres or invisible beings—invisible in the sense that they were seen by none but the victims themselves.[22]

Nor, as some critics contended, could the bewitchings be dismissed as purely imaginary. "*Brimstone* even without a metaphor," Mather assured his readers, "is making a hellish and horrid stench in our Nostrils." Writing to Judge John Richards, he replied to the critics in detail. He granted that the witchcraft was "very much transacted upon the Stage of the Imagination," yet insisted that it could not properly be called imaginary, since "the Effects are dreadfully real." Victims were tortured, even murdered, and were acquainted with secrets which afterwards "proved plainly to have been Realities."[23] Given such proof of extensive communion between the visible and invisible spheres, the obvious implication was that it was the duty of the churches to maintain that communion through the Supper.

Nowhere in his writings did Mather explicitly state that the witchcraft confuted the advocates of open communion along with

22. Mather, *Memorable Providences*, p. 95; idem, *Wonders of the Invisible World*, pp. 80, 128, 161–63; idem, *Magnalia*, 1: 186–87.
23. Mather, *Wonders of the Invisible World*, p. 95; Mather to John Richards 31 May 1692, in *Selected Letters of Cotton Mather*, ed. Kenneth Silverman (Baton Rouge: Louisiana State University Press, 1971), p. 37. Mather's reasoning here invites comparison to the conclusion reached by William James two centuries later. In *The Varieties of Religious Experience*, James wrote that "the unseen region . . . is not merely ideal, for it produces effects in this world. That which produces effects within another reality must be termed a reality itself, so I feel as if we had no philosophic excuse for calling the unseen or mystical world unreal." James summed up by observing that "God is real since he produces real effects" ([New York: Longmans, Green, and Co., 1902], pp. 516–17).

atheists and Sadducees. Yet it does seem clear that what was at issue for him at Salem was the Puritan cast of mind, and its renewal was certain to have bearing upon the standards for church admission. The advent of the witches, as he suggested in his letter to Judge Richards, showed that the realm of spirit had the power to exert pressure on the world of men and to enter it with tangible effect. His conception of grace and ultimately the Puritan tension itself rested on an analogous premise. Only the saint, as Mather wrote of John Eliot (using the familiar phrase that John Norton had applied to John Cotton), *"lived in Heaven* while he *was on earth"*;[24] and the saint, by definition, was one who had experienced a work of the supernatural world. It was grace, coming from the Holy Spirit, which enabled the godly Puritan to dwell in both spheres—the visible and invisible—at once. And without grace, without the invasion of nature by the supernatural, the middle way perished.

———————•———————

This interpretation of Mather's role in the witchcraft, if correct, suggests that there are important lines of connection between him and the later romancers. It provides additional evidence for the growing appreciation of his central place in the emergence of our national literature.[25] Hawthorne, for example, was aware of an affinity between himself and Mather. He acknowledged as much in "Alice Doane's Appeal," which for all its manifold ambiguities

24. Mather, *Magnalia*, 1: 483.
25. Many scholars have contributed to the radical revision of Mather's reputation. I have found especially stimulating the studies by Austin Warren, "Grandfather Mather and His Wonder Book," *Sewanee Review* 72 (1964): 96–116; Daniel Hoffman, *Form and Fable in American Fiction* (New York: Oxford University Press, 1965), pp. 23–24, 31–32, 290–92; Robert Middlekauff, *The Mathers: Three Generations of Puritan Intellectuals, 1596–1728* (New York: Oxford University Press, 1971), pp. 191–367; Richard Slotkin, *Regeneration Through Violence: The Mythology of the American Frontier, 1600–1860* (Middletown, Conn.: Wesleyan University Press, 1973), pp. 128–45; Sacvan Bercovitch, "Cotton Mather," in *Major Writers of Early American Literature*, ed. Everett Emerson (Madison: University of Wisconsin Press, 1972), pp. 93–149; and Bercovitch, *The Puritan Origins of the American Self* (New Haven: Yale University Press, 1975), pp. 136–62, passim.

memorializes the witchcraft as a source of imaginative power. The narrator of the tale, who accompanies two young ladies to Gallows Hill, reads them a manuscript of his own composition, an outright fantasy which leaves his audience unmoved. Whereupon he proposes to make "a trial whether truth were more powerful than fiction." This turns out to involve Hawthorne's familiar strategy of combining the actual and the imaginary, for the narrator, aided by the obscurity of the twilight, summons up a highly fanciful vision of the Salem witches filing past on their way to the gallows. As he proceeds with the story, his companions interrupt him by seizing his arm in fright; this time he has succeeded in reaching "the seldom trodden places of their hearts" and moving them to tears. Hawthorne concludes by expressing his regret that no relic exists on the hill "to assist the imagination in appealing to the heart."[26]

What attracted Hawthorne to Mather, as he stated elsewhere, was the Puritan chronicler's capacity to endow "true events and real personages" with "the dreamy aspect which they wore in [his] singular mind." He realized that this ability derived from Mather's belief in the existence of spirits—derived, in the end, from his Calvinist creed. In a sentence equally applicable to himself, Hawthorne wrote that Mather supposed not only that demons inhabited the external world, but that "they were hidden in men's hearts, and stole into their most secret thoughts." Although he disapproved of the minister's part in the Salem tragedy, he implicitly assented to the attitude which lay behind it—an attitude which made Mather a critic of his age just as it made Hawthorne a critic of his own. "There was great need of the prayers of Cotton Mather," he concluded, ". . . because the old moral and religious character of New England was in danger of being utterly lost."[27]

26. Nathaniel Hawthorne, "Alice Doane's Appeal," in *The Works of Nathaniel Hawthorne*, Centenary Edition, ed. William Charvat et al. (Columbus: Ohio State University Press, 1962–), vol. 11, *The Snow-Image and Uncollected Tales* (1974), pp. 278, 280.

27. Nathaniel Hawthorne, *The Whole History of Grandfather's Chair*, in *The Works of Nathaniel Hawthorne*, Centenary Edition, ed. William Charvat et al. (Columbus: Ohio State University Press, 1962–), vol. 6, *True Stories from History and Biography* (1972), pp. 92, 94, 96. For a different view of

This is not to suggest that Mather's importance consists in the fact that he was mined by writers like Hawthorne. It is to insist, rather, that his significance lies in his commitment to the survival of the founders' faith, and in his effort to exploit episodes such as the witchcraft in order to revitalize American Puritanism. He was not, to be sure, a self-conscious artist in the way that Hawthorne or Melville was, and he left behind no aesthetic theory to account for what he had done in the witchcraft narratives. The nineteenth-century romancers went far beyond him in that they sought to translate the world of their fiction into an aesthetic, an aesthetic that constituted a reformulation in literary terms of the theological balance of the founders. At the same time, the romancers wished to reclaim the spiritual stance of their ancestors as a viable human option, a still relevant article of belief. Mather anticipated them in important respects. As a writer in his own right, he pictured a world akin to theirs, and he did so for comparable reasons: in order to keep alive the metaphysical alternative of living in the world without being of it.

The "dying power of godliness"[28] mourned by Cotton Mather was interred by Poor Richard's proverbs and the *Autobiography* of Benjamin Franklin. Rejecting Calvinist theology, Franklin retained the Puritan social ethic and propounded it in his memoirs as a secular gospel, a gospel whose cardinal tenet was "Avoid Extreams" (p. 150).[29] The son of a professing member of Mather's own

Hawthorne's attitude toward the Puritan conception of visible sainthood, see Michael J. Colacurcio's "Visible Sanctity and Specter Evidence: The Moral World of Hawthorne's 'Young Goodman Brown,'" *Essex Institute Historical Collections* 110 (1974): 259–99.

28. Mather, *Magnalia*, 2: 285.

29. Benjamin Franklin, *Autobiography of Benjamin Franklin*, ed. Leonard W. Labaree et al. (New Haven: Yale University Press, 1964). Page references included in the text are from this edition. For other information on Franklin's life I have relied principally on Carl Van Doren, *Benjamin Franklin* (New York: Viking Press, 1938), and Alfred Owen Aldridge, *Benjamin Franklin: Philosopher and Man* (Philadelphia: J. B. Lippincott Co., 1965). Critical studies which I have found useful include J. A. Leo Lemay's "Benjamin Franklin," in *Major Writers of Early American Literature*, ed. Everett Emerson (Madison: University of Wisconsin Press, 1972), pp. 205–43; John F. Lynen's *The Design*

congregation, Franklin had planned to enter the ministry until
financial hardship forced his father to withdraw him from grammar
school. As an old man, he composed a new bible which replaced
the Decalogue with the standard of utility and which was calculated to supplant his father's faith.

The mentality exemplified by Mather is represented in the *Autobiography* by Franklin's father Josiah. Franklin's ancestors, we
learn at the beginning of his memoirs, were early converts to the
Reformation, zealous in their opposition to popery and sufficiently
Puritan in outlook to keep an English Bible in defiance of Queen
Mary's edict. They remained within the Church of England, however, until the reign of Charles II, when Josiah broke with family
tradition and turned nonconformist. In 1683, he emigrated to
Massachusetts for religious reasons—conventicles being forbidden
at home by law—and sometime after his arrival he was admitted
to full communion in Boston's Old South Church. Even a cursory
reading of the *Autobiography* confirms that Josiah was a devout
Christian whose social preferences were unmistakably Puritan.
He regularly attended public worship, gave his children a strict
religious upbringing, and destined Benjamin as the tithe of his
male offspring for the service of the church. Without being pros-
perous, he was never so poor as his son implied when the latter
boasted of his own rise from "the Poverty and Obscurity in which
I was born and bred" (p. 43). A modest tradesman, Josiah discouraged Benjamin's efforts at poetry on the grounds that "Verse-
makers were generally Beggars" (p. 60). With the help of his wife
Abiah, he managed to maintain "a large Family Comfortably"—
according to the inscription on the tombstone which Benjamin
himself erected in memory of his parents (p. 56). Nor was Josiah
obscure for a man of his education and income. Prominent men
in Boston respected his judgment and fairness and often appealed

of the Present: Essays on Time and Form in American Literature (New
Haven: Yale University Press, 1969), pp. 119-52; David L. Minter's *The In-
terpreted Design as a Structural Principle in American Prose* (New Haven:
Yale University Press, 1969), pp. 77-85; Robert F. Sayre's *The Examined Self:
Benjamin, Franklin, Henry Adams, Henry James* (Princeton: Princeton Uni-
versity Press, 1964), pp. 3-43; and, in particular, James A. Sappenfield's *A
Sweet Instruction: Franklin's Journalism as a Literary Apprenticeship* (Carbon-
dale: Southern Illinois University Press, 1973), pp. 178-214.

to him to mediate between contending parties. His character was captured in the epitaph supplied by his youngest son: "He was a pious and a prudent man" (p. 56).

Josiah was not, however, pious and prudent in equal degree, since for him the love of God took precedence over worldly moderation. His library was stocked with volumes of polemic divinity, and in matters of faith he showed little disposition to bend. Thus Benjamin recalled that when he lived under his father's care he was compelled to attend the church services which he afterward made it his custom to evade.

The inclusion of such material in the *Autobiography* establishes the religious and family background against which Benjamin was to revolt. The youthful Franklin portrayed in part one was intent upon repudiating the values of Boston and his immediate relations. He originally renounced *both* sides of Josiah's creed, the prudence as well as the piety, and became a skeptic and deist who engaged in "indiscriminate Disputations about Religion" which undermined his good standing with the churchgoers of his native city (p. 71). Instead of composing quarrels, he was at the center of them: he fought with both his brother and father, and incurred the enmity of the municipal authorities because of his penchant for controversy. When he quit Boston against his family's wishes, Benjamin assumed the first of the numerous identities he was to don throughout the period of his life covered in part one. He chose a persona which perfectly expressed the nature of his rebellion and forecast what he was increasingly to become: a sinner with an appetite for the lusts of the flesh. He brashly told the captain of the sloop that carried him to New York that he had gotten a girl pregnant and was fleeing in order to avoid having to marry her.

As the flight by ship suggests, Benjamin tended to associate his rejection of his father's values with the sea. According to the *Autobiography,* his earliest differences with Josiah arose over his desire to become a sailor, a desire which his father, having already lost one son in this fashion, was determined to prevent. He was bound over to his brother James at the age of twelve precisely in order to frustrate his urge to ship before the mast. Allusions to water tend to crop up in the *Autobiography* whenever Benjamin is reprimanded by his father or the two of them disagree. Every

reader will recall the famous incident in which he was punished
for stealing some workmen's stones in order to build a wharf. Even
his penchant for poetry, of which Josiah cured him by raising the
spectre of beggary, fits into this pattern. He refers to two ballads
of his own composition: one, entitled the *Light House Tragedy*,
contained the account of a drowning, while the other consisted of
a description of the seizure and execution of the famous pirate,
Blackbeard. And Franklin first mentions his fondness for swimming
in speaking of his refusal to enter his father's business of chandlery:
"I dislik'd the Trade and had a strong inclination for the Sea;
but my Father declared against it; however, living near the Water,
I was much in and about it, [and] learnt early to swim well" (p.
53).

Franklin devoted himself to "forgetting Boston as much I could"
(p. 79), and he thoroughly identified his birthplace with his father's
beliefs. Once having made his way by sea to Philadelphia, he
continued to shed his Puritan inheritance. His friendship with John
Collins reflected this process inasmuch as Collins represented the
first of the cautionary doubles in whom he was to see his own
transgressions magnified and with whom he was to enjoy a brief
intimacy. Collins was as bookish as Franklin and the closest friend
he had in Boston; when they moved to Philadelphia, they lived
together in the same house. Collins borrowed money from Franklin
which he was unable to repay; Franklin broke into the money
he was holding for Vernon and only managed to repay it after
several years had elapsed. But Collins' deterioration—he was so
often drunk that he was unable to hold a regular job—was a constant reminder of Josiah's reproaches, and made a falling-out between the two young men inevitable.

In the printer Keimer, Franklin subsequently found an older
model who was neither pious nor prudent, and in whose presence
he freely indulged the habits his real father abhorred. Like Benjamin himself, Keimer was a poet, albeit an indifferent one, and
he originally hired the young Bostonian to help him set the type
for an elegy. He was also a religious enthusiast who invited Franklin
to be his colleague in forming a new sect. Since he loved to quarrel,
he and his employee had many arguments, the younger man
invariably outwitting the older with his Socratic method. Josiah

Franklin had little interest in food but rather made use of meal times to improve the minds of his children. Keimer, in contrast, was a glutton and womanizer who was incapable of resisting "the Flesh Pots of Egypt" (p. 89).

As he grew more intimate with Keimer, Franklin's relations with his real father apparently worsened. Josiah was dubious about his son's maturity and refused to lend him the money he needed to open a printing shop of his own. He admonished Benjamin to avoid the "lampooning and libelling to which he thought I had too much Inclination" (p. 83). The almost inevitable upshot was that Franklin once again took to the sea and sailed for England in the company of his friend James Ralph, thereby reversing the course that Josiah had followed when he fled the Old World in order to enjoy Congregational liberties in the New World. If Boston represented Puritanism and parental restraint, London was to become identified in the *Autobiography* with theological and personal irresponsibility. Franklin was further to associate such irresponsibility with his companion, Ralph, who now took the place of Collins as a cautionary double.

Ralph was an extreme version of the youthful Franklin. He was a poet, but unlike his friend who tried in vain to dissuade him, he was resolved to earn his livelihood by writing verse. His morals were as lax as his religious views, and when he went to England he left behind a wife and child whom he intended to desert. Thus he was doing in fact what Franklin had only pretended to do at the time he left Boston, when he made up the story about abandoning a pregnant girl. But the resemblance went even deeper than that, since in leaving Philadelphia for London, Franklin was actually deserting his wife-to-be, Deborah Read. The two young men were growing so close as to be virtually interchangeable. This process of identification was already well under way in Philadelphia where Franklin, at Ralph's request, had palmed off the latter's verses as his own. London simply accelerated the process, for once abroad the Americans proved to be "inseparable Companions" and took lodgings in the same house in Little Britain (p. 95). They acquired the habit of spending their evenings together at places of amusement, with the result that Franklin regularly exhausted his weekly earnings and was unable to save enough to pay for

passage home. It was also in London that he composed the deist
pamphlet, *A Dissertation on Liberty and Necessity, Pleasure and
Pain*, which he later came to regard as an erratum. He dedicated
the pamphlet to Ralph.

Eventually Franklin's identification with Ralph became all but
complete. Unable to find employment in London, Ralph went to
Berkshire to teach at a country school, and deeming such work
beneath him, according to Franklin, "he chang'd his Name, and
did me the Honour to assume mine" (p. 98). The man bearing
the name Benjamin Franklin, in short, was now James Ralph;
and soon after Ralph left the city, Franklin attempted familiarities
with his friend's mistress, as if under the impression that the change
of identities was more than a matter of names. When Mrs. T.
repulsed his advances and informed her lover of them, Ralph
terminated the friendship and used the breach as an excuse for
refusing to repay the sums he had borrowed. Whereupon Franklin
confessed that "in the Loss of his friendship I found myself reliev'd
from a Burthen" (p. 99). The burden was the part of himself that
identified with Ralph.

What ensued was a reaction to Ralph and Ralph's ways which
impelled Franklin in the direction of asceticism and ethical preci-
sion. He now began to practice an austerity that far exceeded his
father's and almost severed his ties to society. One incident in
particular in the *Autobiography* shows Franklin in his new ascetic
role. He declined to contribute a second time to his fellow workmen's fund for drink and was excommunicated for his singularity.
The lesson he drew from the experience was "the Folly of being
on ill Terms with those one is to live with continually" (p. 100)
—a lesson in prudence and accommodation that Josiah had endeavored to impress upon his son long ago.

Surely it is no accident that at this time Franklin gave up the
lodgings he had formerly shared with Ralph in order to take rooms
near a "Romish chapel" (p. 101). Having scouted the sins of excess
in the presence of his friend, he now tested the extreme of otherworldliness represented by the monastic strain in Roman Catholicism. The connection between his needlessly stubborn stand for
principle with his fellow compositors and the monkish excesses
of the Catholic religion is highlighted by the fact that the workmen

were accustomed, so Franklin disclosed in both the text and a footnote, to refer to the printing house as a "chapel" (p. 101). While situated at his new lodgings, moreover, he visited an English Catholic spinster who dwelt in the garret of the same house and who had vowed to "lead the life of a Nun as near as might be done" in a country without nunneries. She had donated her estate to charity and renounced her fellowship in society, limiting outside contact to a priest who confessed her each day. Franklin, though he admired her frugality, drew back from the otherworldly isolation which such extreme fidelity to principle produced.

He was now ready to return to Philadelphia and accept his father's social philosophy without adopting his religion. What he was on the verge of embracing, in other words, was the inner-worldly asceticism of Puritanism shorn of its theological framework. He made the transition all the more easily because he had been taken under the protection of a father figure who practiced the Puritan business ethic but appeared to have little interest in religion—albeit that he was nominally a Quaker. This agent of secular conversion was the merchant, Thomas Denham, whom the young man professed to love. Denham persuaded Franklin to accompany him to America, the prospects there being better than in England. He is described in the *Autobiography* almost exclusively in terms of his material achievement and financial probity, and Franklin delineates his character by recounting how he had recovered from bankruptcy and paid back every creditor the full amount outstanding with interest. The difference between Denham and the elder Franklin is perfectly illustrated by the fact that the merchant emigrated to the New World in order to recoup his fortune, whereas Josiah had come for the sake of religion.

It was while he was with Denham at sea on the way to Philadelphia that Franklin drew up his plan for the conduct of his life, a plan, according to the *Autobiography*, which still regulated his behavior in old age. The plan itself is not printed in the book, and only the preamble and heads have been preserved, but these are sufficient to show that Franklin was more conversant with Puritan usage than is commonly assumed. He commented on the confusion and lack of fixed design which had characterized his life prior to 1726, the year of his return to America, and he added that since he was "now entering upon a new one," he wished to form a "scheme of action, that, henceforth, I may live in all respects like a rational creature." A new life founded on order and purpose, where formerly all had been chaos—the similarities to a conversion experience are evident. The difference, of course, is that grace played no part in Franklin's rebirth; the virtues he resolved to acquire were purely secular. With the exception of piety, however, they were identical to the virtues which he commemorated on the tombstone of his parents: thrift, honesty, industry, and a spirit of conciliation.[30]

Franklin summed up his relationship with Thomas Denham by saying that the merchant "counsell'd me as a Father" (p. 107), and in submitting to the older man's guidance he was implicitly making a partial peace with Josiah. The organization of the *Autobiography* supports this conclusion, for it reveals a new attitude on Franklin's part toward swimming, a sport he had associated with his rejection of his father's values. During the very period when he made up his mind to return to America, he was offered a handsome remuneration if he would teach swimming to a nobleman's two sons. The overture convinced him "that if I were to remain in England and open a Swimming School, I might get a good deal of Money"; but he was steadfast in his resolution to accompany Denham and informed the nobleman that he was unable to comply (pp. 105-6). While the Franklin of the memoirs rejected swimming as a physical activity, however, he began to relate it metaphorically to business in general and financial solvency in particular. In describing the printers with whom he worked at Watts's, for example, he dwelt on their addiction to beer and the expense of the habit: "And thus these poor devils keep themselves always under" (p. 100). Somewhat later, speaking of a trip he and Keimer had taken to New Jersey to print paper money, he said that the sum paid for the work enabled his employer "to keep his Head much longer above Water" (p. 112). As such examples suggest, swimming and material success were becoming

30. Benjamin Franklin, *Papers of Benjamin Franklin*, 19 vols. to date, ed. Leonard W. Labaree et al. (New Haven: Yale University Press, 1959–), 1:99–100.

synonymous in Franklin's mind at this period of his life. Reconciled by Thomas Denham to his father's Protestant ethic but not to his piety, he was hereafter to confine his "swimming" to business. In the *Autobiography*, he never again mentions his proficiency in the actual sport, and in part two he announces that he spent no further time "in Taverns, Games, or Frolicks of any kind" (p. 143).

The remainder of part one documents Franklin's transformation into Max Weber's rational capitalist. Repudiating his religious heresies, he took the lead in forming the Junto, a sect of an altogether different order from the one he had launched with Keimer. Membership in the Junto was limited to an apostolic twelve, and the rules strictly forbade warmth of expression or an argumentative tone. Without withdrawing from society, Franklin embarked on a regimen almost as ascetic as that of the English nun. He dressed plainly, allowed himself no diversions beyond an occasional book, and took care to acquire the appearance as well as the substance of an industrious and frugal character. He also undertook to repair his numerous "errata" by discharging his debt to Vernon—here the example of Denham could not have been far from his mind—and marrying Deborah Read.

Franklin's forsaking of his former ways is underscored by his experience with Meredith, the last of the doubles from whom he separates in the course of part one. Meredith resembled the Franklin of old in that he was a disappointment to his father because of the bad habits he seemed powerless to break. As with Collins, his besetting vice was drink, a weakness that threatened to drag Franklin into bankruptcy when the two friends entered into a business partnership. When Meredith persisted in his drinking to their mutual discredit, Benjamin dissolved the partnership and assumed sole control of the business. In casting off Meredith, he was figuratively shedding the vestiges of that part of himself which had first rebelled against Josiah nearly fifteen years earlier. Part one thus comes to an end with Franklin in full sympathy with his father's social values, a diligent and prudent young man bent on prosperity. In his own suggestive words, "I went on swimmingly" (p. 126).

———————•·———————

Part one of the *Autobiography* belongs to the genre of confessional literature. In the manner, say, of Saint Augustine's *Confessions*, it tells the story of a young man's gradual disenchantment with sin—which Franklin called errata—and his painful conversion to the philosophy which was to guide him through life.[31] There are differences, however; most obvious is that Augustine converted to Christianity, whereas Franklin had as little use for conventional religion at the conclusion of part one as he had had at the beginning. In part two, accordingly, he addressed himself to the task of spelling out the precise nature of the creed to which he had given his allegiance, and he replaced Christianity with his table of virtues.

By virtue Franklin did not mean, as Jonathan Edwards meant, love of being in general. He meant instead a policy of enlightened self-interest such as Edwards, his exact contemporary, had defined as disguised self-love. He expounded his scheme for personal success through "the practice of Virtue, or what in the religious Stile are called Good Works" (p. 167)—an equation which the truly religious would have found abhorrent. Franklin wished to inspire the youth of America to emulate the industry, temperance, and frugality which had characterized his ascent to prosperity and eminence. He saw the Republic's collective destiny mirrored in his own success, and he was persuaded that his system of secular values was more relevant to the needs of "a *rising* people" than the outmoded Calvinism of churchmen like Edwards (p. 135).

There is no little significance in the fact that Franklin settled on thirteen virtues rather than ten or fifteen. The most obvious explanation is that four cycles of thirteen conveniently total fifty-two, the number of weeks in a year. According to Franklin, however, his original list contained only twelve virtues, and he did not add the thirteenth until admonished by a friend for insolence and

---

31. This accounts, incidentally, for the artful narrative technique to which writers on Franklin have recently called attention. It was a common practice in confessional literature for the author to present himself simultaneously from two points of view, looking back from the vantage of his altered consciousness upon his former unregenerate self.

pride. Only then did he include humility, giving as its precept "Imitate Jesus and Socrates" (p. 150).

Less than humble motives may well have entered into Franklin's calculations. He probably wanted to remind his readers of the thirteen colonies and to dramatize his identification of the nation with himself. To Franklin's contemporaries, who were steeped in the Scriptures, there was nothing unusual about the idea of representative men. They were familiar with the Old Testament method of recounting the affairs of an entire people as those of a single individual, the tribal patriarch. They had also been taught by their ministry that the community of believers has its corporate identity in Christ. And they knew from such classics of ecclesiastical history as Mather's *Magnalia* that the life of each saint exemplifies in miniature the collective epic of society. "I shall now invite my reader," Mather had written, "to behold at once the *wonders* of *New-England*, and it is in one Thomas Hooker that he shall behold them."[32]

In Mather's hagiographies, the hallmark of the saint is his conformity to Christ. In his table of virtues, Franklin adopted and radically revised this fundamental Christian concept. The twelve original virtues, with the addition of "Imitate Jesus," pointedly recall the apostles and the Savior, but Franklin's Christ was a very different figure from the Christ of Mather or Edwards. In an early piece entitled "Dialogue between Two Presbyterians," Franklin, speaking in the person of Socrates, ascribed to Jesus his own beliefs. "Our Savior," he argued, "was a Teacher of Morality or Virtue" who recommended faith only as "a Means to obtain that End." Thus was Christianity emptied of its spiritual significance. In the *Autobiography*, the historic ideal of *imitatio Christi* was transformed by Franklin into the injunction to imitate himself.[33]

———— • ————

In the threefold division of the Puritan sermon, as preached in America in the eighteenth century, the second section announced the minister's "Doctrine" and the third expounded the "Applica-

32. Mather, *Magnalia*, 1: 302–3.
33. Franklin, *Papers*, 2: 29–30.

tion" or "Uses." So with Franklin's *Autobiography*. By 1788, when
he again resumed writing, he had returned to Philadelphia for
good. Part three demonstrates the effectiveness of his creed in
action, while it also shows a renewed acquaintance with American
realities.

The decades covered in part three witnessed the greatest out-
pouring of religious fervor in the history of the colonies. It is
apparent that the Great Awakening was not without its influence
on Franklin. On the first page of the third installment, he proposed
"Raising an United Party for Virtue" to be composed of the good
and wise men of all nations, thus anticipating Jonathan Edwards's
appeal for the visible union of God's people. Franklin candidly
labeled his United Party for Virtue a sect, and the evangelical
cast with which he endowed it obviously owed much to the pietistic
stirrings of the age (pp. 161-63). Although the demands of business
forced him to abandon his plan, he maintained a continuing interest
in the revivals which swept America throughout the century. In
part three, he makes a point of calling attention to the extraordinary number of revivalists who crossed his path. Six ministers
appear in this section, and others are mentioned by name: with
the exception of Edwards, they include some of the leading divines
of the period, among them Gilbert Tennent and George Whitefield.
It was against such figures that Franklin measured—and encouraged
his readers to measure as well—his success as a doer of good.[34]

Even as he sought to divest himself of his orthodox heritage,
Franklin remained in its debt. His secular teachings, as com-
municated through such vehicles as *Poor Richard's Almanack* (and
the *Autobiography* itself), were calculated to foster the bourgeois
habits of industry and thrift; for only by acquiring such habits,
he believed, could the average citizen procure the modicum of
wealth without which a virtuous carriage remained a shadowy
ideal—"it being more difficult for a Man in Want to act always
honestly" (p. 164). Franklin's reasoning invites comparison to the

34. The most thorough treatment of Franklin's attitude toward the Calvinist
clergy is Melvin H. Buxbaum's *Benjamin Franklin and the Zealous Presbyterians* (University Park: Pennsylvania State University Press, 1975). Buxbaum argues, wrongly I believe, that although Franklin long bickered with the religious
establishment, he suppressed his anticlerical feelings in the *Autobiography*.

social thought of the emigrant Puritans, whose mentor William
Perkins had long ago voiced a preference for the middle class. But
whereas Perkins had believed that the middling sort—as opposed
to beggars or the rich—were the more apt to be saved and numbered
among the saints, Franklin was convinced that they were the backbone of a virtuous citizenry.

This consideration took on special urgency when Franklin con-
templated the future of America. Believing that the survival of
freedom depended upon the virtue of a nation's people, he composed his most sustained panegyric on behalf of the middling folk,
Information for Those Who Would Remove to America, in late
1782 or 1783, at a time when independence was assured. Prospective
emigrants were showering him with enquiries about conditions in
the New World. Franklin replied by picturing America as a land
of labor and opportunity where a "general Mediocrity of Fortune"
prevailed, and he warned away both the idle pauper and the useless
aristocrat who had "no other Quality to recommend him but his
Birth."[35] While such sentiments were commonplace enough among
the French physiocrats who flocked to Passy, they had a precedent
nearer to home in the literature of dissuasion that had issued from
Plymouth during the early years of the settlement. The *Information for Those Who Would Remove to America*, with its paean
to "Happy Mediocrity," can be read as an eighteenth-century restate-
ment of Robert Cushman's 1621 discourse on "The Sin and Danger
of Self-Love," in which Cushman had written off "beggary and
gentry" as equally unwanted in the New World.[36]

35. Benjamin Franklin, *The Writings of Benjamin Franklin*, ed. Albert Henry
Smith, 10 vols. (New York: Macmillan Co., 1907), 8: 603–14; quotations from
pp. 605, 613.
36. Franklin differed from the physiocrats more than he agreed with them.
According to Alfred Owen Aldridge, they saw "America as a paradise of
prosperity without arduous individual labor." The *Information for Those
Who Would Remove to America*, adds Aldridge, "was written in part to
counteract such rapturous impressions as this one." See *Franklin and his
French Contemporaries* (New York: New York University Press, 1957), p.
30. Franklin's stress on frugality and economic independence was more com-
patible with the assumptions of the so-called Commonwealthmen or radical
Whigs, a group of eighteenth-century English intellectuals whose writings
helped to inspire the American Revolution. The similarity between Puritan
and Whig social ideas is discussed by Gordon S. Wood in *The Creation of the*

Franklin's secular appeal to those with middle-class aspirations
did not make him contemptuous of the competing efforts of
organized religion to foster the bourgeois virtues. Insofar as conventional creeds served to stimulate civic responsibility and to
inculcate the Puritan social ethic—his devout father, after all, had
cherished that ethic too—he approved of them and contributed
to the support of their ministers. He even continued his annual
subscription to the Presbyterian congregation of the Reverend Mr.
Andrews, and he maintained a sincere if "mere civil Friendship"
with George Whitefield until the minister's death (p. 178). He
could no more accept Whitefield's theology than his father's, and
he rebuffed the former's periodic attempts to convert him. Yet he
did not hesitate to give the great preacher his due. He was impressed
and personally stirred by Whitefield's efficacy as an orator, as
shown by the famous experiment in which he calculated that the
evangelist's stentorian voice had the range to be heard by "25000
People in the Fields" (p. 179). Since his own *Almanack,* as he
remarks in the *Autobiography,* sold ten thousand copies annually,
Whitefield's words ostensibly reached the larger audience. In view
of the minister's overpowering delivery, he might have been
expected to generate an unrivaled force for good.

Yet Franklin did not regard George Whitefield as an altogether
successful figure. The religious enthusiasm he kindled during his
infrequent visits to Philadelphia apparently had a way of waning
after his departures; by 1749, according to Franklin, the fervor
Whitefield had aroused in 1740 had "long since abated" (p. 194).
Whitefield's powers were simply too tied to his own physical
presence to result in lasting benefits. Moreover, the brilliance of
his oratory was not duplicated in his printed sermons. Filled with
erroneous facts and unguarded opinions, they exposed him to

American Republic, 1776-1787 (Chapel Hill: University of North Carolina
Press, 1969), pp. 53-70, 114-18.

The view that Americans were predominantly middle-class in the latter half
of the eighteenth century has been called into question by numerous demographic studies. It should be pointed out, however, that Franklin was articulat-
ing an ideology—an ideology whose appeal may have derived from its insistence on American uniqueness and middle-class homogeneity at the very
period when America was ceasing to be either socially homogeneous or particularly unique in comparison to Europe.

violent sectarian criticism and ultimately decreased the number of his followers. *"Litera scripta manet,"* Franklin tersely observes: the written word endures, and in the case of Whitefield it endured to his permanent discredit (p. 180). In reading such a passage, we are apt to think of Franklin's own success as a writer and propagandist, to which he called repeated attention. Though Franklin also committed errata, he was flexible enough to confess and correct them; the zealous Whitefield's published mistakes were the cause of his decline.

Franklin's prudence thus proved a more effective means of advancing the social welfare than the evangelist's piety. While revivalists and other clergymen were busy spreading religion, and often embroiling themselves in disputes over doctrinal niceties, Franklin was hard at work disseminating his secular gospel and bettering the lives of his countrymen—spreading citizenship and progress, as it were. In these endeavors he had no peer in the colonies, and much of part three is taken up with listing his now familiar contributions in the area of "public Affairs" (p. 173). Even ministers had occasion to profit from his expertise. The Reverend Gilbert Tennent, second only to Edwards among native American "awakeners," appealed to Franklin for advice in the technique of fundraising. He applied Franklin's shrewd counsel with such success that "he obtain'd a much larger sum than he expected" for the construction of the Second Presbyterian Church (p. 202). The clergy obviously had more to learn from Franklin than to teach him, and their own experiences only testified to the superiority of his utilitarian ethic. Franklin himself emerges from the *Autobiography* as the embodiment of what was most constructive in the native spirit.

With the completion of part three, however, there arose a serious difficulty for Franklin—a difficulty which cannot simply be brushed aside with the explanation that the author was now an old man, past eighty, and unable to continue with his memoirs because of the infirmities of age. He terminated this section with the flat sentence, "We arrived in London the 27th of July 1757" (p. 259), and England, the scene of the worst of his youthful errata, had witnessed their recrudescence. Shortly after his arrival in London, for example, he had taken up residence with Mrs. Margaret

Stevenson, who remained his mistress for some eighteen years. He also had sought out and resumed his friendship with James Ralph, and cooperated with Ralph's wish to conceal his first marriage from his present wife. In England, then, and later in France, Franklin had systematically if privately betrayed the social and moral philosophy he was propounding in the *Autobiography*. Doubtless for this reason the brief fourth installment, which he composed during the winter of 1789-1790, carries the narrative only into the following year and casts him entirely in the role of a public figure, with no glimpse at all into his personal life. The outline in which he projected the remainder of the book consists primarily of a dry, stacatto recitation of political events: "Congress, Assembly. Committee of Safety. Chevaux de Frize. Sent to Boston, to the Camp. To Canada. to Lord Howe. To France, Treaty, &c." (p. 272). Nowhere are Franklin's ideological motives cast into bolder relief than in this monotonous catalogue. He could not go into detail about his life abroad without betraying his personal recidivism, and to do so, of course, would have been to defeat his very purpose in writing.

———◆———

The last year covered in the *Autobiography*, 1758, was also the year in which Franklin published *The Way to Wealth*. The coincidence is appropriate because the piece is a clever attack on the Calvinist clergy. It features "a plain, clean old Man" called Father Abraham who advocates at interminable length Franklin's own gospel of industry and thrift. Franklin was not making light of his teachings, however, so much as the drab method of their exposition. By putting them in the mouth of an Old Testament figure whose delivery rendered them useless, he was saying in effect that even the best of precepts could be made unpalatable if they were preached rather than taught by example. Indeed, no sooner has Father Abraham finished his discourse than his hearers proceed to practice "the contrary, just as if it had been a common Sermon."[37] But there was a serious intent beneath the satirical surface of Franklin's "sermon," and a calculated reason for his choice of

37, Franklin, *Papers*, 7: 340, 350,

Father Abraham as the spokesman for his utilitarian ethic. In the Old Testament, God covenanted with Abraham as the father of Israel, and Americans of Franklin's day regarded themselves as the descendants of the biblical Hebrews. As the new chosen people, they believed they were destined to establish a paradise on earth. Franklin was telling his countrymen that it was not God but rather his maxims for achieving prosperity that had the power to transform America into the Promised Land. "If the Lord be with a people," Cotton Mather had stated a generation earlier, "they shall prosper in all their affairs." In Franklin's revision of the covenant, *"God helps them that help themselves."* Let us practice Poor Richard's virtues, he advised his readers, if we wish to prosper both individually and as a people.[38]

Not all Americans were ready, however, to accept Poor Richard's proverbs as a national orthodoxy. Franklin's harshest critics included the American romancers, and they had good reason to fear the spread of his ideas. Prizing progress above all else, he assumed the primacy of an economic individualism which devalued all "other modes of thought, feeling and action"[39]—including spiritual salvation, the joys of recreation, and artistic achievement. If the principle of delayed gratification, the crown of Franklin's system, built libraries and paved the streets, it also denied man's deepest needs. Its inevitable consequence was the faceless, dehumanized public servant of the last pages of the *Autobiography*, the Franklin whom Melville called "the type and genius of his land" and whose spirit still broods over America.

Despite the cosmopolitan elements of his thought, Franklin remained—in Carl Becker's words—"pungently American,"[40] and his greatest impact was upon America's social and cultural traditions. The famous scene of his entrance into Philadelphia is reminiscent of William Bradford's equally famous description of his arrival at

38. Mather, *The Way to Prosperity* (1690), in *The Wall and the Garden: Selected Massachusetts Election Sermons, 1670–1775*, ed. A. W. Plumstead (Minneapolis: University of Minnesota Press, 1968), p. 124; Franklin, *Papers*, 7: 341.

39. The phrase is used by Ian Watt in *The Rise of the Novel* (Berkeley: University of California Press, 1957), p. 64.

40. *Dictionary of American Biography*, s.v. "Benjamin Franklin."

Plymouth after the *Mayflower*'s stormy crossing to America. Both men paused in later life to call attention to the moment: Franklin, poor, dirty, and worn out from his journey, knowing no soul "nor where to look for Lodging," asked his readers to "compare such unlikely Beginnings with the Figure I have since made there" (p. 75). Bradford wrote that

> here I cannot but stay and make a pause, and stand half amazed at this poor people's present condition; and so I think will the reader, too, when he well considers the same. Being thus passed the vast ocean, and a sea of troubles before in their preparation . . . they had now no friends to welcome them nor inns to entertain or refresh their weatherbeaten bodies; no houses nor much less towns to repair to, to seek for succour.

Where could these weary pilgrims turn for sustenance, Bradford cried, but to "the Spirit of God and His Grace"? Franklin emphasized the contrast between his humble origins and his present eminence in order to dramatize his material ascent and dazzle the youth of "a *rising* people" with the utility of his acquisitive ethic; Bradford, praising the Lord for his mercies to a generation in adversity, implored "the children of these fathers" to remember Him for "His loving kindness and His wonderful works before the sons of men."[41] The difference in their appeals brings starkly into focus the displacement of a vision of piety and prudence by a narrowed creed of prudence alone. Franklin himself made this point in *The Way to Wealth* when he struck off an aphorism which recapitulates the whole of his philosophy: "*In the Affairs of this World*," he had Father Abraham say, paraphrasing from the *Almanack*, "*Men are saved, not by Faith, but by the Want of it*."[42]

41. William Bradford, *Of Plymouth Plantation*, ed. Samuel Eliot Morison (New York: Alfred A. Knopf, 1952), pp. 61–63.
42. Franklin, *Papers*, 7: 344.

IV

Nathaniel Hawthorne

Hawthorne has been much celebrated, in the phrase of one critic, as a "champion of the middle way." According to this school of thought, he conceived of the "good life" as lying "midway between the extremes in an acceptance of the normal" and was a staunch "advocate of moderation, even of pedestrianism."[1] Another school of thought, however, finds Hawthorne's fiction singularly barren of synthesis, and pictures him as "a dualist of good and evil" whose "only reconciliation is acceptance of life's differences and contradictions." According to this view, his art furnishes a classic illustration of the Manichean sensibility which is the legacy of Puritanism to the American literary imagination.[2] These two approaches or variations thereof, which have tended to dominate Hawthorne scholarship over the past century, have naturally given rise to a host of conflicting interpretations. They need not be seen as mutually exclusive, however, since they both call attention to important and even complementary aspects of his work. We can gain some idea of the relationship between Hawthorne's proclivity for moderation and his impulse toward radical extremes if we glance briefly at the sketch of Benjamin Franklin that he included in his *Biographical Stories for Children* (1842).

1. Chester E. Eisinger, "Hawthorne as Champion of the Middle Way," *New England Quarterly* 27 (1954): 29–30, 52.
2. Richard Harter Fogle, *Hawthorne's Fiction: The Light and the Dark*, rev. ed. (Norman: University of Oklahoma Press, 1964), pp. 132–33, 220.

This slim volume, intended, as its title indicates, for the perusal of juvenile readers, proves a surprisingly rich introduction to a number of themes which persist throughout Hawthorne's writings. It is built around a simple formal device. Young Edward Temple, afflicted with a sight disorder at the age of eight or nine, is instructed by his physician to bandage his eyes and keep to a darkened chamber. Unable to read, he is told stories by his father about the childhoods of famous men and women in the hope that he will learn "to see things within [his] own mind."[3] The book, in short, is about the growth of the imagination, and it inevitably brings to mind Henry James's famous remark concerning "Hawthorne's cat-like faculty of seeing in the dark."[4]

Hawthorne's sketch of Franklin is among the least complimentary in the *Biographical Stories*. The fact that it directly follows his description of Oliver Cromwell suggests a decline in stature, since the portraits are not otherwise arranged in chronological order. While Hawthorne shows a sympathetic understanding of the Calvinist saints who spearheaded the English Revolution, depicting Cromwell in particular as a champion of brotherhood and equality, his contempt for Franklin is barely disguised by a mask of qualified respect. The future sage, who gives the appearance even in boyhood of holding "very sagacious opinions," is first employed at his father's trade of making candles; and "thus, you see, in his early days, as well as in his manhood, his labors contributed to throw light upon dark matters." As a foe of darkness and mystery for whom light means only "enlightenment," Franklin is the very antithesis of the artist. He is forever going on about "schemes for the public benefit," and Hawthorne recounts the incident of his stealing the workmen's stones in order to build a wharf for his playmates. Franklin's reasoning in justification of the theft is the crassest utilitarianism:

3. Nathaniel Hawthorne, *Biographical Stories for Children*, in *The Works of Nathaniel Hawthorne*, Centenary Edition, ed. William Charvat et al. (Columbus: Ohio State University Press, 1962-), vol. 6, *True Stories from Biography and History* (1972), p. 220.
4. Henry James, *Hawthorne* (1879; London: Macmillan and Co., 1887), p. 99.

You see these stones. The workmen mean to use them for the underpinning of a house; but that would be for only one man's advantage. My plan is, to take these same stones and carry them to the edge of the water, and build a wharf with them. This will not only enable us to carry on the fishing business with comfort, and to better advantage, but it will likewise be a great convenience to boats, passing up and down the stream. Thus, instead of one man, fifty, or a hundred, or a thousand, besides ourselves, may be benefitted by these stones.

Franklin, according to Hawthorne, is the soul of the enterprise, contrives methods to "lighten" the labors of his schoolfellows, and brings the project to successful completion. It occurs to none of his friends, and to himself least of all, to question the justice and propriety of "building a wharf, with stones that belonged to another person."[5]

It does, however, occur to the master mason, who is one of those "unreasonable" persons who jealously guards his rights and privileges and who hastens to report the theft to Ben's father. When Ben pleads the public welfare in his own defence, Josiah admonishes his son that it is a moral wrong "to violate what is eternally right for the sake of a seeming expediency." This lesson, which conveys something of the heritage of Puritanism to the Enlightenment, is said to make a lasting impression on Ben, whose subsequent rise to fame and riches is swiftly summarized. Yet at the end of the tale, when Edward asks his father why Franklin became so celebrated, Mr. Temple attributes his reputation almost entirely to Poor Richard's proverbs. Edward, the incipient romancer, protests that he doesn't care for Franklin's maxims, which are "all about getting money, or saving it," and Mr. Temple agrees that "they teach men but a very small portion of their duties."[6]

Mr. Temple's remark goes to the source of Hawthorne's attitude toward Franklin and the whole system of values that he represents —thrift, moderation, business acumen, and the substitution of the standard of utility for the rule of right. As Mr. Temple observes, Poor Richard's proverbs do teach men a part of their duties, and

5. Hawthorne, *Biographical Stories for Children*, Centenary Edition, 6: 263–66.
6. Ibid., pp. 269–71, 274.

"they were suited to the condition of the country" at the time of their popularization.[7] Once enshrined as absolutes in the national pantheon, however, they come into conflict with the imagination and pose a threat to the survival of the Puritan vision treasured by Cromwell and Josiah alike. Brotherhood, after all, is a very different thing from a mindless idolatry of the public and its putative "benefit," and if expediency and the commonplace have their uses, they have their dangers as well.

Hawthorne's thinking here is perfectly illustrated by his treatment of two characters in *The House of the Seven Gables:* Judge Jaffrey Pyncheon and Uncle Venner. For all their differences, the two have much in common. It is not by chance, after all, that they make their respective appearances in the same chapter of the book, appropriately entitled "A Day Behind the Counter." Both are firm believers in the philosophy of Poor Richard, and share the conviction that it behooves an eminent man in a republic to adopt an air of humility, apologizing, "as it were, to the people, for [one's] wealth, prosperity, and elevated station."[8] The Judge has an imposing country seat where he spends what time he can spare from public service. Uncle Venner speaks of retiring to his "farm," by which he means the public workhouse, and passing his last years there in well-deserved leisure. Venner, indeed, is presented as almost a caricature of Franklin, and since he is both ancient and poor, it seems likely that Hawthorne patterned him directly after Father Abraham and Poor Richard. He is said to have pretensions to "no little wisdom," and he favors Hepzibah with "sage counsel" and "golden maxims" which smack of *The Way to Wealth:* "Give no credit! . . . Never take paper money! Look well to your change!" and so forth.[9]

If Venner represents the harmless side of Franklin's creed, however, the Judge's career is proof of its more insidious implications.

7. Ibid., p. 274.
8. Nathaniel Hawthorne, *The House of the Seven Gables,* in *The Works of Nathaniel Hawthorne,* Centenary Edition, ed. William Charvat et al. (Columbus: Ohio State University Press, 1962-), vol. 2 (1965), pp. 63, 108.
9. Ibid., pp. 61, 65. Daniel Hoffman has noted some of the resemblances between Venner, Judge Pyncheon, and Franklin. See *Form and Fable in American Fiction* (New York: Oxford University Press, 1965), p. 200, n. 4.

As the parallels between them suggest, moreover, Venner's "wisdom" helped to spawn the Judge and his ilk. Jaffrey has all the worst traits of Franklin and none of his virtues: he carries Poor Richard's gospel to monstrous lengths. He is immersed in financial transactions, thoroughly identified with the rampant commercialism of the age, and driven by an insatiable desire to amass riches—riches, as Hepzibah reminds him in vain, for which he can no longer have any possible use. He is reputed to "be as close-fisted as if his gripe were made of iron." A zealous doer of good who takes care to maintain a front of "unimpeachable integrity," he is active in such civic projects as the "Widow's and Orphan's fund" and the local temperance movement. Like Franklin himself, he suffers from the gout and is distinguished for the "snowy whiteness of his linen." And he is in line for the governorship of Massachusetts, an indication, as Henry Nash Smith points out, that "business interests are already in control of society."[10]

Hawthorne's portrait of the Judge brings into focus his deepest fears concerning the virtual deification of Franklin's ethic in mid-nineteenth-century America. It also helps to explain why his romances have generated such conflicting readings. The "pedestrianism" of an Uncle Venner has its place in that America, Hawthorne believes, and he rewards the "venerable" old soul by including him in the triumphant party of survivors who will shortly assume possession of the Judge's wealth. But at the same time he grasped the existential tension at the core of Puritan thought, and he gave it priority over the social and political creed whose apotheosis threatened its extinction. What has been called Hawthorne's Manicheanism is in reality his attempt to break free of the confines of the national cult of "getting money, or saving it" that Franklin helped inspire and that assumes grotesque proportions in the Judge. Hawthorne is indeed a "champion of the middle way," but by "middle way," as we shall see, he did not mean the sagacious pieties of a Benjamin Franklin. He meant instead the

10. Hawthorne, *House of the Seven Gables*, Centenary Edition, 2: 122, 230–31; Henry Nash Smith, "The Morals of Power: Business Enterprise as a Theme in Mid-Nineteenth-Century American Fiction," in *Essays on American Literature in Honor of Jay B. Hubbell*, ed. Clarence Gohdes (Durham, N.C.: Duke University Press, 1967), p. 96.

vision of inner-worldly sainthood which was carried to New England by the emigrants of whom he wrote in his first full-length work of fiction, *The Scarlet Letter*.

The Scarlet Letter

Hawthorne's "Introductory" to *The Scarlet Letter* has been a source of puzzlement to readers since the book's appearance in 1850. Although its importance as a statement of literary theory is readily conceded, its connection to the romance proper still remains something of a mystery after a century of critical exegesis.[11] The mystery is more apparent than real, however, and one way to unravel it is to bear in mind that the action of the romance is set at the time of the founding of Massachusetts Bay. The work that ushers in the decade commonly known as the American Renaissance begins, in other words, with an extended look in the direction of the Puritan past. And it begins with an autobiographical sketch which relates Hawthorne's own undertaking as an artist to the usages and theology of the first generation Puritans whose world he sought to re-create.

Two influences in particular seem to have shaped Hawthorne's thinking in "The Custom-House," and the first of these is the Gospel of Matthew. Hawthorne makes at least two explicit references to the apostle, alluding to him directly in the "Introductory" and then quoting from his Gospel in accounting for Pearl's name,

11. Attempts to relate Hawthorne's preface to the action and characters of the story have been made by many critics. Of special interest is Nina Baym's *The Shape of Hawthorne's Career* (Ithaca: Cornell University Press, 1976), pp. 123–51. Baym draws an intriguing parallel between Hawthorne's artistry and Hester's defiance of society. I have also found useful the studies by Paul John Eakin, "Hawthorne's Imagination and the Structure of 'The Custom-House,' " *American Literature* 43 (1971): 346–58; Charles Feidelson, *Symbolism and American Literature* (Chicago: University of Chicago Press, 1953), pp. 6–16; Frank MacShane, "The House of the Dead: Hawthorne's Custom House and *The Scarlet Letter*," *New England Quarterly* 35 (1962): 93–101; Joel Porte, *The Romance in America: Studies in Cooper, Poe, Hawthorne, Melville, and James* (Middletown, Conn.: Wesleyan University Press, 1969), pp. 98–114; and Larzer Ziff, "The Ethical Dimension of 'The Custom-House,' " *Modern Language Notes* 73 (1958): 338–44.

"as being of great price" (p. 89).[12] His indebtedness to Matthew is hardly surprising in light of the fact that the apostle was also employed in a custom-house. Indeed, Hawthorne follows the Scriptures in describing Matthew as seated at the receipt of custom. General Miller, the single custom-house officer who quickens Hawthorne's imagination and commands his respect, is the Collector of Revenue. Slowed by age and infirmity, he is pictured as spending his days seated "in his customary chair beside the fireplace" (p. 20). Hawthorne indulges a similar habit when he retires to his study at the Old Manse. He is fond of sitting and musing beside the coal fire whose genial glow supplies the element of human warmth necessary to the composition of his romances. It is noteworthy, too, that Matthew leaves the custom-house upon being called to his mission by Jesus with the words "Follow me" (9:9). Jesus' command and the apostle's willing compliance are twice echoed in the course of Hawthorne's personal sketch: first by General Miller's response, "I'll try, Sir!" (p. 23), on being ordered to take a British battery during the War of 1812; and then again by Hawthorne himself when he says "I will" to the ghost of his ancient predecessor, Mr. Surveyor Pue, whom he imagines exhorting him to tell the story of Hester Prynne (p. 33). A parallel is accordingly established between the apostle, the author, and the old General, one notable consequence of which is to relate Hawthorne's role as an artist to the religious imperative to imitate Christ.

This brings us to the second and major source that Hawthorne was drawing upon in the "Introductory," and it is a source that figures importantly in the romance as well. Much of the drama of *The Scarlet Letter* turns, after all, on the dilemma of whether the Reverend Mr. Dimmesdale will confess his complicity in the adultery of Hester Prynne: whether he will bring himself to make a public relation of his secret sin.[13] And the crucial point to be

---

12. Nathaniel Hawthorne, *The Scarlet Letter*, in *The Works of Nathaniel Hawthorne*, Centenary Edition, ed. William Charvat et al. (Columbus: Ohio State University Press, 1962-), vol. 1 (1962). All quotations are from this edition; page references are included in the text.

13. Henry James was the first to focus on Dimmesdale (*Hawthorne*, pp. 107-22). James's lead has been followed by, among others, Roy R. Male,

made about the preface is that it derives its structure from the
Puritan practice of requiring the candidate for visible sainthood
to make a narration of his spiritual autobiography. Hawthorne's
self-portrait, in short, has all the earmarks of what the Puritans
called a confession of saving grace.

The confession procedure adopted by the New England colonists
conformed to specific rules that became standardized during the
first decade of settlement. Every American Calvinist who underwent conversion and made a relation of his experience was assumed
to have passed through a number of stages on the route from
sin to holiness. As formulated by William Perkins, the "morphology
of conversion" consisted of ten steps, the crucial ones being
humiliation, despair and assurance.[14] Although under Congregationalism wording differed from church to church, no confession
was considered complete unless it included an acknowledgment of
inability on the part of the believer—an acknowledgment, that
is to say, of his depravity—and a conviction, however imperfect,
that he had been reborn through the agency of Christ. To judge
from the irritation of Thomas Shepard, a confessor might sometimes abuse the custom by entertaining his church with a voluble
account of his conversion. Shepard responded by laying down the
bare outlines of an acceptable relation:

> Thus I was humbled, then thus I was called, then thus I have
> walked, though with many weaknesses since, and such special
> providences of God I have seen, temptations gone through, and
> thus the Lord hath delivered me, blessed be his Name &c.[15]

It is unlikely that Hawthorne was familiar with Shepard's prescription, but since he was steeped in Puritan literature, he would almost

---

Hawthorne's Tragic Vision (Austin: University of Texas Press, 1957), pp.
90–118; and Frederick C. Crews, *The Sins of the Fathers: Hawthorne's Psychological Themes* (New York: Oxford University Press, 1966), pp. 136–53.

14. On the morphology of conversion see Edmund S. Morgan, *Visible Saints:
The History of a Puritan Idea* (New York: New York University Press, 1963),
pp. 64–112, passim; Norman Pettit, *The Heart Prepared: Grace and Conversion in Puritan Spiritual Life* (New Haven: Yale University Press, 1966), pp.
86–124; and Darrett B. Rutman, *American Puritanism: Faith and Practice*
(Philadelphia: J. B. Lippincott Co., 1970), pp. 97–107.

15. Thomas Shepard, *The Parable of the Ten Virgins Unfolded* (1659), in
Works, 3 vols., ed. John Albro (Boston, 1853), 2: 631.

certainly have been acquainted with the general format of the confession as it was developed in New England during the seventeenth century.[16] A careful scrutiny of "The Custom-House" confirms that he was writing with the confession model in mind.

It is suggestive, for instance, that Hawthorne calls attention to the difficulty of the task that he has set himself in the preface. In order to screw up his courage to speak of his personal circumstances, he requires "some true relation with his audience"—a sense of kinship and sympathy that frees him from his native reserve without violating the sanctity of his self, the "Me behind its veil." His tone is mildly apologetic; he frankly counts on his reader's indulgence for yielding to the autobiographical impulse which has now visited him a second time. (It first possessed him "for no earthly reason" in 1846, when he prefaced his *Mosses from an Old Manse* with a sketch of his abode.) Reluctant as he is to intrude, he nevertheless proposes to share his three years' experience in the Salem Custom-House: to lay bare his private life for our "kind and apprehensive" inspection. The reason for his constraint is not far to seek: contemporary readers, even friendly ones, are not in the habit of listening to confessions (pp. 3–4).

It comes as no surprise, therefore, that Hawthorne allies himself with the past in general and the Puritan past in particular. He declares at once that his loyalties belong to a scorned and forsaken world, the Salem of his forebears, a once bustling port that has fallen into ruin and decay. And he adds that "the sentiment has likewise its moral quality" (p. 9), for unlike the merchants who flock to Boston and New York, his attachment is to a forgotten vision as well as a physical locality. The local Custom-House displays the heraldry of an eagle clutching in each claw "a bunch of intermingled thunderbolts and barbed arrows" (p. 5) and symbolizes the authority of the American republic; but it does not, as Hawthorne hastens to tell us, open "on the road to Paradise" (p. 13). In this respect, the Salem of the present resembles the

16. See Marion L. Kesselring's *Hawthorne's Reading: 1828–1850* (New York: New York Public Library, 1949), for evidence of his knowledge of Puritan literature. Hawthorne's reading included Cotton Mather's *A Companion for Communicants*, which spells out the necessary qualifications for partaking of the Lord's Supper.

Boston of the seventeenth century, whose founders, whatever their original utopianism, have made provision for a graveyard and a prison, the primal transgression having brought death and sin into the world. To Hawthorne, as to the Puritans, these are the realities of the human condition.

In a fallen world, salvation is apt to be a personal and tentative affair, subject to the willingness of the individual to avow his own fellowship in the community of sin. Thus Hawthorne invokes his ancestors William and John Hathorne, whose persecutions of the Quakers and witches have blackened the family name in the annals of New England. Although generations of shipmasters separate Hawthorne from the progenitors of his line, it is the two Puritan magistrates and not their commercial posterity that bind him to his birthplace. The guilt-stained soil of Salem holds him "as powerfully as if the natal spot were an earthly paradise": he inhabits an Eden thoroughly despoiled by ancestral sin. When he volunteers to take upon himself the family shame, he writes of the "curse" that "the dreary and unprosperous condition of the race, for many a long year back, would argue to exist" (pp. 9–11). As used here, the word "race" suggests mankind and "curse" the primal sin. Several pages later, describing the gluttonous Inspector, Hawthorne observes of him that he is sure to remember a dish "which had adorned his board in the days of the elder Adams . . . while all the subsequent experience of our race . . . had gone over him with as little permanent effect as the passing breeze" (p. 19). In this instance, "race" plainly does refer to mankind; but now Hawthorne is punning on the name "Adams." The pun resurfaces in the romance proper, during the scene in which Hester asks Pearl if she knows the meaning of the scarlet letter, and the child replies, "It is the great letter A. Thou hast taught it to me in the horn-book" (p. 178). Pearl is speaking of the alphabetical tablet that the Puritans used to teach reading. Hawthorne asserts elsewhere that as a result of her upbringing she "could have borne a fair examination in the New England Primer" (pp. 111–12). Each letter in the *Primer* was accompanied by a doggerel verse to facilitate word memorization, and the rhyme for A was the familiar "In Adam's Fall/ We sinned all." Since Hawthorne himself dons the letter in the preface, it should be clear that his subject is metaphysical as well as historical guilt, and that he has completed the first decisive step of his confession. For by assuming responsibility for inherited crime, he has given his assent to the doctrine of original sin. He alludes, it will be noticed, to crimes perpetrated long before the composition of the "Introductory" proper. His personal sketch and the ensuing romance are in substantial agreement on this score. As every reader is aware, *The Scarlet Letter* deals with the consequences of a sin committed prior to the actual events described in the text.[17]

Hawthorne's three years in the Custom-House—and his repeated emphasis on the number three is significant—mark a period of spiritual deadness which saps his character of its force and creative energy. He has lost the power to write, and he fears that he is in danger of becoming "much such another animal as the old Inspector," without a shred of moral endowment (p. 40). The Inspector offers an ominous contrast to General Miller. Stolidly ignorant of his soulless condition, he strikes Hawthorne as scarcely more human than the animal flesh on which he loves to dine: "He had no soul, no heart, no mind; nothing, as I have already said, but instincts" (p. 18). Though surprisingly sprightly for his eighty years, the old gourmand is completely at home in the spiritually dead world of the Custom-House. It is impossible, according to Hawthorne, "to conceive how he should exist hereafter, so earthly and sensuous did he seem" (p. 18). Indeed, "were he to continue in office until the end of time," he "would be just as good as he was" when Hawthorne first encountered him, "and sit down to dinner with just as good an appetite" (p. 19). He literally gives the impression of being able to live forever. Hawthorne's point is that the "permanent Inspector"—for such is his official title—will not die in order to be reborn. The past has left him untouched, the future stretches endlessly before him, and he has no existence beyond the meaningless present. His absorption in the material and his utter indifference to the spiritual side of life amount to a denial of the possibility of redemption.

The Inspector is the rule rather than the exception among the

---

17. Roy R. Male says of the adultery, "Of course it is prior; it is the literal, the Original Sin" (*Hawthorne's Tragic Vision*, p. 99).

aging figures who people the Custom-House. Hawthorne, who holds a political appointment as Surveyor, can see no way to extricate himself from his predicament by means of his own endeavor, "it being hardly in the nature of a public officer to resign." Few if any of his fellow functionaries manage to escape the baleful effects of bartering their self-reliance for employment in the service of the Republic. Once having succumbed to the temptation of "the Devil's wages," they become helpless dependents and cling to the forlorn hope of tenure in office. "This faith," according to Hawthorne, "more than anything else, steals the pith and availability out of whatever enterprise [they] may dream of undertaking." Reviewing the fate of those who toil in the Custom-House, his thoughts inevitably turn to ruin and death; he imagines the posthumous torments of the ejected officer, for whom even the grave offers no relief from the "hallucination" of being restored to office (pp. 38–39). In Calvinist terms, Hawthorne is overcome by fear of the punishment for sin. Mired in inability, he cannot save himself, and he trembles on the brink of extinction. He has touched the depths of despair that the Puritans hopefully regarded as preparatory to the infusion of grace.

And indeed his situation is not so grim as it appears, for he has before him the impressive example of gallant General Miller. What sets the General apart from the other inmates of the Custom-House is the powerful spirit that still breathes within his massive frame. Although he has slain men with his own hands and wears "the bloody laurel on his brow," he is without a trace of personal cruelty and cherishes an almost girlish fondness for flowers (pp. 22–23). It is important to notice, however, that unlike the ancient Inspector, who is in fact some ten years his senior, the General has already begun to show the signs of age. This detail, which is stressed at considerable length, suggests in part that the Collector has submitted to the ravages of time in a way that the gourmand, being oblivious to the Fall and its consequences, has not. And yet General Miller, trapped though he is in the colorless present, has not been vanquished by decay. Like Hawthorne himself, for whom "the past was not dead" (p. 27), he is rich in memories of better days. If his heroic powers are dormant, they are still capable of resurrection, and it seems to Hawthorne's fancy that

> under some excitement which should go deeply into his con-
> sciousness,—roused by a trumpet-peal, loud enough to awaken
> all of his energies that were not dead, but only slumbering,—
> he was yet capable of flinging off his infirmities like a sick man's
> gown, dropping the staff of age to seize a battle-sword, and
> starting up once more a warrior (p. 21).

Summoned by an external call, a call such as that which he answered in seizing the British battery—a call, indeed, like the one that stirred Matthew to do Jesus' bidding—the General will spring dramatically to life and sally forth from the Custom-House in the confidence that his powers are unimpaired. The inspiration of his example is not lost upon Hawthorne, for whom a similar reawakening is at hand.

Hawthorne's fear that he has thrown away his soul in exchange for becoming "a tolerably good Surveyor of the Customs" (p. 38) proves groundless, although it should be emphasized that he is spared the fate of the brutish Inspector through no effort of his own. "Providence," he says, "had meditated better things for me than I could possibly imagine for myself" (p. 40). Divinity intervenes to rescue him from the damnation of immurement in the Custom-House. With the election of General Taylor, he is expelled from office; and election, needless to say, is a theological as well as a political term. Again, there is an obvious parallel between the "Introductory" and the tale that follows, since Dimmesdale delivers an Election Sermon moments before his death on the scaffold. The parallel is heightened by Hawthorne's disclosure that the scaffold was formerly held "to be as effectual an agent in the promotion of good citizenship, as ever was the guillotine among the terrorists of France" (p. 55). In the "Introductory" he likens his own expulsion from the Custom-House to a beheading: "My own head," he exclaims, "was the first that fell" (p. 41). What is involved here is a symbolic dying to the things of this world, and the fact that Hawthorne describes that death as a form of decapitation is charged with theological significance. His reference is manifestly to John the Baptist, a figure whom he later invokes

in observing that the elaborate ruff worn by Governor Bellingham
causes the magistrate's head "to look not a little like that of John
the Baptist in a charger" (p. 108). The main Biblical source for
the familiar story of Salome demanding John's head on a platter
from Herod is Matthew 14:6–11; the episode is one of the relatively
few that disrupt the harmony of the Gospels. Since John's ministry
prepares the way for the coming of the Lord, Hawthorne's dismissal
from the Custom-House, associated as it is with the prophet's
beheading, can be viewed as preparatory to his own salvation. And
following his discharge, he does in fact claim to be "in the realm
of quiet" and to write "from beyond the grave" (p. 44).

His irony veils his meaning, but there can be little doubt that
Hawthorne has entered upon the final stage of his confession. He
dons "the crown of martyrdom" (p. 42)—an apparent allusion
to the crown of thorns placed upon Jesus' head by the Roman
soldiers in Matthew 27:29—and is restored the artistic gifts whose
loss he has interpreted throughout as the seal of perdition. The
"crown of martyrdom" further recalls the "bloody laurel" on the
General's brow, suggesting that Hawthorne, like the old soldier,
has emerged from his spiritual sleep to find his powers intact.
Heeding the summons to "Follow me," which in his case involves
complying with the request of Surveyor Pue, he resumes his life
as a man of letters, the ordeal of his three years' interment in
the Custom-House fading from his memory "like a dream" (p. 44).
On the last page of the "Introductory," his thoughts revert to
his forefathers, and he asks to be remembered as he has remembered
them. Speaking of Salem, he adds that "henceforth, it ceases to
be a reality of my life. I am a citizen of somewhere else." (p. 44).
The Calvinist framework of his personal narrative is unmistakable
in these concluding sentences. Hawthorne has attained the state
of assurance that the Puritans identified with spiritual rebirth.
He is one with the saints.

———————————•━•••———————————

In describing General Miller, Hawthorne alludes to the warrior's
remarkable fondness for flowers. This allusion is picked up in the
very first chapter of *The Scarlet Letter*, where Hawthorne himself
plucks a flower from the rosebush planted at the threshold of the

prison and presents it to the reader. His gesture amplifies the meaning of the regeneration experience whose morphology he traces in the preface. Rich as it is in theological resonance, and vital as it proves to be as a link between the romance and the sketch that precedes it, Hawthorne's rebirth is not simply or even primarily religious. He is not, after all, making a literal confession of grace or seriously entering his name into the book of the saints. Rather, he is attempting to associate his theory of fiction with the doctrinal content of American Calvinism: to establish a line of descent from the Puritan faith of his forebears to his own undertaking as a romancer. His art is what is reborn in "The Custom-House," and his art, it must be stressed, takes its form as well as its content from the past. Herein lies the importance of his renewing his identification with the old soldier at precisely the moment when he embarks on his literary mission and is once again in full possession of his creative talent. The General, we are told, dwells in an "inner sphere of contemplation" where the bustle of the Custom-House intrudes only as a distant murmur and the "scenes and sounds" of ancient battles are "all alive before his intellectual sense." To Hawthorne, he seems to lead "a more real life within his thoughts, than amid the unappropriate environment of the Collector's office" (pp. 19–23). It is, in brief, the General's devotion to a bygone era that Hawthorne aspires to in his capacity as romancer. For he too seeks to exhume a buried world and to revive an allegiance that his countrymen have lost sight of in their pursuit of more worldly goals.

This is not to suggest that Hawthorne himself was a Puritan in the way that his ancestors were, or to deny that he harbored profound reservations about the system of beliefs that they transported to the New World.[18] Indeed, the lightness of tone that he adopts throughout the "Introductory" may well be his way of dispelling some of the gloom that has attached itself to the family

18. The most extensive account of Hawthorne's view of Puritanism appears in Michael Davitt Bell, *Hawthorne and the Historical Romance of New England* (Princeton: Princeton University Press, 1971). Although I disagree with him at many points, I am indebted to Bell's study for its thorough examination of Hawthorne's attitude toward the founders. See also Michael J. Colacurcio, "Footsteps of Ann Hutchinson: The Context of *The Scarlet Letter*," *ELH* 39 (1972): 459–94.

name as a result of the misdeeds committed by William and John
Hathorne. But precisely because he bears that family name, Hawthorne cannot disown his ties to the protagonists of his tale, and he
is irrevocably bound to the Puritan past where the tragedy of their
lives unfolds. His surname brands him with ancestral guilt as surely
as Hester is branded by the scarlet letter, Chillingworth by his
misshapen figure, and Dimmesdale by the mark on his breast. And
yet it is not guilt alone that keeps fresh the Puritan inheritance that
Hawthorne is tapping in "The Custom-House." In speaking of his
progenitors, he freely admits that "strong traits of their nature have
intertwined themselves with mine." He is mindful, of course, that
his "stern and black-browed" ancestors would be aghast at his
manner of earning a livelihood, and he pictures them reproaching
him for his idle and useless existence:

> "What is he?" murmurs one gray shadow of my forefathers to
> the other. "A writer of story-books! What kind of a business
> in life,—what mode of glorifying God, or being serviceable to
> mankind in his day and generation,—may that be? Why, the
> degenerate fellow might as well have been a fiddler!" (p. 10).

Hawthorne's self-mockery should not be allowed to obscure the
serious claim that he is making for his art in this passage. For
it is exactly as "a writer of story-books" that he is carrying on
the tradition of American Puritanism, thereby glorifying God and
doing service to humanity in a form that the Puritans themselves
were at pains to suppress. Scorn him as they will, he nevertheless
denominates himself "as their representative" (p. 10) in the present;
and his fictions, like those of Charles Brockden Brown, the only
one of his compatriots to whom he awarded a niche in the Hall
of Fantasy,[19] are sermons in disguise.

What concerns us here, therefore, is Hawthorne's conception
of the romance. He is quite explicit about laying down the metaphorical conditions necessary for the creation of his art. He requires,
according to the preface, "a neutral territory, somewhere between

---

19. Nathaniel Hawthorne, "The Hall of Fantasy," in *The Works of
Nathaniel Hawthorne*, Centenary Edition, ed. William Charvat et al. (Columbus: Ohio State University Press, 1962–), vol. 10, *Mosses from an Old Manse*
(1974), p. 174.

the real world and fairy-land, where the Actual and the Imaginary may meet, and each imbue itself with the nature of the other" (p. 36). As Terence Martin points out, "a similar concern for a middle ground may be seen" in Irving, Cooper and Poe.[20] In the case of Hawthorne, it is directly related to his interest in Puritanism and the metaphysical issues that Puritanism embraced.

For if it is true, as we have suggested, that the source underlying the "Introductory" is the confession of saving grace, then Hawthorne's "neutral territory" is his equivalent of the state of weanedness that the Puritans attributed to the elect. The New England Calvinist who experienced grace endeavored to strike a balance between the demands of the spirit and the prohibition against spurning the world; he strove to "live in heaven, while he lived on earth." Correspondingly, Hawthorne's fiction comes into being at a point where history, fact and the everyday realities of human existence merge with the shadowy and unknown realm which is inaccessible to ordinary or "unregenerate" sense. The romancer is one who can dine with equal relish on the airy visions of Bronson Alcott and the earthy reminiscences of the old Inspector, but who soon tires of a steady diet of either. Avoiding on the one hand the pitfall of excessive spirituality, he declines on the other to lose himself in the rude "materiality of this daily life" (p. 37). He is wary of the extremes, yet he is not indifferent to them. Rather, he seeks to moderate their force by imbuing each "with the nature of the other." His art honors the world and exalts the spirit by recognizing the legitimate claims that each makes on the character of man.

But the neutral region where the "Actual" and the "Imaginary" interpenetrate is not the whole of Hawthorne's aesthetic, which is incomplete without the glimmering embers of the hearth fire. The warmer glow that the fireside diffuses throughout the study of the Old Manse "mingles itself with the cold spirituality of the moonbeams, and communicates, as it were, a heart and sensibilities

20. Terence Martin, *Nathaniel Hawthorne* (New York: Twayne Publishers, 1965), p. 42. On the critical background to Hawthorne's distinction between the romance and the novel, see John Caldwell Stubbs, *The Pursuit of Form: A Study of Hawthorne and the Romance* (Urbana: University of Illinois Press, 1970), pp. 3–48.

of human tenderness to the forms which fancy summons up. It converts them from snow-images into men and women" (p. 36). This passage, so crucial to Hawthorne's theory of art, sustains and enhances the metaphoric equation between the romance genre and the Puritan sensibility; its implications are moral as well as aesthetic. It can be seen, for example, as a repudiation of the excessive legalism of his persecuting progenitors, affirming as it does the value of "human tenderness." Without exculpating the victims that they sent to the stocks or the gallows, it impeaches them for their inflexibility in applying the letter of the law. Hawthorne's ancestor, William, the first of his line to emigrate from England, is portrayed in "The Custom-House" as appearing at Salem "with his Bible and his sword," the one emblematic of religion, the other of statecraft and the law. Hawthorne is careful to explain that William "had all the Puritanic traits, both good and evil," and he adds that his ancestor's "better deeds . . . were many" though largely forgotten. They have been forgotten, he continues, because of William's "hard severity" toward the Quakeress Mary Dyer (pp. 9–10). The burden of his indictment accordingly falls on William's rigid code of justice, which was too often implemented with a fine disregard for Christian charity. He does not suggest William was wrong to wield the sword, nor does he deny that the law and its machinery have their place in the human community. What he objects to, rather, is that William mistook the sword for the Bible and sacrificed religion in his zeal to uphold the public order. Hawthorne then goes on to repeat this charge in the romance itself, flatly accusing the Puritans of being "a people amongst whom religion and law were almost identical" (p. 50), and he dramatizes the point by having Wilson the minister and Bellingham the magistrate invariably appear in the book together. Interpreted in this fashion, his concern with the ruddy gleam cast by the coalfire is prescriptive as well as descriptive: it amounts to a caveat against violating the brotherhood of man.

Yet it also rounds out his definition of the romance, and in this respect its bearing is primarily on the nature of art. Once again, however, the aesthetic and the theological converge in order to form a unified statement. For the authentic Calvinist, it will be recalled, was as much averse to antinomianism as he was to its legalistic opposite. He did not seek or desire an unmediated relationship with the Deity, such as that presumably enjoyed by the Catholic mystic or Protestant pietist. Instead he belonged to a church, remained within the community, and worked to promote the welfare of his brethren. Hawthorne, for all his misgivings about the America of the 1850s, basically shared these convictions, and his declaration on behalf of the human dimension in art is a coming to terms with the dangers inherent in a literary form that avowedly has difficulty in animating the "ordinary characters" who inhabit the Custom-House (p. 37). By emphasizing the warmth shed by the hearth fire, Hawthorne distinguishes his own writing from that of the Transcendentalists, whom he elsewhere describes as being wholly out of touch with the "intellect and sympathies of the multitude."[21] What he means in part, when he takes the Transcendentalists to task, is that their utterances are too remote and otherworldly to suit the popular taste; but he also has in mind a second point of difference that emerges from the "Introductory" and that obliquely relates the "dreamy" exponents of the new philosophy to the separatists and enthusiasts of the seventeenth century.

Hawthorne refers to the movement spawned by Emerson in his discussion of his former habits. He briefly alludes to the "impracticable" experiment of Brook Farm and the "wild, free days on the Assabeth" when he consorted with the likes of William Ellery Channing. The flight from an impure society in the hope of founding a perfect one, and the exhilaration of "wild" conjecture—here Hawthorne parts ways with his Transcendentalist contemporaries, whose "fantastic speculations" overstep even the imaginative boundaries of the romance. For even the romance, as Hawthorne will later acknowledge in the preface to The House of the Seven Gables, "must rigidly subject itself to laws."[22] Notice that he labels the schemes of his erstwhile associates "impracticable," and that he accounts it a tribute to his "well-balanced" constitution that

21. See Hawthorne's preface to "Rappaccini's Daughter," in The Works of Nathaniel Hawthorne, Centenary Edition, ed. William Charvat et al. (Columbus: Ohio State University Press, 1962–), vol. 10, Mosses from an Old Manse, p. 91.
22. Hawthorne, House of the Seven Gables, Centenary Edition, 2: 1.

he can take the loss of their company in stride. It is significant, though, that he does not condemn them outright; he merely states that their fellowship satisfies but a part of his nature (pp. 24–25). Another part, it appears, can adapt to—if not exactly thrive in—the more regular and confining atmosphere of the Custom-House, where, as the overseer of the revenue, his official reading material consists of the "Acts of Congress, and a bulky Digest of the Revenue Laws" (p. 7). Insofar as his duties involve enforcing such laws and thereby servicing the social machinery, his position as Surveyor is more in keeping with the temper of his lineal progenitors than with that of the heretics who drew down their wrath. But neither extreme in itself is sufficient for the production of his art or the welfare of his being: he finally has no more in common with his brother officers, General Miller excepted, than he does with the progeny of the *Dial*. What he requires, in order to find fulfillment as both a writer and an individual, is the range of insight and experience that can take the measure of the multitude without disdaining its laws: that can sojourn at Brook Farm and hold public office in Salem "and never murmur at the change" (p. 28). To borrow the lexicon of Calvinism, it is precisely at the point of intersection between "the Legalist, on the one hand, and the Antinomian, or loose gospeler, on the other" that Hawthorne attains the pitch of creativity essential for the composition of romance.

What all this reduces to is that for Hawthorne, the "topmost bough" of the family tree (p. 10), art takes over the function that religion served for his forebears. He stakes out a position as romancer that is precisely analogous to the metaphysical middle way, constituting a kind of aesthetic correlative for the vital strain in Calvinism that gave priority to grace over works but still retained the edict of the law—the strain that cherished the spirit as well as the world and tempered justice with mercy and love.[23] That aesthetic is also his theme: the form that he appropriates for his

23. Compare Hyatt H. Waggoner's comment on Hawthorne: "The strongest way of putting the case for Hawthorne's 'Puritanism' is to say that he thought there were truths at the center of the Puritan faith that, when suitably translated, were still viable." See *Hawthorne: A Critical Study*, rev. ed. (Cambridge: Harvard University Press, 1963), p. 15.

fiction and the values that his fiction espouses are at bottom the same. But this is simply to say that Hawthorne's deepest commitment as an artist is to the ideal of inner-worldly sainthood, and that he measures the heroes of his romances against the Puritan standard of living in the world without being of it.

It is important to remember, however, that Hawthorne's talent eludes him so long as he is employed in the service of the Republic. The implication, though he hesitates to draw it, is that there is something in the nature of American political authority that is uncongenial to art. There is one figure described in the preface who can be said to capture perfectly the ethos of the Custom-House, and who accordingly embodies the temperament that is anathema to the creative spirit in general and the romantic genre in particular. Much as the old Inspector flourishes in the Custom-House setting, he is no match for the unnamed functionary who stands in Hawthorne's estimation as "the ideal of his class," that of public servant. This person, whose "gifts were emphatically those of a man of business," is the cog that keeps the machinery of the Custom-House in working order. He is also the very incarnation of the Protestant ethic, and the catalogue of his virtues reads like a rehash of Benjamin Franklin's prescription for the exemplary American. He is industrious, orderly, punctual, forbearing towards his blundering associates, highly regarded by the merchants whose affairs he dispatches with unrivaled efficiency, and congenitally incapable of an act of dishonesty:

> His integrity was perfect; it was a law of nature with him, rather than a choice or a principle; nor can it be otherwise than the main condition of an intellect so remarkably clear and accurate as his, to be honest and regular in the administration of affairs.

Although Hawthorne professes to admire this model bureaucrat, he cannot resist poking holes in his mechanical and narrow-minded morality; there is something decidedly amiss, after all, about a man who would be discomforted in roughly the same way by a blot on his conscience and "an error in the balance of an account." The "man of business" is clearly a case of Franklinianism run wild in the body politic; his prominence in the Custom-House is suggestive of the ascendancy of his type in American life. The constellation of values that he represents, having banished the Puritan vision to the past, now threatens its reemergence in the present as a form of art. For the "man of business," according to the preface, is "the Custom-House in himself," and he must therefore be held accountable for Hawthorne's failure to write (pp. 24–25).

———•—•———

The opening chapters of *The Scarlet Letter* scout the extremes of lawlessness and legalism, of otherworldliness and materialism, that the Hawthorne of the "Introductory" deemed inimical to the spirit of romance. He immediately sets up a polarity between the "wild rose-bush," which he associates with Ann Hutchinson, and the "black flower of civilized society, a prison" (p. 48). The polarity is figuratively resolved by Hawthorne's gesture of placing the rose in the context of the tale's "darkening close" (p. 48). But otherwise his emphasis is on the gulf that separates Hester, the unrepentant adulteress, from the hard-hearted onlookers who speak of "Scripture and the statute-book" in the same breath (p. 52); it is on the contrast between the "spectral images" called up by Hester's "preternaturally active" memory (p. 57) and the substantial Puritan matrons, born and bred in England and nourished on the "beef and ale of their native land," who throng about the public scaffold (p. 50); and finally it is on the jarring contradiction between the Boston magistracy as personified by Governor Bellingham, with his black tunic and air of worldly experience, and the ethereal presence of the youthful Reverend Mr. Dimmesdale. These are the divisions that inform the opening mood of *The Scarlet Letter*, and they help to define the challenge that Hawthorne faces as a romancer. His object is to bring the action and tenor of his story into some degree of conformity with his concept of the romance, to curb the intensity of opposition between the extremes that beset his characters in order to vitalize the metaphysical middle way that parallels—and is the source for—the "neutral territory" of his fiction.

The obstacles to overcoming the stark contrarieties of *The Scarlet Letter* are formidable indeed, and they converge at the outset on the Puritan community's mistreatment of Hester, which elicits one of Hawthorne's most outspoken attacks on the colony's lack of compassion:

> There can be no outrage, methinks, against our common nature, —whatever be the delinquencies of the individual,—no outrage more flagrant than to forbid the culprit to hide his face for shame; as it was the essence of this punishment to do (p. 55).

Although Hawthorne's specific reference is to the stocks, a penal device that Hester is spared, the real target of his censure is the "dismal severity of the Puritanic code of law" (p. 52), founded as it is on the false belief that dragging iniquity into the marketplace can constrain sincere contrition in the offender. The effect is exactly the opposite: Hester's three hours on the platform leave her defiantly impenitent and fail to bring about the spiritual rebirth demanded by the authorities. Like Eve after the Fall, she craves only death and wishes to assume full responsibility for the sin committed by herself and Arthur.[24]

For Hester has quite literally been victimized by the "letter" of the law, and she has consequently hardened her heart against the need for penitence and grace. Hawthorne does not excuse her sin—he writes that "the world was only the darker for this woman's beauty, and the more lost for the infant that she had borne" (p. 56)—but neither does he overlook the culpability of her judges, who in the manner of Hawthorne's progenitors, William and John, confuse the Bible with the sword. Hester has broken the seventh commandment, and the action of *The Scarlet Letter* covers the seven years from 1642 to 1649,[25] a coincidence that is quite deliberate on Hawthorne's part and that bears directly on the draconian nature of Puritan law. Seven is also the number of years for which indentured servants contracted to labor in exchange for passage across the Atlantic. It is the term of the bondsman—

24. The Miltonic theme is central to Male's study. See also F. O. Matthiessen, *American Renaissance: Art and Expression in the Age of Emerson and Whitman* (New York: Oxford University Press, 1941), pp. 305–12.

25. For documentation see Edward Dawson, *Hawthorne's Knowledge and Use of New England History: A Study of Sources* (Nashville: University of Tennessee Press, 1939), p. 17.

"a free-born Englishman, but now a seven years' slave" (p. 104) —who ushers Hester into Governor Bellingham's mansion when she makes her impassioned plea to keep Pearl. This is the status to which Hester has been reduced in the eyes of her fellow Bostonians, who regard her as "the people's victim and life-long bond-slave" (p. 227). According to Calvinist dogma, hers is the plight of fallen man in general, who is in bondage to the law until ransomed by Christ. Thus the townspeople's view of Hester is essentially correct, in spite of her outward humility, because she remains unrepentant and estranged from society; but Hawthorne's point is that Puritan justice, administered without regard to mercy, has helped to make her that way, and must share responsibility for her failure to experience the change of heart that signifies redemption.

And so the crime of the town of Boston is not that it has penalized Hester for adultery, but rather that it can offer so little in the way of assistance to deliver her from her fallen condition.[26] Her spiritual counselor, the Reverend Mr. Dimmesdale, is the secret partner to her sin; and even the venerable John Wilson, who commands her to confess from his perch overlooking the scaffold, is said to have no right to "meddle with a question of human guilt, passion, and anguish" (p. 65). To argue that Hawthorne was preoccupied with the "falling-off from the manhood of the first generation" is to overstate the case for the Puritan elders, whose strengths are invariably balanced against their shortcomings.[27] The paragraph in which Hawthorne describes the assemblage on the balcony furnishes an apt illustration. On the one hand, he credits the founders with the practical wisdom that accomplishes much "precisely because it imagined and hoped so little," while on the other he condemns the "rigid aspect" that renders them incapable of "sitting in judgment on an erring woman's heart" (p. 64). Most

26. Compare Randall Stewart's remark on Boston: "The Puritan community in Hawthorne's novel was un-Christian in its unforgiving attitude and be-havior—its bigotry and cruelty—but it was not un-Christian in its doctrine." See *American Literature and Christian Doctrine* (Baton Rouge: Louisiana State University Press, 1948), p. 87.

27. Bell, *Hawthorne and the Historical Romance of New England*, p. 80. See also pp. 137–39.

devastating of all, however, is his portrait of Governor Bellingham, "a gentleman advanced in years" (p. 64) and the very embodiment of the civil authority. As numerous commentators have noted, John Winthrop was actually in office during June of 1642, the date when Hester is supposed to have been punished on the scaffold. Given Hawthorne's thorough knowledge of New England history, his choice of Bellingham as governor is somewhat curious; unfortunately the reasons usually given for the substitution have not been very convincing. Hawthorne did have sound reasons for making the change, however, and the best of them are supplied by Winthrop himself, in the *Journal* that he kept during the first nineteen years of Boston's existence.

The *Journal* was originally published in its entirety in 1825, and was often consulted by Hawthorne while he composed his romance. Winthrop had a good deal to say about his contemporary Richard Bellingham, and little that he says is to the latter's credit. Bellingham, it seems, had the bad habit of picking quarrels with his fellow magistrates, and Winthrop criticizes him for his "stiffness," "singularity in opinion," and general lack of Christian spirit.[28] In *The Scarlet Letter*, Hawthorne draws heavily on this characterization, showering Bellingham with adjectives like hard, stern, rigid, and severe. He thoroughly identifies the Puritan magistrate with the law, going far beyond his sources in stressing the Governor's legal training. Dr. Caleb Snow's *History of Boston*, from which Hawthorne apparently derived much of his material, merely states that Bellingham "was by education a lawyer,"[29] but Hawthorne makes him out to have been a figure of note in his field, being "accustomed to speak of Bacon, Coke, Noye, and Finch, as his professional associates" (pp. 105-6). The Governor's background has not done much to acquaint him with "the truth of the human heart."[30] Hawthorne calls attention to the fact that he was the

---

28. *Winthrop's Journal: "History of New England,"* 2 vols., ed. James Kendall Hosmer (New York: Barnes and Noble, 1966), 2: 117. The 1825 edition prepared by James Savage is identical to Hosmer's in its description of Bellingham.

29. Charles Ryskamp, "The New England Sources of *The Scarlet Letter*," *American Literature* 31 (1959): 264, n. 18.

30. The quotation is from the preface to *House of the Seven Gables*, Centenary Edition, 2: 1.

originator of the cruel design to remove Pearl from her mother's care, and during the interview at his mansion it is Wilson, not the Governor, who enthusiastically seconds Dimmesdale's arguments on Hester's behalf.

Thus Hawthorne's use of Bellingham at the beginning of *The Scarlet Letter* serves in part to underscore the harshness of the Puritan magistracy without tarnishing the reputation of John Winthrop, who was universally revered as the most humane of the founding fathers. But what must especially have caught Hawthorne's notice as he perused the *Journal* is the passage in which Winthrop comments on Bellingham's strange marriage. The passage deserves quotation at length:

> The governor, Mr. Bellingham, was married, (I would not mention such ordinary matters in our history, but by occasion of some remarkable accidents). The young gentlewoman was ready to be contracted to a friend of his, who lodged in his house, and by his consent had proceeded so far with her, when on the sudden the governor treated with her, and obtained her for himself. He excused it by the strength of his affection, and that she was not absolutely promised to the other gentleman. Two errors more he committed upon it. 1. That he would not have his contract published where he dwelt, contrary to the order of the court. 2. That he married himself contrary to the constant practice of the country.[31]

Winthrop's misgivings about bringing this incident to light do not alter the fact that he is all but accusing Bellingham of stealing another man's betrothed. With this in mind, Hawthorne's rationale for rewriting colonial history and bestowing the principal dignity of the Bay on a near adulterer for the entire seven years of his story yields its full significance. The law, he is reiterating, is administered by men, and men are invariably corrupt. In personal terms, the law is powerless to alter the soul, and cannot even generate a righteous exertion to comply with the commandments. Hawthorne imparts symbolic force to this truth, which applies to Hester as well as Governor Bellingham, by alluding obliquely to the Fall and its consequences. His allusions purposely duplicate

31. *Winthrop's Journal*, Hosmer edition, 2: 43-44.

but also depart from those which he invokes with regard to himself in "The Custom-House." He explains that the Governor, who retains "the native English taste for ornamental gardening," has attempted to re-create an Edenic setting in his adopted country but has had to abandon the effort because of the cabbages and pumpkin vines that overrun his estate. Whereupon he immediately likens Bellingham's head to that of John the Baptist on a platter (pp. 106-8). Like Hawthorne himself, then, the chief magistrate dwells in a fallen Eden and has suffered a figurative death; but unlike Hawthorne, there is nothing in *The Scarlet Letter* to indicate that he will be reborn. Certainly it is no accident that Hawthorne goes out of his way, again without basis in historical fact, to emphasize that Bellingham is the brother of a witch, and that he resides together with his sister in the governor's mansion. In the world of *The Scarlet Letter*, as in Calvinist theology, those who rely on the false security of the legal covenant are closely related to the damned.

Q. D. Leavis, in her study, "Hawthorne as Poet," has commented on his frequent use of the "labyrinth" motif as a metaphor for Puritan society, and she has argued that "there is no escape but in death" for the protagonists of his tale, given the narrow confines of the environment in which they are trapped.[32] The difficulty with this reading is that it removes responsibility from the characters themselves, and reduces metaphysical issues to exclusively social ones. This is not to say that Hawthorne is indifferent to the question of social identity, but merely to reaffirm that he poses that question in a context that is theological and quintessentially Calvinist. What interests him, consequently, is the way in which an individual's relation to his society illuminates his spiritual condition. The figure of the labyrinth to which Leavis calls attention refers to the religious quandary in which Hawthorne's protagonists find themselves mired for the major part of the book, a quandary that strikingly resembles the state of confusion endemic to *Wieland* and common to the Gothic novel in general. Indeed,

32. Q. D. Leavis, "Hawthorne as Poet," *Sewanee Review* 59 (1951): 439.

there is good reason to believe that Hawthorne's reading of Godwin
and Brown directly influenced his conception of the romance, and
that he borrowed extensively from the idiom and situation of
Wieland in composing his own version of *le genre noir*. The
unidentified stanza that Brown used as the epigraph for his
"American Tale" may have supplied some of the inspiration for
the maze imagery of *The Scarlet Letter:*

> From Virtue's blissful paths away
> The double-tongued are sure to stray;
> Good is a forth-right journey still,
> And mazy paths but lead to ill.[33]

Hawthorne's affinity for the Gothicists takes the form of an
analogous concern with the familiar Calvinist drama of sin and
redemption. It is not his purpose, as Leavis contends, to vindicate
his protagonists by focusing exclusively on the injustices fostered
by the New England commonwealth. The Puritan state is a
contributing factor but it is not the cause of the spiritual crises
that proliferate throughout *The Scarlet Letter*. If, for example,
the attempt to force Hester to name her fellow sinner is ill-advised
—sincere repentance of necessity being voluntary—it does not
excuse her determination never to divulge the secrets of her heart
on earth. Indeed, it is her misguided attitude toward the confession
in general that sets apart the wearer of the scarlet letter from
the narrator of "The Custom-House." For whereas Hawthorne
publicly relates his personal circumstances, Hester twice refuses
to do so within the opening pages of the romance: first, of course,
on the scaffold, and then again only hours later when she accedes
to Chillingworth's request to conceal his identity as she has kept
the secret of her lover's. In both instances, she presumably acts
out of concern for the welfare of Arthur. Yet she is quite right

---

33. The labyrinth or maze as an image of spiritual bewilderment and lost
direction is a common one in Western literature; it has been studied in detail
by Angus Fletcher, *The Prophetic Moment: An Essay on Spenser* (Chicago:
University of Chicago Press, 1971). As Fletcher points out, "Christian dogma
blamed this bewilderment on a blindness beginning with the Fall" (p. 24).
Both Brown and Hawthorne were familiar with the use of such imagery by
Spenser and Milton.

to fear that the oath of silence extorted by Chillingworth endangers her soul.

The danger is graver by far than Hester suspects. Her desire to protect her fellow sinner, however well-intentioned and commendable in itself, is only symptomatic of her deeper failure to find a "neutral territory" between the claims of the world and her forbidden longings to break free of the world's constraints. It attests to her estrangement from the integrated faith that anchors the confession. On the one hand, she does penance on earth—not "genuine and steadfast penitence"—by making garments for the poor and humbling herself before the haughty gentlewomen who covet her needlework but otherwise treat her with contempt (pp. 83–84). On the other, she clings to the hope that she will be restored to Arthur in the afterlife: that they will stand "together before the bar of final judgment, and make that their marriage altar," thereby resuming the adulterous union that the laws of society proscribe (p. 80). Between these extremes lies the elusive middle way of visible sainthood, and Hester, although she is a martyr, is not a saint. She cannot even forgive her enemies, unlike Hawthorne, who freely pardons the Whigs when they eject him from office. The irony of her situation is obvious enough: condemned by an overly legalistic society, Hester has responded by seeking to expiate her sin through good works; like the Puritan magistracy itself, she has mistaken the covenant of the law for the covenant of grace.

And so Hawthorne quite naturally associates his heroine with Catholicism and the Arminian heresy. He writes:

Had there been a Papist among the crowd of Puritans, he might have seen in this beautiful woman, so picturesque in her attire and mien, and with the infant at her bosom, an object to remind him of the image of Divine Maternity (p. 56).

But Hawthorne hastens to add that in fact Hester has been guilty of the deepest crime. As time wears on, and her acts of kindness overshadow the scandal of her past, she acquires the reputation of a "Sister of Mercy," and even her badge of shame has the "effect of a cross on a nun's bosom," enabling her to pass unharmed in the midst of peril. Her penance, as opposed to penitence, is an article of Catholic rather than Protestant faith. To some of her townsmen, those most impressed by her "power to do," Hester's scarlet letter loses its original meaning and comes to stand for "Able," in recognition of her ability to lighten suffering and cheer the afflicted. But ability, as an author versed in the creed of his Calvinist forefathers would be sure to know, is theological short-hand for the heretical notion that man can overcome his fallen nature without divine assistance: that good deeds are the means of election and foolproof evidence of a gracious character. Without directly contradicting this view of Hester, Hawthorne manages to undercut it by suggesting that her demeanor—though it passed for humility—yet "might be pride," and that the gratitude of the public was more than she desired, "or, perchance, than she deserved" (p. 162).

These qualifications are not simply instances of what Yvor Winters called Hawthorne's "formula of alternative possibilities."[34] They build to the climactic sentence in which he declares outright that "the scarlet letter had not done its office" (p. 166). Hester's antinomian impulses, which first issued in her guilty passion, have not been abjured as the public supposes, but only sublimated. They have resurfaced in a form which the Puritan elders, "had they known of it, would have held to be a deadlier crime than that stigmatized by the scarlet letter," and which prompts Hawthorne to associate his heroine with Ann Hutchinson, as the potential founder of a new and essentially lawless sect. Hester's submission to the civil authority of Boston, resting on nothing more solid than the performance of good works, has not effected the change of heart that separates the hypocrite from the elect—the change without which there can be no genuine striving to fulfill the commandment of the law. Convinced that "the world's law was no law for her mind," Hester has imbibed the spirit of perfection-ism, then rampant in Europe but still alien to her countrymen, that

34. Yvor Winters, *Maule's Curse: Seven Studies in the History of American Obscurantism*, in his *In Defense of Reason* (Denver, Colorado: Alan Swallow, 1947), p. 170. The case for Hawthorne's ambiguity has been made most effectively by Frank Kermode, "Hawthorne's Modernity," *Partisan Review* 41 (1974): 428–41.

would tear down the whole social system in order to structure it anew (p. 164). Here Hawthorne virtually spells out the link between the wild theories of his heroine and the "fantastic speculations" of the Transcendentalists. In both cases, the impetus for their thought comes from abroad, and Hester's schemes, it is clear from the text, are quite as "impracticable" as those hatched by the "dreamy brethren of Brook Farm."

The separatist side of Hester, which places her in defiant if covert opposition to the Puritan town on whose outskirts she dwells, is given tangible life in Pearl, who is a "natural" child in the double sense that she is both illegitimate and unsocialized. Her lawless behavior, while partly the product of Dimmesdale's failure to acknowledge his paternity, is also the legacy of her mother's impenitence. When Hester vows on the scaffold that Pearl "must seek a heavenly Father; she shall never know an earthly one" (p. 68), she effectively denies her daughter a social existence, with results that can be traced in Hawthorne's description of the child. She is worthy, he writes, to dwell in Eden after the "first parents were driven out," an indication of her isolation and lack of reference to the actual and fallen world into which she has the misfortune to be born. This "outcast of the infantile world" has no friends among the other children of the settlement, and when she is taunted for her singularity, she responds with outbursts of rage in which Hester can discern the reflection of her own tempestuous nature (pp. 90–93). And indeed Pearl literally acts out her mother's lawless speculations, giving vent in her solitary play to Hester's desire to overthrow the present constitution of society. Her fertile imagination seizes upon commonplace objects and converts them into "imaginary personages": the pine trees become Puritan elders, and the "ugliest weeds of the garden were their children, whom Pearl smote down and uprooted, most unmercifully." She never conjures up a playmate for whom she feels affection but pictures instead a hostile and "adverse world," peopled by a host of enemies against whom she wages her child's warfare (pp. 95–96). And she even seems to intuit that her "seclusion from human society" (p. 94) condemns her to seclusion from God. She emphatically protests to Hester that "I have no Heavenly Father" (p. 98); and when Wilson asks her who made her, she replies that she was plucked by her mother from the wild rosebush growing in front of the prison. The second exchange occurs in the third year of Pearl's life, a fact of which we are reminded repeatedly; like Hester on the scaffold, she has not arrived at the state of spiritual rebirth that Hawthorne himself attains in the preface.

It is difficult, in view of this portrait, to follow the argument, advanced by a number of critics, that Pearl embodies Hawthorne's theory of fiction, or that she herself is a symbol of romance.[35] It would be more accurate to say that she is like a tale such as might have been written by a Transcendentalist. Her lawless antics and the fact that she cannot "be made amenable to rules" (p. 91) go far beyond what Hawthorne allows in the way of aesthetic license, and the sympathy for mortal frailty and error that he insists upon in "The Custom-House" surely precludes the savage antagonism with which she regards "the offspring of her own heart and mind" (p. 95). A child who laughs like "a thing incapable and unintelligent of human sorrow" (p. 93) makes a poor symbol indeed for "a tale of human frailty and sorrow" (p. 48).

From the foregoing discussion it should be clear that Hester and Pearl are representative of a pervasive theological confusion—a confusion that engulfs not only themselves but also Chillingworth and Dimmesdale. The leech's efficacy as an agent of evil, like the comparable villainy of Brown's mysterious biloquist, is a corollary to that very confusion; hence when it is dispelled, he vanishes too. In the meantime he is able to exploit the contradictory impulses that bedevil his victim and wife and thwart their efforts at repentance only because they are as spiritually twisted as he is. It is no accident, for example, that he is associated with both lawlessness and legalism. When he first appears in Boston, it is in the company of a wild Indian, and he himself is clad "in a strange disarray of civilized and savage costume" (p. 60). He expressly reassures Hester that he will not betray her lover to the civil authority of Boston. As she rightly surmises, however,

---

35. See, for example, Rudolph Von Abele, *The Death of the Artist: A Study of Hawthorne's Disintegration* (The Hague: Martinus Nijhoff, 1955), p. 53; Richard Chase, *The American Novel and Its Tradition* (Garden City, N.Y.: Doubleday and Co., Anchor Books, 1957), p. 78; and Porte, *Romance in America*, pp. 105–6.

his speech conveys no promise of Christian charity. On the contrary, he tends to speak in the legalistic idiom of the Puritan magistracy, and his philosophy, if he can be said to have one, partakes more of the Old Testament code of an eye for an eye than it does of the spirit of forgiveness enjoined by Christ. During the interview with Hester after her exposure on the scaffold, he says, "Between thee and me, the scale hangs fairly balanced" (p. 75). These are the words of a man who thinks in terms of strict retribution. Accordingly, when Hester later implores him to cease tormenting Dimmesdale, he rebuffs her plea on the grounds that the minister "has but increased the debt" (p. 172). And the debt, he implies, will be repaid in full, for he pointedly disclaims any will or power to pardon.

Chillingworth's quest for vengeance is the dark offshoot of the legal covenant, but it is not incompatible with the performance of good works. In a community where physicians are scarce, his professional skills are much in demand, and he is even present at the bedside of John Winthrop when that worthy expires on the night of "The Minister's Vigil." His outward comportment in matters concerning religion is "exemplary," and he is soon regarded as a "brilliant acquisition" to the fledgling Puritan town (pp. 119–20). Knowing himself to be a wanderer, and one "isolated from human interests," he finds in Boston "a woman, a man, a child, among whom and myself there exist the closest ligaments." His decision to settle in their midst can be viewed as a pathetic if warped attempt to find the society that he otherwise lacks. In the same breath in which he utters these words, however, he swears Hester to silence, renouncing any intention of confessing his true identity to his adopted townsmen. He adds that it is his wish to vanish "from the world as one already dead, and of whom no tidings shall ever come" (p. 76). Thus he repudiates the very social ties that he appears to crave. The irony is that he is already dead in spirit, and when he takes up residence with Dimmesdale, their abode appropriately borders on the local graveyard.

Chillingworth, of course, nurses demonic schemes more terrible than anything meditated by Hester or Arthur, yet it is nevertheless striking that he resembles them in so many respects. They are all three branded or disfigured; they all spurn the confession; and

they are all alienated from society, but give every appearance of
conforming to social law. The fact that Chillingworth is married
to Hester and becomes inseparable from the minister simply confirms their spiritual kinship. In the case of Dimmesdale, the inner
division that can only be healed by grace is the more noticeable
because as a man of the cloth he is committed to the very system
of values that his actions belie. Hawthorne writes of him that
he was

> a true priest, a true religionist, with the reverential sentiment
> largely developed, and an order of mind that impelled itself
> powerfully along the track of a creed, and wore its passage
> continually deeper with the lapse of time (p. 123).

When he entreats Hester to confess for him in the marketplace,
Dimmesdale willfully betrays his office and trust, for as he well
knows, every sinner must confess for himself. The youthful minister
has wandered far indeed from the track of the creed to which
he pays such fervent lip service. Like his accomplice in sin, he
has stumbled into a labyrinth of religious uncertainty, and he
cannot find the middle way to lead him out to salvation. On the
one hand, he takes refuge in the covenant of works, discharging
his pastoral duties with an earnestness that wins him the love
of his flock and the esteem of his brother clergymen. On the other,
he exhibits an otherworldliness so intense that he seems to his
adoring parishioners to hover on the verge of translation into pure
spirit. Seeing him waste away, they conclude that the world is
"not worthy to be any longer trodden by his feet" (p. 120). Fearing
to confess on earth, he longs to die and to present himself before
his Maker at the bar of final judgment. This is a refrain to which
he often returns, using it as an excuse, for example, when Pearl
presses him to stand with her and her mother before the public
gaze. They will not meet again, he tells the stubbornly inquisitive
child, until eternity: "Then, and there, before the judgment seat,
thy mother, and thou, and I, must stand together! But the daylight
of this world shall not see our meeting!" (p. 153). In the chapter
"The Leech and his Patient," Dimmesdale casuistically argues that
the antithetical sides of his nature are perforce related: that the

good deeds he performs on earth and in time are made possible
precisely because he will not bare his soul until the world's end.
A zeal to promote man's welfare, he reasons, justifies the duplicity
of which he secretly knows himself guilty, since without a spotless
exterior "no good can be achieved . . . no evil of the past be redeemed by better service" (p. 132).

Dimmesdale's reasoning is the product of his divided sensibility,
and it is reminiscent of the theological confusion that his Reformation contemporaries attributed to the medieval church. Wherefore
Hawthorne associates the minister with Catholicism, again bringing out his resemblance to Hester. He writes that Dimmesdale's

> inward trouble drove him to practices, more in accordance with
> the old, corrupted faith of Rome, than with the better light
> of the church in which he had been born and bred (p. 144).

This Puritan divine rejects every suggestion of marriage, "as if
priestly celibacy were one of his articles of church-discipline" (p.
125); he lacerates his flesh with a bloody scourge, and fasts until
he trembles from weakness; and he keeps nightlong vigils that
cause his reeling brain to summon up a host of spectral visions.
As Hawthorne points out, these are acts of penance, not signs
of sincere penitence (pp. 144–45). The point is not lost on Dimmesdale himself, whose Protestant faith has been too deeply ingrained
in his being for him to cast it out utterly in the span of seven
years. In the great forest scene, he reverts, if only for the moment,
to the creed of Calvin, overpowering Hester's faulty logic when
she tries to persuade him of "the penitence thus sealed and
witnessed by good works." He can find no relief, he bitterly tells
her, in the good that he appears to do, for "it must needs be a
delusion," coming as it does from a soul as ruined as his. And
he adds, in words that would certify his redemption if he could
but act on them, that his deeds are

> cold and dead, and can do nothing for me! Of penance I have
> had enough! Of penitence there has been none! Else, I should
> long ago have thrown off these garments of mock holiness, and
> have shown myself to mankind as they will see me at the
> judgment-seat (p. 192).

Here Dimmesdale fleetingly grasps the clue that will eventually solve the maze of *The Scarlet Letter*. The self that he unbosoms to his fellow men on earth, he declares in effect, must be the same self that he shows to the Almighty on the day of final reckoning. Thus he resolves the split between time and eternity, this world and the next.

The resolution whose possibility Dimmesdale glimpses in the forest is not realized, however, until the penultimate chapter of the romance, and it is deferred, at least in part, for reasons that bear once again on the nature of the New England commonwealth. All the principal actors in Hawthorne's Calvinist drama are spiritually lost and at odds with society, but a distinction must be made with regard to the minister. The distinction consists in exactly the fact that he is a member of the clergy. He is introduced in his public role, and his unrivaled influence over the people is stressed from the first. In a settlement, according to Hawthorne, where "even political power . . . was within the grasp of a successful priest" (p. 238), such influence entails considerable responsibility. As the foremost preacher in the Bay, Dimmesdale ideally cannot work out his own salvation until he has found a way to make that salvation meaningful for the colony at large: until he can translate the integrated faith that underlies the confession into terms that are as valid for the Puritan state as they are for himself.

What this means, as Hawthorne poses the problem in *The Scarlet Letter*, is that in order to fulfill his pastoral obligation Dimmesdale must reconcile the competing claims of the New Testament and the Old. These are religious categories but in the romance they are social as well, for they are inseparably bound up with Dimmesdale's singular position within the Boston community. That community, as Hawthorne often reminds us, is the creation of elderly men, and it thoroughly reflects the character of its ruling elders. He does not neglect to give the founders their due. They are to a man competent, grave, and "distinguished by a ponderous sobriety." Their self-reliance and physical courage in times of peril safeguard "the state like a line of cliffs against a tempestuous tide" (pp. 237–38). They tend to be identified in general with materiality, political power, and the rule of law, which they rightly recognize as indispensable in any society composed of fallible men. And they give the impression, therefore, of being cast in the mold of the patriarchs of the Old Testament, rather than the divinely inspired apostles of the New, a point that is underscored by their "father-hood" and longevity.

Having been shaped by long and "sad-colored experience" (p. 238), and steeped in the Mosaic code, the Puritan fathers are not inclined to put much stock in the power of brotherly love. Even the best of them, true saints such as the Reverend Mr. Wilson, are ignorant in matters pertaining to the heart. This deficiency is the more noticeable in light of the fact that Wilson himself is not bereft of generosity or personal kindness. Yet when he speaks in his official capacity and addresses the populace, it is the Decalogue and not the gospel of Christ that breathes in his words. Surely it is with this consideration in mind that Hawthorne alludes in passing to a tapestry

> representing the Scriptural story of David and Bathsheba, and Nathan the Prophet, in colors still unfaded, but which made the fair woman of the scene almost as grimly picturesque as the woe-denouncing seer (p. 126).

The story of David's adultery with Bathsheba, which is told in the Book of Samuel, affords an Old Testament parallel to *The Scarlet Letter*, with the part of the "woe-denouncing seer" assumed by Wilson, who on the occasion of Hester's public exposure delivers a punitive "discourse on sin, in all its branches, but with continual reference to the ignominious letter" (p. 68). But if the mood of the jeremiad is congenial to Wilson, who is regularly described as the oldest divine in the Bay, it is utterly foreign to the "godly youth" (p. 65) whose popularity as an orator overshadows the reputations of his more substantial and learned elders. For Dimmesdale alone among the pastors of Boston has the "Tongue of Flame," the power of "addressing the whole human brotherhood in the heart's native language." His sorrows, although they virtually sap his will to live, also endow him with an instinctive sympathy for the sufferings of the multitude, enabling him to move his audi-tors as effortlessly as if he spoke with the voice of an angel. Such eloquence, according to Hawthorne, is "Heaven's last and rarest attestation" of the apostolic office: it is the gift that descends from the Holy Spirit "upon the chosen disciples at Pentecost," as described in the Acts of the Apostles (pp. 141–42). Dimmesdale is thus directly linked to evangelical preachers of the New Testament, an identification that is strengthened by his youth and "sonship," which is implicitly contrasted to the fatherhood of his aging fellow divines.

Seventeenth-century Boston, as it appears in *The Scarlet Letter*, resembles nothing so much as the Salem Custom-House writ large. Dimmesdale's "Tongue of Flame"—which roughly corresponds to Hawthorne's artistic power—and his compassion and spirituality, are beleaguered values in a community more Hebraic than Christian. Yet those values are rooted in the fact of his sin. In order to redeem his soul and alter society, therefore, Dimmesdale must heal the breach between himself and the Puritan fathers. He must somehow acquire their strengths without forsaking the positive qualities that are uniquely his own.

For much of the romance the emphasis falls on Dimmesdale's failure to measure up to his elders. It is obvious, for example, that he lacks their imposing presence and solidity of character. There is "an apprehensive, a startled, a half-frightened look" about him that is almost childlike in comparison to the unruffled composure of the colonial magistrates (p. 66). He is elsewhere described as a person for whom it is essential "to feel the pressure of a faith about him, supporting, while it confined him within its iron framework" (p. 123). This description recalls Hawthorne's remarks on the habit of dependence that enervates the political appointees who toil overlong in the service of the Republic. But whereas the timidity of the Custom-House officers is clearly related to their old age, the equivalent trait in Dimmesdale is attributable to his youth. It suggests a lack of self-reliance that is incompatible with a forthright assumption of the burdens of maturity. His betrayal of the fathers is shown most conspicuously, perhaps, by his flouting the Old Testament law in the act of adultery. But it is also shown by his craven refusal to face up to the consequences of that act. And it is shown, too, in his attitude toward time, from which he is constantly trying to escape by courting his own demise. His

wish for an early grave, precluding as it must the possibility of
his ever growing old, inevitably marks him off from the ruling
elders, whose wisdom and endowments are the harvest of age.
Dimmesdale's divergence from the Puritan fathers is dramatically
highlighted by his three denials of public trust, each of which
occurs under circumstances that invite unfavorable comparison
to his older brethren. The first denial takes place when Hester is
exposed in the marketplace, and the minister chooses to conceal
his own fatherhood by declining to acknowledge Pearl as his
daughter. The second occurs when he "discloses" his secret sin
on the very night of John Winthrop's death. A gigantic A appearing in the sky, Dimmesdale interprets the letter as a reference to his
own adultery, while the townspeople take it to mean that Winthrop
has been transformed into an angel. The events of the night make
for a telling contrast between the cowardice and vanity of the
young divine and the virtue of the old governor.[36] Finally, the
third denial is enacted in the forest, where Dimmesdale succumbs
to Hester's appeal that he abandon the New England settlement
and flee to Europe with her and Pearl. He is intercepted after
paying a visit to "the apostle Eliot, among his Indian converts"
(p. 183); and when he later proceeds on his way to Boston, he
has to restrain himself from whispering blasphemous thoughts to,
respectively, a "paternal deacon," "the eldest female member of
his church," and the youngest maiden under his pastoral care (pp.
217–19).

The scene in the wood and its aftermath represent the nadir
of Dimmesdale's descent into spiritual chaos and social irresponsibility. The interview itself is evocative of Eve's temptation of
Adam in *Paradise Lost*, with Hester taking the initiative in urging
the minister to break completely with the Boston community.
Transcendentalist, separatist and antinomian at once, she denies
altogether the doctrine of original sin. Insisting to Arthur that
"what we did had a consecration of its own" (p. 195), she casts
aside the scarlet letter which only moments earlier, hounded by
Pearl for an explanation of its meaning, she had casually but

36. Bell discusses this incident at length (*Hawthorne and the Historical
Romance of New England*, pp. 136–37).

accurately identified as the mark of the Black Man. A corollary
to Hester's position, and of particular relevance here, is her
emphasis on decline and decay in describing the Puritan town.
"Leave this wreck and ruin here where it hath happened" she cries,
and headily proclaims her faith in the opportunity of beginning
anew. In a phrase that might have been uttered by Emerson
himself, and penned by Hawthorne with *Nature* in mind,[37] she
exhorts her dispirited lover to be "up, and away!" (p. 198). Arthur,
meanwhile, regresses to a state of almost infantile dependence on
Hester's vitality. He implores her to "think for me . . . thou art
strong. Resolve for me" (p. 196); and she responds by launching
into her fervent appeal determined "to buoy him up" with the
force of her words (p. 198). "Buoy" in this context suggests a pun
on boy, which is what Dimmesdale has all but become by surren-
dering his will to Hester and abdicating the principles of the fathers.
    There can be little doubt that Hawthorne looks with disfavor
on Hester's rejection of sin and the past.[38] While she and Arthur
exchange vows of love, he intervenes to remind us that her
estrangement from human institutions "had made her strong, but
taught her much amiss" (p. 200). It is evident, moreover, that
he does not participate in the sympathy with which the "unre-
deemed, unchristianized, lawless" wilderness responds to her plan
of escape (p. 201). When we read Hester's triumphant exclamation
that "the past is gone" (p. 202), we should bear in mind what
Hawthorne himself says in the preface concerning his art: "But
the past was not dead" (p. 27). And when she tells her lover to
give up his name and take another, "and a high one, such as thou
canst wear without fear or shame" (p. 198), we should recall that
Hawthorne retains the surname of his ancestors, stained though
it is with the blood of innocent victims, and that the demonic
Roger Chillingworth has done exactly what Hester proposes by
changing his name from Prynne.

37. The theme of youth and age, the sons and the fathers, is central to
Emerson's essay, which begins with the famous sentences: "Our age is retro-
spective. It builds the sepulchres of the fathers . . ."
38. A. N. Kaul, for one, would disagree. See *The American Vision: Actual
and Ideal Society in Nineteenth-Century Fiction* (New Haven: Yale University
Press, 1963), pp. 173–89.

But it is primarily Dimmesdale on whom the author now projects —in Henry James's famous phrase—"the cold, thin rays of his fitfully-moving lantern."[39] And it is also at this point in the narrative that Hawthorne begins to reintroduce the chief source on which he relies in the preface: the morphology of conversion. For what Dimmesdale is compelled to confront in the wood is the depravity of his own nature, and with the felt realization that he, like Hawthorne in the Custom-House, is in jeopardy of losing his soul, the tortuous process commences that eventuates in his redemption.[40] As he wanders in a maze of uncertainty, the minister is conscious of wicked impulses surfacing "in spite of himself, yet growing out of a profounder self than that which opposed the impulse" (p. 217). In the grammar of Calvinism, the "profounder self" is the unregenerate natural man who is helpless to overcome sin without the intervention of grace. Mistress Hibbins instantly recognizes the clergyman as one of her fellowship, and Dimmesdale, startled by the unprecedented familiarity of the witch's greeting, fears that he has indeed entered his name into the book of the damned. Adds Hawthorne:

He had made a bargain very like it. Tempted by a dream of happiness, he had yielded himself with deliberate choice, as he had never done before, to what he knew was deadly sin (p. 222).

Nearing his study, Dimmesdale is overwhelmed by the conviction of his own inability, and he touches a depth of despair that is analogous to Hawthorne's fright at the prospect of permanent

39. James, *Hawthorne*, p. 100.
40. There is considerable disagreement over the question of Dimmesdale's salvation or damnation. Darrel Abel, "Hawthorne's Dimmesdale: Fugitive from Wrath," *Nineteenth-Century Fiction* 11 (1956): 81–105; and Male, *Hawthorne's Tragic Vision*, pp. 115–17, take the position that his regeneration is authentic. Edward H. Davidson, "Dimmesdale's Fall," *New England Quarterly* 36 (1963): 358–70, argues that the minister is damned, as does Porte, *Romance in America*, pp. 108–12, although Porte's view is somewhat qualified. Porte basically agrees with Crews, *Sins of the Fathers*, pp. 136–53, in seeing the Election Sermon and the subsequent confession as sublimations of sexual energy. Crews's interpretation has been sharply challenged by Quentin Anderson, *The Imperial Self: An Essay in American Literary and Cultural History* (New York: Alfred A. Knopf, 1971), pp. 59–87.

interment in the Salem Custom-House. But the moment of dread is preparatory to the onrush of hope, for "another man had returned out of the forest; a wiser one; with a knowledge of hidden mysteries which the simplicity of the former could never have reached" (p. 223).

The "wiser man" whom Dimmesdale has become is no longer the helpless boy whom Hester swayed in the wood. Upon reaching his rooms, he places his hand "on the Hebrew Scriptures" and calls for food which he devours "with ravenous appetite" (pp. 223–24). These are actions that one might expect from the fathers— or even, indeed, from the old gourmand of the "Introductory." That they are attributed to Dimmesdale at this critical juncture indicates that he is in the grip of an internal revolution, a revolution whose meaning he is about to transmit to the New England settlement by destroying his unfinished Election Sermon and inditing a fresh one,

> which he wrote with such an impulsive flow of thought and emotion, that he fancied himself inspired; and only wondered that Heaven should see fit to transmit the grand and solemn music of its oracles through so foul an organ-pipe as he (p. 225).

Hawthorne's language in this passage is deliberately ambiguous, and numerous critics have hastened to conclude that Dimmesdale is deceiving himself when he "fancies" that his inspiration is divine. But from the perspective of Calvinism, there is nothing paradoxical about the fact that the Holy Spirit should vouchsafe an influx of grace to "so foul an organ-pipe" as a sinner who has experienced humiliation and knows that he is too thoroughly polluted to redeem himself. Accordingly, when we next see Dimmesdale, his hand no longer rests "ominously upon his heart" (p. 238), he is marching proudly in the company of the fathers, and it is quite clear that he has been "reborn" in the three days that have elapsed since his meeting with Hester—just as Hawthorne himself is reborn after his three years in the Custom-House.[41] Watching him pass

---

41. As even Crews notes, "There is little doubt that Dimmesdale has somehow recovered his piety in the three days that intervene between the writing of the sermon and its delivery" (*Sins of the Fathers*, p. 148).

in the procession, Mistress Hibbins cannot believe that he is the same man who emerged from the forest, and even she is impelled to admit that he "really looks" like the "saint on earth" whom the people judge him to be (p. 241).

The Election Sermon proper represents Dimmesdale's solution to the problem of integrating—in terms that apply to the Puritan colony—the promise of the New Testament with the truths of the Old. But before examining the sermon, it is necessary to return to the richly suggestive remark that Chillingworth makes in the minister's study just as his erstwhile patient sits down to compose. "A good man's prayers are golden recompense!" the physician declares in taking his leave. "Yea, they are the current gold coin of the New Jerusalem, with the King's own mint-mark on them!" (p. 224). Once before, when the ailing divine was first placed under his care, Chillingworth spoke of the impatience of saintly men to quit this life in order to walk with God "on the golden pavements of the New Jerusalem" (p. 122). He alludes, of course, to the holy city described in Revelation as descending from heaven at the millennium. It is a very different city from the seventeenth-century Boston where Dimmesdale resides, and its evocation inevitably brings to mind the clergyman's frustrated longing for a more Christian community. Why then is it mentioned by the leech at all, and for what presumably sinister purpose? The answer is readily supplied if we recall that Dimmesdale has repeatedly stated his intention of postponing his personal confession until the day of final judgment. Correspondingly the New Jerusalem, according to John, will not materialize on earth until the Second Coming and the end of worldly time. To dwell on the celestial city, therefore, is to encourage the minister to pursue the same course with regard to his social obligation that he has followed in dealing with his spiritual predicament. It is to attempt to deflect him, if only by implication, from envisaging a temporal realization of his hope for a better society.

And yet the dream of the New Jerusalem proves to figure importantly in the official pronouncement that Dimmesdale delivers to the Puritan populace. His discourse differs notably in spirit and content from the jeremiad thundered by Wilson at the romance's inception; we learn of its message in the chapter fittingly

entitled "The *Revelation* of the Scarlet Letter" (italics added).
"As he drew towards the close," Hawthorne writes of the youthful
preacher,

> a spirit as of prophecy had come upon him, constraining him
> to its purpose as mightily as the old prophets of Israel were
> constrained; only with this difference, that, whereas the Jewish
> seers had denounced judgments and ruin on their country, it
> was his mission to foretell a high and glorious destiny for the
> newly gathered people of the Lord (p. 249).

What Dimmesdale has managed to do, in breaking with the tradition of the "woe-denouncing seers" of the Hebrew Bible and rein-
terpreting the millennial vision of Revelation, is to locate the New
Jerusalem in time and on this side of eternity. And in doing so he
has at last fulfilled his pastoral calling. For his prophecy is not, as
one commentator has recently claimed, "a ranting political oration,
a hymn to American progress" on the order of George Bancroft's
corruption of Edwards.[42] Informing Dimmesdale's words is a
plaintive undertone of sorrow and pathos: "the whisper, or the
shriek, as it might be conceived, as of suffering humanity, that
touched a sensibility in every bosom!" (p. 243). The tremor of woe
discernible in Dimmesdale's utterance seems to his listeners to signal
his approaching death; but it conveys something more to the reader
who knows that seven long years of guilt and anguish have gone
into the minister's own search for salvation on earth. It conveys
Dimmesdale's intimate acquaintance with the sin and suffering that
will precede, and are apt to continue in some diminished degree,
into the glorious future that he has foretold for the people of New
England. The epic of the individual soul parallels and prefigures the
history of the entire community; seven, after all, is the number of
the Sabbatism.

Sin, suffering, and death—which shortly awaits the young divine
—these realities, as noted earlier, came into being with the primal
crime. Their unavoidable social consequences are the cemetery and
the prison that the venerable founders provided for almost as soon
as they stepped ashore upon the virgin American soil. Once the

42. Bell, *Hawthorne and the Historical Romance of New England*, p. 142.

fathers, too, were not total strangers to the idea of a "Utopia of human virtue and happiness" (p. 47). But they have lost sight of that hope, and it has fallen to Dimmesdale to restore it to the Puritan commonwealth. With the delivery of the Election Sermon, Dimmesdale discharges his debt to society, and frees himself to make his long overdue personal confession. Again, he invites comparison to Hawthorne, who writes his autobiographical sketch—and makes his own "Revelation of the Scarlet Letter"—only after successfully completing his term as Surveyor of the Revenue. As the colonial procession returns on its way to the townhall, the Reverend Mr. Wilson, observing his youthful colleague's weakened condition, steps forward to offer assistance; but Dimmesdale, we are told, "tremulously, but decidedly, repelled the old man's arm" (p. 251). The import of this gesture becomes clear when we remember what Hawthorne says in the preface concerning the fate that befalls the officer who overstays his tenure in the Custom-House:

> while he leans on the mighty arm of the Republic, his own proper strength departs from him. He loses, in an extent proportioned to the weakness or force of his original nature, the capability of self-support. . . . He usually keeps his ground just long enough for his own ruin, and is then thrust out, with sinews all unstrung, to totter along the difficult footpath of life as best he may. Conscious of his own infirmity,—that his tempered steel and elasticity are lost,—he for ever afterwards looks wistfully about him in quest of support external to himself (pp. 38–39).

Enfeebled though he is, Dimmesdale is able to withstand the temptation of "support external to himself" because he has been transformed by the "grace" of a merciful Providence (p. 253). And he no longer needs to rely on the strength of the fathers because he is about to take his rightful place in their ranks by acknowledging his own fatherhood of Pearl. He beckons to Hester, who "approaches against her strongest will," and asks her help in mounting the platform (p. 252). But whereas in the forest he submitted passively to her direction, the minister now exclaims, "Thy strength, Hester; but let it be guided by the will which God hath granted me" (p. 253). And then, summoning all his energy, he thrusts her aside as well.

Hawthorne uses the occasion of Dimmesdale's final speech to weave together the diverse themes of *The Scarlet Letter*. The minister overcomes the split between this world and the afterlife by standing "out from all the earth to put in his plea of guilty at the bar of Eternal Justice" (p. 254). Accepting what is true in the creed of his elders, he admonishes Hester to turn her thoughts, not to the false hope of a future reunion, but rather to "the law we broke" and "the sin here so awfully revealed" (p. 256). Moments earlier, he showed his compassion by asking God's forgiveness for Chillingworth, the "wretched and wronged old man" whom he could not pardon in the wood (p. 253). Thus he incorporates on a personal basis the values of the fathers and the New Testament injunction that the fathers too often ignore. It is not pride but the assurance of salvation that accounts for the exultation of the minister's dying words. For according to the morphology of conversion, it is only by publicly owning membership in the brotherhood of sin that the believing Christian can hope to attain the state of visible sainthood that Dimmesdale—and Hawthorne—achieve at the last. Surely this is the deeper meaning of the moral "Be true!" (p. 260) that Hawthorne himself draws from the minister's death on the scaffold.

———————•—•———————

Dimmesdale's confession profoundly alters the lives of the three surviving protagonists of *The Scarlet Letter*. As he kisses Pearl's lips, the child is humanized, delivered from her isolation, and assured of the social identity that she previously lacked. Like Hawthorne's own children, who "shall strike their roots into unaccustomed earth" (p. 12), she leaves Boston and settles abroad, eventually to become the wife of a European nobleman.[43] But it would be a mistake to argue that the effect of Pearl's departure

43. Harry Levin writes of Pearl: "When we read . . . that she grew up an heiress and traveled abroad, we realize that we can pursue her further adventures through the novels of Henry James" (*The Power of Blackness: Hawthorne, Poe, Melville* [New York: Alfred A. Knopf, 1958], p. 78).

is to belittle the "Puritan sense of reality," as one critic has put it.[44] Hers is not, after all, a flight like the one advocated by Hester in the forest: she does not sever her ties to the past but keeps them alive by sending gifts and other "tokens of a continual remembrance" to her mother (p. 262). And it is not Pearl herself so much as her contemporaries—that is, the children of the first generation—who forsake the authentic "Puritan sense of reality." For it is the "immediate posterity" of the founding fathers, according to Hawthorne, who "wore the blackest shade of Puritanism, and so darkened the national visage with it, that all the subsequent years have not sufficed to clear it up" (p. 232).

Pearl's travels abroad are made possible, of course, by Chillingworth's unexpected bequest—for Chillingworth, too, is changed when Dimmesdale confesses. His change resembles the one undergone by Pearl herself insofar as it issues in his assumption of a social identity. The generous act that he performs on his death bed amounts to a public acknowledgment of what he went to such lengths to conceal from the moment that he appeared in the Boston marketplace: his intimate relation to the wearer of the scarlet letter and her illegitimate offspring. In summing up the leech's part in the events of the book, Hawthorne comments on his equally intimate relation to the minister, pondering the curious question "whether hatred and love be not the same thing at bottom" (p. 260)—an insight that occurred to Melville as well, who wrote of Claggart's feelings for Billy Budd in similar terms.

As for Hester, after accompanying her daughter to Europe, she returns to the "more real life" that awaits her in New England "than in that unknown region where Pearl had found a home." Here she begins her "penitence"—as opposed to penance—and here, too, she restores "of her own free will" the symbol of sin which she had discarded in the forest (pp. 262–63). The emphasis on Hester's volition in resuming the scarlet letter suggests a willing compliance with the commandment of the law that is possible only for those who have exchanged the covenant of works for the covenant of grace. It is true, however, as several commentators have pointed out, that when Hawthorne speaks of Hester in the

44. Crews, *Sins of the Fathers*, p. 151.

"Conclusion," his orientation is more secular than religious. But
this should not be construed to mean that Hester's stature is diminished in comparison to Dimmesdale's.[45] The point, rather, is
that Hester—like Hawthorne himself—has found a secular equivalent to the theological stance of the American Puritans. The very
location of her home, situated as it is neither quite within the
community nor wholly away from it, constitutes a kind of physical
correlative for the metaphysical ideal of living in the world without
being of it. And it should be noted as well that Hester takes to
heart the message of Dimmesdale's Election Sermon. Like her
former lover, she masters the gift of addressing her fellow creatures
"in the heart's native language." She consoles and advises the erring
and wounded souls—"women, more especially"—who flock to her
cottage demanding to know the cause of their misery and the
possible remedy. And what she tells them is notably similar in
spirit to the farewell sermon that Dimmesdale preached to the
New England populace. She assures them of her firm belief in
a brighter future, a period when "the whole relation between man
and woman" will be established "on a surer ground of mutual
happiness." Her prophecy is not a repetition of the lawless specula-
tion in which she was secretly wont to indulge while estranged
from the Puritan town. The glorious destiny to which she alludes
will materialize, she says, "in Heaven's own time," and she now
recognizes the folly of expecting that the mission of actualizing
it will be entrusted, as she once vainly imagined, to a woman such
as herself, "stained with sin" and "bowed down with shame" (p.
263). Thus Hester accepts the inevitability of suffering and sin
by counseling patience and trusting in Providence, while holding
out the hope of a more just society in the years to come. Her
disclosure of her views in this matter amounts in effect to a public
confession.

There still remains one character whose final sentiments we have
yet to consider—a character who occupies an important place
in *The Scarlet Letter*, albeit not in the romance proper. This, of
course, is Hawthorne himself. In a sense, he also "returns" by

45. See, for example, Male's observation that "where Hester's ascension was
limited, Dimmesdale's is complete" (*Hawthorne's Tragic Vision*, p. 98).

going back to the color scheme of his opening gesture: the offer
of the wild rose against the background of the tale's "darkening
close." The juxtaposition of red and black, with their symbolic
connotations of love and law, clearly prefigures the heraldry of
the scarlet letter against its sable field that adorns the common
tombstone of the guilty lovers. The way in which the romance
concludes invites comparison to the circular journeys undertaken
by Hester and Dimmesdale, both of whom grow to a measure of
self-realization as a result of their sin and sorrow. Since the book
is composed of twenty-four chapters, in the manner of an epic,
we may even describe it as a Christian *Odyssey* in which the end
is the beginning transformed. Yet the gloom at the close of *The
Scarlet Letter* is somehow disproportionate to the theodicies of
the two central protagonists, who leave us, after all, with promises
of a better future. It conveys something more than an awareness
on Hawthorne's part of the educational value of suffering. It hints,
indeed, at a deep-seated dissatisfaction with the nature of contemporary American society. For the America of Hawthorne's day—
the America of which he writes in "The Custom-House"—has
obviously not realized—indeed it has betrayed—the hopes of Hester
and the minister.

Hester foretold a richer life for women in general; but Hawthorne, in describing his heroine's genius for needle-work, observes
that the art was "then, as now, almost the only one within a
woman's grasp" (p. 81). Dimmesdale prophesied a "glorious destiny"—a New Jerusalem—for the settlers of the Bay. But instead
of a New Jerusalem, we are given an account of nineteenth-century
Salem, a crumbling seaport whose Custom-House is staffed by
superannuated public servants more dead than alive, more damned
than holy. Chillingworth likened a good man's prayers to "the
current gold coin of the New Jerusalem, with the King's own
mint-mark on them"; and Dimmesdale's sermon, we are told, so
stirred his auditors that they imagined a passing angel "had shed
down a shower of golden truths upon them" (p. 249). The narrator
of the preface, however, comments on the fever for riches that
impels his countrymen to seek their fortunes in California. They
might have spared themselves the trouble, he adds, and stayed
at home to earn their livelihood in the employment of the Republic.

Whereupon he identifies "Uncle Sam's gold"—as opposed to the gold of the New Jerusalem—with "the Devil's wages"; and he expresses his fear that he has bartered his soul and his art for "a little pile of glittering coin out of his Uncle's pocket" (p. 39).

The implicit judgment that Hawthorne thus passes on contemporary America gains force from the fact that in composing the "Introductory" he borrows extensively from the Gospel of Matthew. For we know that Hawthorne was also familiar with the *Journal* of John Winthrop, and that Winthrop was one of the chief sources he turned to when he wrote *The Scarlet Letter*. Winthrop, of course, was a prophet in his own right, who admonished his brethren aboard the *Arbella* that "wee shall be as a Citty upon a Hill, the eies of all people are uppon us." As Hawthorne was certainly aware, the conceit used by Winthrop derives from the Bible, specifically Matthew's Gospel. It is during the Sermon on the Mount, according to Matthew, that Jesus declares to the apostles: "Ye are the light of the world. A city that is set on an hill cannot be hid" (5:14). It seems safe to infer that Winthrop's vision furnished Hawthorne with the inspiration for Dimmesdale's prophetic Election Sermon. But it seems equally clear from the preface that neither the Puritan ideal advanced by Winthrop, nor the dream of a Christian community cherished by Dimmesdale, has fared very well at the hands of posterity. And so the last word properly belongs to Matthew. "A prophet," the apostle quotes Jesus as saying, "is not without honor, save in his own country, and in his own house" (13:57).

The House of the Seven Gables

As A. N. Kaul has pointed out, *The House of the Seven Gables*, "makes a bridge, as it were, between the seventeenth century and the author's own time."[46] The point is worth emphasizing because Hawthorne goes out of his way to establish a continuity between his first two romances; or to put it differently, between the Puritan past where the action of *The Scarlet Letter* takes place and the

46. Kaul, *American Vision*, p. 142.

nineteenth-century American background described in "The Custom-House." On the most obvious level, the continuity is supplied by the Pyncheon dwelling whose history is told in the introductory chapter. But the house does more than simply carry the narrative into the present, thereby welding the temporal progression into an organic whole. It also re-creates something of the mood and setting of the earlier romance and its prefatory sketch. Its dismal aspect is an appropriately forceful reminder of both the blackened prison from which Hester emerges to stand in the marketplace and the scene of Hawthorne's own three years' immurement as Surveyor of the Revenue. As the central symbol of the book, it speaks with renewed urgency to the issue of the contemporary relevance of the Calvinist vision that underlies Dimmesdale's confession and Hawthorne's theory of art.[47]

The same vision underlies the preface to *The House of the Seven Gables*. It is there, in a much reduced compass, that Hawthorne speaks of the necessity of subjecting even his own unorthodox art form to rules, insisting in particular on conformity to "the truth of the human heart"—a variation on his original effort to define the romance by disavowing Transcendental license while stressing the importance of endowing his creations with "a heart and sensibilities of human tenderness." And it is in the preface, too, that he distinguishes his fictions from novels by claiming the latitude "to mingle the Marvellous" with the real "as a slight, delicate, and evanescent flavor" (p. 1).[48] This also is a variation on his former apology for his art as a "neutral territory" between the "Actual" and the "Imaginary," and his present task as romancer can accordingly be seen as part of a continued endeavor to body forth his aesthetic in the development and characters of his tale.

Given this fact, it is necessary to take some account of the changes which Hawthorne shows to have occurred between 1642,

47. The centrality of the symbol of the house has been discussed by Maurice Beebe, "The Fall of the House of Pyncheon," *Nineteenth-Century Fiction* 11 (1956): 1–17; and Porte, *Romance in America*, pp. 114–25. Hawthorne's use of Calvinist ideas in *House of the Seven Gables* has been examined perceptively by Ursula Brumm, *American Thought and Religious Typology*, trans. John Hoaglund (New Brunswick, N.J.: Rutgers University Press, 1970), pp. 128–40.

48. Quotations are from Hawthorne, *House of the Seven Gables*, Centenary Edition; page references are included in the text.

when *The Scarlet Letter* opens, and the last decade of the seventeenth century, which ushers in the events of *The House of the
Seven Gables*. It is evident from the first, for example, that the
polarities rife at the outset of the earlier book have been greatly
sharpened by declension. The class divisions which were largely
absent from Winthrop's Boston now make their appearance in the
persons of Pyncheon and Maule. Indeed, the only redeeming
feature of the witch persecutions, according to Hawthorne, is that
they fell with impartiality on rich and poor, victimizing persons
of every rank. American Calvinism itself, secularized and perverted
by the children of the first settlers, has lost its unity and splintered
into literally warring camps. Its respect for the world has become
the pretext for an unprincipled pursuit of material gain, while its
hunger for the spirit has degenerated into the wizardry of Matthew
Maule. Its recognition of the value of law has hardened into the
hypocritical legalism personified by Colonel Pyncheon, who exploits the machinery of the state to further his own rapacious
ends. Its New Testament message of forgiveness has vanished
altogether, and in its stead we are given the chilling curse that
Maule hurls from the gallows at his relentless persecutor: "God
will give him blood to drink!" (p. 8). Most significant of all, perhaps, the effect of the witchcraft has been to discredit the clergy,
who are among the "loudest to applaud the work of blood" (p. 8)
and whose representative spokesman, the Reverend Mr. Higginson,
extols his "distinguished parishioner's earthly career" and pronounces him a saint (p. 17). There is no Arthur Dimmesdale in
The House of the Seven Gables to give religious utterance to the
Puritan synthesis which Hawthorne seeks to restore through the
medium of his art. There is no Election Sermon, no dying confession on the scaffold. Within the tale itself, therefore, art becomes a
substitute for the sermon, and it falls to the figure of the artist
to teach the truths that it was once the province of the ministry
to preach.

   That Hawthorne sees his own function in precisely these terms
is suggested by his allusion, in the second paragraph of the story,
to "the little regarded truth, that the act of the passing generation
is the germ which may and must produce good or evil fruit, in
a far distant time" (p. 6). The truth in question is the "truth

of the human heart," and it is little regarded for reasons that
emerge from Hawthorne's treatment of the symbol of the house.
Quite early in the narrative he compares the house to "a great
human heart, with a life of its own" (p. 27), and he dwells on
the comparison throughout the romance. The house is tainted by
crime from the moment of its inception, having been purchased
with the blood of Matthew Maule and callously erected over his
grave. Its original owner is the ruthless Colonel Pyncheon, who
bears a pronounced likeness to Hawthorne's own ancestor William
—he is represented in his portrait as clutching a sword in one
hand and a Bible in the other—and who is similarly described
as the progenitor of his race. As might be expected, he is punished
for his greed by the sentence of death, which is the wages of sin.
In commenting on the Colonel's demise, Hawthorne invites his
readers to ponder the question whether each inheritor of the house
"did not commit anew the great guilt of his ancestor, and incur
all its original responsibilities" (p. 20). Since the house is an emblem
of the corrupt heart of man, he is referring to the primal transgression and its perpetual reenactment by the posterity of Adam.
Here it is instructive to glance once again at the preface where
Hawthorne, "not to be deficient" in professing "some definite moral
purpose" (as he puts it), adopts as the moral to his tale the precept
that "the wrong-doing of one generation lives into the successive
ones." He accordingly renews his consent to the Calvinist doctrine
of innate depravity, and imparts to his art the office of impressing
"mankind (or indeed, any one man)" with the reality of original
sin (p. 2).[49]

Hawthorne admits to little expectation that his moral will be
"any more evident, at the last page than at the first" (p. 3)—
a disclaimer that is perhaps inevitable in a world which bestows
its highest honors on the present-day Judge. The consequences
of the Fall are social as well as individual, and they are especially
virulent in the wake of the witchcraft. It is worthy of note, for

49. Evert A. Duyckinck pointed out long ago that the house "may be no
unmeet adumbration of the corrupted soul of man," adding with shrewd insight
that Hawthorne "of all laymen . . . will preach to you the closest sermons."
See his review of *House of the Seven Gables* printed in *Literary World* 7 (26
April 1851): 334–35.

example, that Hawthorne calls repeated attention to the resemblance between the Judge and his ancestor the Colonel, and that he turns the full blast of his irony on Jaffrey's palpably contrived "look of exceeding good-humor and benevolence" (p. 116). Presumably he is inviting us to recall his forebodings about the descendants of the founding fathers as expressed in *The Scarlet Letter*, and to recall in particular his pronouncement concerning his contemporaries: "We have yet to learn again the forgotten art of gayety."[50] Jaffrey's bogus smile is what passes for merriment in modern Salem, and his eminent standing in the community is a measure of the failure of Dimmesdale's prophecy of a glorious future for the New England commonwealth.

The failure of that prophecy can be measured in other ways as well, most strikingly in the spread and worsening of the un-Christian attitude which governed the Puritans' treatment of Hester, causing them to regard her as their "life-long bond-slave." Colonel Pyncheon's zeal in purging the land of evil spirits brings about the imprisonment and subsequent execution of Matthew Maule; but according to the local townspeople, the Colonel's haughty descendants are repaid in kind, for they are rumored to be "no better than bond-servants to these plebian Maules, on entering the topsyturvy commonwealth of sleep" (p. 26). Otherwise opposites, the Maules and the Pyncheons are equally guilty of abusing their powers for the purpose of subjugating others. The family traditions have been handed down with disastrous results for the individual members and far-reaching implications for the nation at large. In the manuscript supposedly written by Holgrave, Matthew Maule, the grandson of the wizard, is greeted at the door of the Pyncheon mansion by a Negro slave; and Gervayse Pyncheon himself knowingly sells his daughter into "a bondage more humiliating, a thousand fold, than that which binds its chain around the body" (p. 208). According to the Savage edition of Winthrop's *Journal*, the slave trade was first introduced to Massachusetts by "the Salem ship, the *Desire*" in 1637,[51] and it seems

50. Hawthorne, *Scarlet Letter*, Centenary Edition, 1: 232.
51. *Winthrop's Journal: "History of New England,"* 2 vols., ed. James Savage (Boston, 1825), 1: 254. Savage has the date wrong: it was actually 1638. It is now much debated whether this was in fact the first shipment of slaves to

likely that Hawthorne intended a criticism of his fellow New
Englanders for having participated in the social evil whose reper-
cussions were threatening to destroy the Union by the time he
composed *The House of the Seven Gables*. He strongly suggests
the North's complicity in slavery by giving his archetypical Yankee
the revealing name of Dixey. It is with this specific criticism in
mind that we can appreciate the irony of the scene in which
Hepzibah is driven by poverty to sell gingerbread miniatures of
Jim Crow to little Ned Higgins. As a general point, Hawthorne's
target is the pervasive rot of exploitative ownership and enslavement which he finds at the core of American society.

The principal carrier of the contagion of slavery into the present
is Hepzibah's cousin, the Judge. Closely associated with the law,
and a figure to reckon with in local politics, Jaffrey is a Governor
Bellingham *redivivus* who combines all the worst features of the
Puritan magistracy with the soulless materialism of the old gourmand of "The Custom-House." He is coarse-grained and elderly,
possessed of an iron energy of will that brooks no impediments,
and endowed with an "ogre-like appetite" (p. 275). His wife, we
are told, met with an early grave because the Judge "compelled
her to serve him coffee, every morning, at his bedside, in token
of fealty to her liege-lord and master" (p. 123). And he is responsi-
ble, of course, for Clifford's thirty years' imprisonment on the false
charge of having murdered their uncle. In portraying the Judge—
whose imposing title is itself significant—Hawthorne occasionally
slips into a religious idiom which hints at an identification of his
subject with the Old Testament conception of a wrathful and
despotic God. It is Jaffrey who keeps up the pretense that Clifford
is a sinner whose fate is deserved; and emulating his progenitor
the Colonel, whom he so markedly resembles, he fully intends
to hunt his long-suffering victim "to death for his spoil" (p. 8).
In the confrontation scene with Hepzibah, the Judge's anger gets
the better of him, and he relaxes his mask of "free and christianlike
forgiveness" to reveal a "frown which you at once feel to be eternal"

---

arrive in Massachusetts. It seems probable, at all events, that the date 1637
stuck in Hawthorne's mind, since he often draws to our notice the fact that
the Pyncheon house was exactly thirty-seven years old when Maule reduced
Alice to servitude.

(p. 232). Recovering his composure, he declares that he is Clifford's "only friend and an all-powerful one" (p. 233). When Hepzibah asks him what possible motive her brother could have for concealing evidence of their uncle's missing property, he piously lays the cause to mankind's "fallen nature," and adds in accents that might have been uttered by the wrathful Deity of the legal covenant:

> He looked upon me as his enemy. He considered me as the cause of his overwhelming disgrace, his imminent peril of death, his irretrievable ruin (p. 235).

If Clifford is indeed, as Hawthorne writes elsewhere, "a thunder-smitten Adam" (p. 150), it is abundantly clear that he will receive no mercy from the Judge.

Jaffrey lacks not only compassion but also an understanding of the heart. In the same chapter in which the interview with Hepzibah occurs, Hawthorne draws a sustained metaphoric equation which serves to underscore the Judge's ignorance of human nature, his own in particular. Though he is acclaimed by church and state, the Judge's inner being contains some "evil and unsightly thing" which is hidden from the eyes of the world and forgotten or ignored by himself. Hawthorne likens his daily life to a splendid palace, "a tall and stately edifice, which, in the view of other people, and ultimately in his own view, is no other than the man's character, or the man himself." But in an obscure corner or room of this magnificent dwelling

> or beneath the marble pavement, in a stagnant water-puddle, with the richest pattern of mosaic work above—may lie a corpse, half-decayed, and still decaying, and diffusing its death-scent all through the palace (p. 230).

When we read this passage, with its reference to "marble pavement" and "a stagnant water-puddle," we are surely meant to recall Hawthorne's earlier observation, "Life is made up of marble and mud" (p. 41). Obviously the Judge is too preoccupied with his marble palace to notice the muddy foundation on which it is built. According to Hawthorne, however, the decaying corpse within its stagnant pool is "the true emblem" of Jaffrey's corrupted soul, and his refusal to acknowledge its presence amounts to a denial of original sin (p. 230). Inured to the stench of his own depravity, Jaffrey vainly places his trust in works and outward obedience to the law; and he smugly repudiates his membership in the sinful brotherhood of man. His legalism seals his spiritual death and purchases him only perdition; and if he tyrannizes others, he is also a slave, for what dungeon, writes Hawthorne, "is so dark as one's own heart! What jailor so inexorable as one's self!" (p. 169).

It is the calling of the artist, and the mission of his art, to unlock the prison of selfishness and arrest the infection of enslavement by laying bare the "truth of the human heart" which Jaffrey endeavors to hide. The obvious candidate for the figure of the artist in *The House of the Seven Gables* is Holgrave, the reformer and daguerrotypist, who makes "pictures out of sunshine" (p. 91) and writes stories which he contributes to local periodicals.[52] But the stridency of Holgrave's zeal for reform, and his immersion in fashionable idealism, otherwise ill equip him for the part that he is eventually destined to play. From the moment that he is introduced to the reader, he invites comparison to Hester Prynne as the "dark lady" of *The House of the Seven Gables*, a spokesman, as numerous commentators have pointed out, for the Transcendental outcry against the past and its legacy of social injustice. Hepzibah says of him, more on faith than from any actual knowledge, that "he has a law of his own" (p. 85), but whatever code it is that he follows, he clearly belongs to Hester's party in believing that "the world's law was no law for [his] mind." His philosophy, according to Hawthorne, is "crude, wild, and misty" (p. 181). He rails against social restraints, wishes to tear houses down—in sharp contrast to the Judge, who metaphorically builds a house—and shares Hester's error in supposing that the "golden era" into which he is said to possess prophetic insight will be "accomplished in his own lifetime" and through his own efforts (pp. 179–80). Here we should bear in mind what Hawthorne says in the preface concerning his art: "It must rigidly subject itself to laws."

52. On Holgrave as artist see Porte, *Romance in America*, pp. 114–25; Von Abele, *Death of the Artist*, pp. 58–69; and Richard H. Brodhead, *Hawthorne, Melville, and the Novel* (Chicago: University of Chicago Press, 1976), pp. 84–90.

The most serious flaw in Holgrave's radicalism, from Hawthorne's point of view, is that it impels him to reject the reality of evil in general and original sin in particular. When he first appears in the book, he reassures Hepzibah that the sinister shapes who people the world are as little to be feared "as the giants and ogres of a child's story-book." Cribbing a thought from Emerson, he explains that "I find nothing so singular in life, as that everything appears to lose its substance, the instant one actually grapples with it" (p. 144). He seems almost as perplexed as Phoebe by his initial daguerrotype of the Judge, which brings out his subject's uncanny likeness to the Colonel and which he has taken "over and over again, and still with no better result" (p. 91). What the miniature reveals, of course, is the Old Adam, the progenitor of the race, lurking just beneath the surface of the Judge's beaming smile, but its full significance is as yet a mystery to Holgrave, who is indeed "much struck" by Phoebe's offhand assurance that the face belongs to her Puritan ancestor (pp. 91–92). His attitude manifests itself most dramatically, perhaps, in his judgments on houses and the Pyncheon house especially. To Holgrave, habitations like that of the seven gables, built of "such permanent materials as stone or brick," are concrete monuments to the dead weight of the past, hateful symbols of institutions which have outlived their time. To level them and replace them at regular intervals is to root out corruption and speed the advent of a purified world:

> If each generation were allowed and expected to build its own houses, that single change, comparatively unimportant in itself, would imply almost every reform which society is now suffering for (pp. 183–84).

It is instructive to juxtapose this outburst with Hawthorne's own sentiments as they are spelled out in "Earth's Holocaust" (1844), a story which ridicules the shallow optimism of reform. The "dark-visaged" stranger who materializes at the tale's end to deliver the moral might be addressing Holgrave himself when he observes:

> There is one thing that these wiseacres have forgotten to throw into the fire, and without which all the rest of the conflagration

is just nothing at all—yes; though they had burned the earth
itself to a cinder!

Asked what he has in mind, the stranger replies, "What, but the
human heart itself!"[53]

The mention of the heart naturally takes us back to the house
of the seven gables. When Phoebe interrupts Holgrave to inquire
why he bothers to live in the old Pyncheon mansion at all, he
replies "that I may know the better how to hate it" (p. 184). His
answer, interpreted in light of the pervasive symbolism of the book,
betrays his ignorance and fear of his innermost self. As Phoebe
notes, he is altogether too cold and detached an observer; she "felt
his eye often; his heart seldom or never" (p. 177). Most damaging
of all is his uncritical interest in mesmerism, which Hawthorne
seems to have regarded as a nineteenth-century version of witchcraft, enabling its practitioners to violate the sanctity of the individual soul by reducing their subjects to involuntary servitude.
Such power, of course, is the imaginative correlative of the Judge's
legal authority, and can be the instrument of an equally terrible
form of enslavement over others.

But it is also true, as several critics have insisted,[54] that Hawthorne tends to associate his own creative energies with witchcraft,
and that his animus against its abuses is coupled with an awareness that when transmuted into art it has the power to free as
well as to bind. As art it can free, that is, because it can awaken
us to our fallen natures and take over from the sermon as the
means of "grace," thereby effecting that transformation of the
heart which alone makes possible the redemptive act of caring
for others. This, at all events, is what happens to Holgrave when
he reads Phoebe his manuscript on Alice Pyncheon and for the
first time grasps the deeper meaning of his art. The story dramatizes the unsuspected capacity for evil that resides within men's
hearts, specifically the Maules' and thus by implication Holgrave's,

53. Nathaniel Hawthorne, "Earth's Holocaust," in *The Works of Nathaniel
Hawthorne*, Centenary Edition, ed. William Charvat et al. (Columbus: Ohio
State University Press, 1962-), vol. 10, *Mosses from an Old Manse* (1974),
p. 403.
54. On this point see especially Daniel Hoffman's chapter on *House of the
Seven Gables* in *Form and Fable in American Fiction*, pp. 187-201.

who as the sole surviving representative of his race is heir to its
"great guilt" of vengeance. According to the manuscript, young
Matthew Maule "was popularly supposed to have inherited some
of his ancestor's questionable traits." He is fabled to be privy to
the secret of entering "other people's dreams, and regulating matters there . . . pretty much like the stage manager of a theatre."
He shares with Holgrave the family disposition of habitual reserve,
and he is similarly suspected by his neighbors of "holding heretical
tenets in matters of religion and polity." It is not by chance, surely,
that Hawthorne includes the detail that he is not "a church-com-
municant," for as it turns out, Maule is as little mindful as the
present-day Judge of his inward corruption (pp. 189–90). When
he makes himself "despot" over Alice's spirit (p. 209), he does so
without thought for the consequences, and proceeds to "commit
anew" the crime of his progenitor. Daniel Hoffman's allegation
that Maule is overcome by frustration because "death has cheated
his of his revenge" is certainly mistaken.[55] What makes him the
"wofullest man that ever walked behind a corpse" is rather the
discovery, which comes too late to save him, of Hawthorne's "little
regarded truth" concerning human nature:

> He meant to humble Alice, not to kill her;—but he had taken
> a woman's delicate soul into his rude gripe, to play with;—
> and she was dead! (p. 210).

As for Alice, by repenting her pride, she manages to escape the
blight that descends upon Maule. Hers is the same family sin that
Jaffrey later neglects to repent, as Hawthorne makes clear by alluding to the bust of "a marble woman" which stands in a corner
of Gervayse's apartment (p. 193). The statue is an emblem of Alice
herself, and looks ahead to Hawthorne's evocation of the Judge's
marble palace. It is a detail of considerable importance, therefore,
that Alice contracts the fever which kills her while treading "the
muddy sidewalks" on her way home from "the mean dwelling"
where she is summoned to wait on Maule's bride. No longer proud,
Alice accepts the mud whose existence Jaffrey denies, and she is

55. Ibid., p. 198.

forthwith delivered from the bondage which imperils her soul (pp. 209–10).

The effect of this story on Holgrave can fairly be likened to a conversion experience. Observing that he has almost mesmerized Phoebe by the spell of his words, he swells with "the consciousness of power" and fleetingly toys with the idea of "acquiring empire over the human spirit" (pp. 211–12). Yet the moral of his tale, which is all but identical to the moral of *The House of the Seven Gables*, is not lost upon Holgrave, who senses as never before his potential for evil. He resists the impulse to become a slaveholder like his ancestor Maule—or indeed like the Judge—and he is liberated from his fear and hatred of the heart:

> After all, what a good world we live in! How good, and beautiful! How young it is, too, with nothing really rotten or age-worn in it! This old house, for example, which sometimes has positively oppressed my breath with its smell of decaying timber! . . . Could I keep the feeling that now possesses me . . . it would be like a bower in Eden, blossoming with the earliest roses that God ever made. Moonlight, and the sentiment in man's heart, responsive to it, is the greatest of renovators and reformers (p. 214).

It is a whole new way of seeing the world that Holgrave affirms in this speech, and it is reminiscent of Jonathan Edwards' discovery, at a comparable stage in his own spiritual development, that "the appearance of every thing was altered; there seemed to be, as it were, a calm, sweet cast, or appearance of divine glory, in almost every thing."[56] In the context of the romance, Holgrave's acceptance of the house of the seven gables signals the first step toward his being able to love and to feel compassion. Moreover, his recognition that the heart is the "greatest of renovators" will eventually set realistic limits to his haste for reform and reconcile him to the necessity of living in society and abiding by its laws.

The change that comes over Holgrave as a result of reading his manuscript aloud is not shared by Phoebe, however, who

56. Jonathan Edwards, "Personal Narrative," in *Representative Selections*, ed. Clarence H. Faust and Thomas H. Johnson, rev. ed. (New York: Hill and Wang, 1962), p. 60.

admits that she can't "remember the incidents quite distinctly" and professes not to understand his subsequent effusion (p. 212). Representing modified versions of their antagonistic ancestors, Holgrave and Phoebe are initially portrayed as a study in contrasts. Whereas he espouses idealism and belongs to what Jaffrey derisively calls "the dreaming class of men" (p. 235), her sphere, according to Hawthorne, is emphatically "the Actual" (p. 140). Without being a materialist like her cousin the Judge, she has the "stern old stuff of Puritanism" in her veins and excels at such mundane chores as housework and shopkeeping (p. 76). In her presence even the ghostlike Clifford feels that "the world was no longer a delusion" (p. 141). As befits a Pyncheon—the family hallmark, after all, is its legalism—she is "orderly and obedient to common rules" (p. 168), and she regards the unconventional Holgrave with deep misgivings, it being her essence "to keep within the limits of law" (p. 85). And she is puzzled and slightly alarmed by whatever strikes her as unusual or strange; "for she was by nature as hostile to mystery, as the sunshine to a dark corner" (p. 218).

As the foregoing description suggests, Phoebe is also an innocent in matters of sin and the heart. She instinctively turns away her eyes when Holgrave shows her his original daguerrotype of the Judge, and she is profoundly discomforted by the thought, which occurs to her when Jaffrey flushes in anger because she shrinks from his kiss, that human "weaknesses and defects . . . are handed down from one generation to another, by a far surer process of transmission than human law has been able to establish" (p. 119). It is Holgrave's task to strengthen her to accept the intuition of original sin that she is otherwise "fain to smother" (p. 131). This he does by showing her a photographic image of the dead Judge seated in the same ancestral chair where the Colonel met his fate. The full import of this climactic moment in the book becomes clear when we remember Hawthorne's earlier metaphor of the stately palace with its hidden secret. The Judge's rotting carcass in the house of the seven gables is "the true emblem" of the corruption in the heart of man, and Holgrave himself has become the "seer"—the artist as prophet—"before whose sadly gifted eye the whole structure melts into thin air, leaving only . . . the decaying corpse within" (p. 230). It is only by facing this truth at the last, with all that it implies about her own fellowship in the community of sin, that Phoebe is able to love.[57]

The House of the Seven Gables is nothing less than Hawthorne's defense of "the great Christian doctrine of original sin." It thoroughly reflects his conviction, which he held in common with his Calvinist forefathers, that a heartfelt assent to universal depravity tends to foster humility, love, and joy in one's fellow men, whereas (to quote Edwards):

> our *disowning* that sin and guilt, which truly belongs to us, and endeavoring to persuade ourselves that we are vastly better than in truth we are, tends to a foolish *self-exaltation* and *pride*.[58]

It is, to be sure, a secularized Calvinism that informs Hawthorne's tale, a Calvinism that is reconstituted and preserved in his theory of the romance. The outcome of *The House of the Seven Gables*, although it has seemed unconvincing to many readers, is clearly intended as a realization of the aesthetic articulated in Hawthorne's preface. Holgrave's "conversion," which is anchored in his knowledge of the heart, issues in the vow that he will conform himself "to laws, and the peaceful practice of society" (p. 307). His resolution, implying a recognition of his own "helplessness" in the work of historical redemption (p. 180), and of the inevitability of social and individual evil in a fallen world, is reminiscent of the spirit, if not the mood, of Hester's return to New England at the close of *The Scarlet Letter*. Even the decision to take up residence in the Judge's "elegant country-seat" (p. 314) has a logic consistent with the "moral" of the book. Here it is helpful to glance once again at the sentence in which Hawthorne "provides" himself with his theme. He writes in the preface of

57. Regarding this scene, Porte writes: "Phoebe's introduction into an active awareness of death represents her introduction to knowledge of human evil—corruptibility—in others and at least potentially within herself, and the emotional and psychological depth obtained thereby will purchase her adult sexuality" (*Romance in America*, p. 124).

58. Jonathan Edwards, *The Great Christian Doctrine of Original Sin Defended*, ed. Clyde C. Holbrook (1758; New Haven: Yale University Press, 1970), p. 424.

the folly of tumbling down an avalanche of ill-gotten gold, or real estate, on the heads of an unfortunate posterity, thereby to maim and crush them, until the accumulated mass shall be scattered abroad in its original atoms (p. 2).

As this passage suggests, the family curse incurred by the Pyncheons is lifted with the death of the Judge and the redistribution of his unjustly acquired wealth. But the obvious pun on the phrase "original atoms" also suggests that the universal curse incurred by mankind as a result of the Fall continues intact.

It is shortly after Jaffrey's death that Holgrave produces the deed to the vast territories coveted by the Pyncheons and discloses that he himself is descended from the Maules. "In this long drama of wrong and retribution," he says, "I represent the old wizard" (p. 316). Since Phoebe, as we are reminded repeatedly, stands for the real, her betrothal to Holgrave can be seen as embodying that union of the "Actual" and the "Imaginary" which for Hawthorne defines the romance. The antithetical extremes epitomized in the first generation are sufficiently moderated by experience and the passage of time to render such union possible. The death of the Judge thus becomes an occasion for honest rejoicing, and the bliss of the lovers forms an ironically appropriate contrast to his sham joviality. For Holgrave and Phoebe, at least, the "forgotten art of gayety" has been revived in the present.

And yet it is, finally, a qualified and personal hope with which Hawthorne leaves us at the ending of *The House of the Seven Gables*. The book was published in 1851, at a time when an expanding and still optimistic nation, swollen with confidence and self-assured of its "power to do," had just wrested Texas and the Southwest from Mexico in a war fought under the jingoistic banner of Manifest Destiny. It was the election of the hero of that war, General Zachary Taylor, which brought about Hawthorne's expulsion from the Custom-House in 1849. It is important to remember that the narrator of the "Introductory" to *The Scarlet Letter* comments with distaste on his countrymen's lust for territory and riches, and that an analogous avarice motivates both Colonel Pyncheon and his contemporary avatar the Judge. To Hawthorne, the rapacity of his fellow Americans has despoiled the Eden of

the New World as surely as the greed of the Pyncheons corrupted
the "garden-ground" of old Matthew Maule (p. 316).

Hawthorne invites this inference by his relentless emphasis on
the number seven and by the fact that he dwells throughout the
romance on the motif of paradise lost and regained. When Phoebe
and Holgrave first declare their love, for example, he writes that
"they transfigured the earth, and made it Eden again, and themselves the first two dwellers in it" (p. 307). It has been pointed
out by several critics, furthermore, that seven generations of
Pyncheons have occupied the family mansion, and that Hawthorne
gives the book an organic unity of sorts by ending it with the
italicized words of its title.[59] The theological and social significance
of these details is immense. Manifest Destiny has been described
as a "nationalistic theology," and to advocates of expansionism it
seemed that the United States was about to fulfill its millennial
mission of restoring mankind to paradise.[60] Behind their triumphant rhetoric lay a reading of Revelation which gained currency
during the Reformation: that history is divided into seven periods
and that the pouring out of the "seventh vial" will be followed
by the apocalyptic marriage of heaven and earth. Hawthorne makes
use of such ideas at the conclusion of *The House of the Seven
Gables* to express his revulsion from the strident, facile, and self-
assertive chauvinism of his compatriots. He rings down the curtain
on his drama "of retribution for the sin of long ago" by emanci-
pating his four central protagonists from the time-drenched house
of the seven gables (p. 41)—and by implication, from the suffering
of history. But insofar as he means us to construe the "departure"—
the last chapter title—as a fulfillment of the prophecy of Revelation,
it is on a purely individual level in which America itself has no part.
Redemption is achieved and paradise regained by Holgrave and
Phoebe through imagination and art; but the nation as a whole,
which prides itself on its indifference to the "moral" of Haw-

59. See, for instance, Beebe's "The Fall of the House of Pyncheon," pp. 7–
8, 17.
60. The phrase "nationalistic theology" appears in Albert K. Weinberg's
Manifest Destiny (1935) and is quoted by Ernest Lee Tuveson on page 91 of
Redeemer Nation: The Idea of America's Millennial Role (Chicago: University of Chicago Press, 1968).

thorne's tale, is unchanged and unlikely to change in the foreseeable future. Unlike his fellow Americans, Holgrave exchanges his "haughty faith" in man's powers for the "far humbler" creed that "God is the sole worker of realities" (p. 180). And his betrothal to Phoebe is linked by metaphoric association with a personal union of heaven and earth, the spiritual and the mundane—in Hawthorne's terms, the "Marvellous" and the real.[61]

There is even something of an apocalyptic quality to the last paragraph of *The House of the Seven Gables*. Uncle Venner is said to imagine that Alice Pyncheon—whose posies erupt into bloom after the September gale—ascends heavenward flushed with happiness at the imminent prospect of marriage between "the descendant of the legendary wizard, and the village-maiden, over whom he had thrown love's web of sorcery" (p. 319). The mention of Alice at the conclusion of the romance is a reminder of the parallel between Hawthorne's own art and that of the daguerrotypist. For it will be recalled that Alice was witness to an earlier wedding, and that she perished as a result of an earlier storm; but her posies, of course, are symbolic of rebirth, and they give promise of a bright future indeed for Holgrave and Phoebe, though hardly for the Republic. The final words actually spoken in the book are ascribed, after all, to those "sagacious" and enterprising Yankees, Dixey and his unnamed companion, who shake their heads in disbelief at "the will of Providence" but agree that the luck of the Pyncheons is "Pretty good business!" (pp. 318–19). To that way of thinking, which instinctively equates material prosperity with divine favoritism, Hawthorne joins Melville in proclaiming "*NO!* in thunder . . . [and] the Devil himself cannot make him say *yes*."[62]

---

61. Two analogous uses of the number seven in Romantic literature might be noted in passing: Coleridge divides "The Rime of the Ancient Mariner" into seven parts; and Emerson speaks of the "seven lords of life" in his essay "Experience." Many of these ideas are discussed with general reference to the Romantic movement by M. H. Abrams in his *Natural Supernaturalism: Tradition and Revolution in Romantic Literature* (New York: W.W. Norton and Co., 1971).

62. Herman Melville, *The Letters of Herman Melville*, ed. Merrell Davis and William H. Gilman (New Haven: Yale University Press, 1960), p. 125.

V

Herman Melville

I t is altogether appropriate that Melville's first
concise statement of his literary theory was written in response
to "Hawthorne and His Mosses."[1] The review is attributed to "a
Virginian Spending July in Vermont," a pseudonym which dramatizes the author's situation as a tourist in search of information
about New England. Numerous references to the local countryside
and produce, to "mountains, old woods, and Indian pools," contribute to the sense of novelty and exploration (p. 536).[2] But the re-
viewer is otherwise bookish in his approach to his unfamiliar environment. We are told that he has been spending his mornings
perusing Timothy Dwight's *Travels in New England*. His cousin,
a native of Vermont, happening to chance upon his copy of Dwight,
informs him that "I have something far better than that—something more congenial to our summer on these hills" (p. 537). Grate-
fully accepting her present of the *Mosses*, Melville bids a farewell
to the *Travels* and hastens to make his acquaintance with New

1. A provocative discussion of Melville's review of the *Mosses* appears in
Edgar A. Dryden, *Melville's Thematics of Form: The Great Art of Telling
the Truth* (Baltimore: Johns Hopkins Press, 1968), pp. 18–29. See also Marvin
Fisher, "Portrait of the Artist in America: 'Hawthorne and His Mosses,' "
Southern Review 11 (1975): 156–66.
2. Melville's essay has been conveniently reprinted in *Moby-Dick*, Norton
Critical Edition, ed. Harrison Hayford and Hershel Parker (New York: W. W.
Norton and Co., 1967), pp. 535–51. Citations are from this edition; page
references are included in the text.

England through "the enchanting landscape" of Hawthorne's fictional world (p. 536).

There is more involved in this shift than simply a movement from a conventional and presumably factual guide book to a collection of imaginary tales. Dwight, the grandson of Jonathan Edwards, was one of a host of "New Divinity" men who helped to recast orthodox doctrine into more palatable form. To a reader of the *Travels*, however, Dwight's Calvinism, diluted as it was, takes a back seat to the socially conservative ideology which made him a first-generation Federalist and an outspoken critic of democratic ideas. Essentially a paean to the Protestant ethic, the *Travels* is pervaded by the spirit of Benjamin Franklin. It opens with a survey of New England manners and history and awards high marks to the original colonists for sobriety, diligence, enterprise, and morality. Everywhere about him Dwight beholds the fruits of their industrious character, finding that a general level of "competence" prevails among the present-day settlers. Moving on to a description of Boston, he notes that the townspeople are distinguished for their "habits of business," and adds in phrases that might have been penned by Franklin himself that "a man who is not believed to follow some useful business, can scarcely acquire, or retain, even a decent reputation."[3]

As Dwight continues his journey into Vermont, he turns a critical eye on the shiftless frontiersmen. Yet the minister does not despair of the woodsmen, for they, too, he believes, can "become sober, industrious citizens, merely by the acquisition of property." This thought gives rise to the notion that "the love of property to a certain degree seems indispensable to the existence of sound morals." A servant who is not desirous of getting ahead, according to Dwight, is unworthy of trust, and it is therefore the duty of those who have the welfare of society at heart to encourage its members to make money. He then goes on to bestow the sanction of religion itself on the pursuit of prosperity, arguing that the

3. Timothy Dwight, *Travels in New-England and New York*, 4 vols. (New Haven, 1821–1822) 1: 169–73, 214–15, 507. A useful summary of Dwight's thought is A. Whitney Griswold, "Three Puritans on Prosperity," *New England Quarterly* 7 (1934): 489–93.

possession of wealth is a powerful incentive to stability, and concluding with the hope that the owner of a modest homestead will
"become in the end a religious man."⁴ For the author of the *Travels*,
the Puritan social code has all but usurped the place of theology,
and with the material blessings of New England in mind he ap-
provingly quotes an anonymous gentleman: "God has never forsaken
that country."⁵

To Melville, Dwight's glowing account of his travels lacks the
veracity of Hawthorne's fiction. What it lacks in particular is the
profound sense of spiritual reality which is the genuine legacy
of New England Puritanism to the American mind. It is not the
Congregationalist divine, promoting his catalogue of secular virtues as a regional orthodoxy, who carries on the tradition of Ed-
wardean Calvinism; that tradition endures instead in the misunderstood and retiring native romancer whose stories are charged
with a "mystical depth of meaning" which is searched for in vain
in the pages of Dwight (p. 539). And precisely because the ministry
has abdicated its function, the reader is obliged to open his *Mosses*
in order to repossess the "power of blackness" which is common
to Edwards and Hawthorne alike. "Certain it is," adds Melville,
that Hawthorne's blackness owes its force and appeal "to that
Calvinistic sense of Innate Depravity and Original Sin, from whose
visitations, in some shape or other, no deeply thinking mind is
always and wholly free" (p. 540).

Here Melville gives his most forthright assent to the creed of
his forebears. And he follows Hawthorne in implicitly opposing
that creed to the prevailing ideology of the day—an ideology which
honors its Dwights while misconceiving, when it appreciates at all,
its tellers of truth. And "the world is mistaken in this Nathaniel
Hawthorne," deeming him a harmless spinner of simple tales (p.
541). It is no less mistaken in its idea of Shakespeare, whose
comparable blackness furnishes the background for "those occasional
flashings-forth of the intuitive Truth" which are the authentic
but little regarded source of his genius (p. 541). Little regarded

---

4. Dwight, *Travels*, 2: 459–63.
5. Dwight, *Travels*, 1: 170.

or heeded they must inevitably be in "this world of lies," a world
where

> Truth is forced to fly like a scared white doe in the woodlands;
> and only by cunning glimpses will she reveal herself, as in Shake-
> speare and other masters of the great Art of Telling the Truth
> —even though it be covertly, and by snatches (p. 542).

What Melville seems to have in mind when he speaks of the
"Truth" is primarily that sense of original sin which in Hawthorne
derives from his Puritan origins. His notion of evil is not, to be
sure, confined to man, and he specifically likens the dark side of
Hawthorne's soul to that "half of the physical sphere" which is
shrouded in blackness (p. 540). Yet his emphasis—and it is a
telling emphasis in an age of optimism about the perfectibility
of human nature—is on man's inherent capacity for corruption
and sin. Thus in commenting on "Young Goodman Brown," which
after the second reading impresses him as the strongest of all the
tales, Melville pronounces it "deep as Dante" in its penetration
into the evil residing in every breast (p. 549).

It is not Dwight, then, but Hawthorne who "shoots his strong
New-England roots into the hot soil of [the narrator's] Southern
soul" (p. 548). And there can be little doubt that in calling for
recognition of Hawthorne, Melville is also recalling his countrymen to a tradition of religious belief. In almost the same breath
in which he banishes the *Travels*, whose title page identifies Dwight
as the author of *Theology Explained and Defended*, the narrator
summons his fellow Americans to glorify Hawthorne in a palpably
scriptural idiom. Let us, he writes, not be remiss like "those
Jewish eyewitnesses" who beheld the Savior in the flesh but were
blind to His spiritual presence (p. 536). And then, in a well-known
phrase, he goes on to hail the author of the *Mosses* as "the literary
Shiloh of America" (p. 550).

Melville's enthusiastic linking of Hawthorne and Christ reiterates his conviction that the gospel mission has passed from the
clergy to writers of fiction who have mastered the "Art of Telling
the Truth." The artist like Hawthorne, not the minister like Dwight,
is the authentic *imitator Christi* of the Republic. It is important
to add, however, that Melville's conception of "Truth," in its

bearing on the character of native letters, is not narrowly or exclusively religious but yields implications which are social as well. It partakes of the assumption that the American people, by virtue of their peculiar heritage and destiny, have been chosen to carry forth the ideals of Christianity into the political realm. The country's literary Shilohs—for Melville postulates "a plurality of men of genius" (p. 550)—are accordingly bound to give utterance to the very "republican progressiveness" which is the birthright and promise of America itself (p. 543). We dishonor only the Republic, he says, when we withhold just tribute from the meritorious writers who are our own, writers who

> breathe that unshackled, democratic spirit of Christianity in all things, which now takes the practical lead in this world, though at the same time led by ourselves—us Americans (p. 546).

As Perry Miller has pointed out, Melville's review of the *Mosses* can be read as an attempt to reclaim Hawthorne from the Anglophiles of Boston, and to muster him into the cause of literary nationalism.[6] But the patriotic effusions are more than offset by a candid assessment of American realities. If Hawthorne is underrated or admired for the wrong reasons, if the country is slow to render respect to its democratic authors, then there is something decidedly amiss in the putative homeland of freedom and justice. A palate for "spiritual truth" (p. 542) is little in evidence among contemporary readers, and the "world of lies" is emphatically not confined to Great Britain. It is for the sake of his fellow citizens, according to Melville, that he would have America be heedful of her writers of worth, and it is for his own sake as one of their number that he lavishes praise on Hawthorne. If his essay thereby makes him a kind of John the Baptist to Hawthorne's Christ, he is "by no means desirous of the glory of a prophet," hoping instead that his countrymen will anticipate posterity by righting their estimate and making good their neglect (p. 551). For otherwise they, like the Jews, will be guilty of praying for the heralded coming

6. Perry Miller, *The Raven and the Whale: The War of Words and Wits in the Era of Poe and Melville* (New York: Harcourt, Brace, and World, 1956), pp. 282–86.

while their Shiloh is already among them. And again like the Jews, they will be running the danger of betraying their historical calling and trust.

Moby-Dick

It is precisely that betrayal to which Melville turned his attention in the romances and stories of the 1850s. Throughout the decade he was acutely conscious of the growing split between the ideals which he celebrated in his essay on Hawthorne and the realities of American life. With the decline of Calvinism—a process, as we have seen, to which Timothy Dwight lent an unwitting hand—a host of optimistic creeds had captured the loyalties of Melville's contemporaries, weaning them from belief in the reality of evil and fostering the smugness and self-importance which are satirized in the "Vivenza" section of *Mardi*. To Melville, such creeds threatened the survival of Christianity and democracy alike, and they consequently struck at the heart of his hopes for his country, hopes to which he gave his most stirring utterance in a famous passage from *White-Jacket:*

> Escaped from the house of bondage, Israel of old did not follow after the ways of the Egyptians. To her was given an express dispensation; to her were given new things under the sun. And we Americans are the peculiar, chosen people—the Israel of our time; we bear the ark of the liberties of the world . . . God has predestinated, mankind expects, great things from our race; and great things we feel in our souls. The rest of the nations must soon be in our rear . . . Long enough have we been skeptics with regard to ourselves, and doubted whether, indeed, the political Messiah had come. But he has come in *us*, if we would but give utterance to his promptings.[7]

As such sentiments indicate, the youthful Melville was deeply stirred by the millennial expectations which gripped his country-

7. Herman Melville, *White-Jacket: or The World in a Man-of-War*, in *The Writings of Herman Melville*, ed. Harrison Hayford, Hershel Parker, and G. Thomas Tanselle (Evanston and Chicago: Northwestern University Press and the Newberry Library, 1968–), vol. 5 (1970), pp. 150–51.

men in the middle years of the nineteenth century. By the time he wrote *Moby-Dick*, however, his awareness of America's wrongs had dimmed his faith in her potential as world redeemer. His criticism of his country, as expressed in the book, is directed, first, against the utilitarian sensibility of Peleg and Bildad and, second, against the destructive millennialism represented by Ahab. It is not by chance that the three captains were formerly shipmates and are now partners in the voyage of the *Pequod*, for Melville's point is that utilitarianism and millennialism are closely related aspects of American thought. Ishmael, in speaking of Ahab, remarks that whereas the ship's investors "were bent on profitable cruises," he himself was "intent on an audacious, immitigable, and supernatural revenge" (p. 162).[8] For Melville's contemporaries the pursuit of profit, in the service of progress, did in fact have a metaphysical end: to regenerate mankind, to reform the world by abolishing want and diffusing the blessings of liberty, and thus to initiate the millennium.

Peleg and especially Bildad personify the bourgeois mentality that Melville was to attack more directly in *Israel Potter*. Their enterprise is informed by the spirit of capitalism, for the natives of Nantucket, according to Ishmael, invest in whaling vessels much as people elsewhere speculate "in approved state stocks bringing in good interest" (p. 71). As we are often reminded, they are also both devout Quakers, though "Quakers with a vengeance" who at some cost to consistency invade the Atlantic to spill "tuns upon tuns of leviathan gore" (pp. 71–72). They are said to have separated the affairs of the world from those of religion; but what is apt to strike us most forcibly is their complete subordination of religion to business, as revealed, for example, by Bildad's hypocritical gloss on the biblical injunction against laying up treasures on earth. Bildad's devotion to profit, so Ishmael tells us, is such that aboard ship "indolence and idleness perished from before him." Spare and economical in appearance, "his own person was the exact embodiment of his utilitarian character" (p. 72). His objections to shipping a savage like Queequeg appear in their true light when we notice

---

8. All citations to *Moby-Dick* are from the Norton Critical Edition; page references are included in the text.

that his own "cannibal of a craft" (p. 67) is named for an Indian
tribe massacred by bloodthirsty white men, and that he and Peleg
oversee preparations from a wigwam pitched on its deck. Cannibals
themselves in spite of, or rather because of, their utilitarianism,
the two captains are hardly strangers to the apocalyptic vision
of Ahab, who is cut, after all, from the same Quaker cloth. Bildad
presses on Queequeg a doomsday tract called "The Latter Day
Coming; or No Time to Lose," and he beseeches the harpooner
to "spurn the idol Bel, and the hideous dragon; turn from the
wrath to come" (p. 85).

It is precisely the utilitarian, capitalist ethos of the two Quaker
owners that accounts for their affinity with Ahab. For them as
for him, ends justify means, and human values are ruthlessly suppressed to ensure success even though their ventures appear to
be otherwise antithetical. In both instances, men are reduced to
the level of things or machines. Ishmael receives his first kick
aboard the *Pequod*, and it is obvious that commercial enterprise
in general has done little to dignify the lives of the New Yorkers
whom he sees on the docks of Manhattan and who spend their
week days "tied to counters, nailed to benches, clinched to desks"
(pp. 12–13). Weber defined the spirit of capitalism as the rational
pursuit of profit; Ahab uses rational measures in pursuit of his
madman's goal. He too must have men to accomplish his object,
and aware that the sailors are untrustworthy tools, he is careful
to allay their suspicions with the promise of cash returns. He is
quite as ready as Peleg, moreover, to enforce his authority by ad-
ministering kicks, and his ideal man is a mechanical monster endowed with a quarter acre of brains and no trace of a heart.

Numerous critics have pointed out that the *Pequod* bears a striking resemblance to the American ship of state which plied the
oratorical seas in Melville's day.[9] As captain of the *Pequod*, Ahab
is entrusted with the fate of the national Israel, and he is himself
representative of the chosen people, having wandered for "forty
years on the pitiless sea" (p. 443). Potentially, of course, he is also
a type of the Savior, since it is from the seed of Israel that the

9. See in particular Alan Heimert, "*Moby-Dick* and American Political Symbolism," *American Quarterly* 15 (1963): 498–534.

Messiah is born. Melville's contemporaries believed in the messianic role of the American people, and they were persuaded, as he put it in *Mardi*, that history had entered "the last scene of the last act of her drama."[10] As recently as *Redburn*, Melville himself had said of his countrymen, "We are the heirs of all time, and with all nations we divide our inheritance. On this Western Hemisphere all tribes and people are forming into one federated whole; and there is a future which shall see the estranged children of Adam restored as to the old hearth-stone in Eden."[11] It is hardly surprising, in view of these sentiments, that in *Moby-Dick* Ishmael characterizes the polyglot crew of the *Pequod* as "an Anacharsis Clootz deputation" drawn from all the ends of the earth and "federated along one keel" under the command of an American skipper (p. 108).

It is revealing to recall in this connection the traditional iconography of Christ as a dragon slayer.[12] The Bible speaks of the sea-serpent or Leviathan that will be destroyed on the day of judgment and whose death will deliver the children of Adam from bondage to sin. An illustration is the verse from Isaiah 27 which Melville quotes in the "Extracts": "In that day, the Lord with his sore, and great, and strong sword, shall punish Leviathan the piercing serpent, even Leviathan that crooked serpent; and he shall slay the dragon that is in the sea" (p. 2). The victory over Satan, which restores mankind to paradise, fulfills God's prophecy in Genesis that the seed of Adam shall bruise the serpent's head. It is a prophecy of special significance for the redeemer nation, and it is cited repeatedly in the writings of the emigrant Puritans. Two hundred years before the sailing of the *Pequod*, for example,

10. Herman Melville, *Mardi: And a Voyage Thither*, in *The Writings of Herman Melville*, ed. Harrison Hayford, Hershel Parker, and G. Thomas Tanselle (Evanston and Chicago: Northwestern University Press and the Newberry Library, 1968–), vol. 3 (1970), p. 525.

11. Herman Melville, *Redburn: His First Voyage*, in *The Writings of Herman Melville*, ed. Harrison Hayford, Hershel Parker, and G. Thomas Tanselle (Evanston and Chicago: Northwestern University Press and the Newberry Library, 1968–), vol. 4 (1969), p. 169.

12. Here I am indebted to the discussion of *Paradise Regained* in Northrop Frye's *The Return of Eden: Five Essays on Milton's Epics* (Toronto: University of Toronto Press, 1965), pp. 118–43.

John Winthrop recorded in his journal that during the synod at
Cambridge a snake appeared in the midst of a sermon and was
promptly killed by one of the elders. Winthrop interpreted the
incident as follows: "The serpent is the devil; the synod, the representative of the churches of Christ in New England. The devil
had formerly and lately attempted their disturbance and dissolu-
tion; but their faith in the seed of the woman overcame him and
crushed his head."[13] The step from Winthrop's confident assertion
to Melville's novel is long historically but short in imaginative
terms; they draw on a common conception of American destiny.
Ahab begins his hunt on December 25, the date of the Savior's
birth, and he is said to have "piled upon the whale's white hump
the sum of all the general rage and hate felt by his whole race
from Adam down" (p. 160). The God of Genesis declares to the
serpent that "thou shalt bruise his heel," and in fulfillment of
the prophecy that he would be dismembered, Ahab lost his leg
to Moby Dick. "I now prophesy," he vows, "that I will dismember
my dismemberer" (p. 147). Appropriately, it is the utilitarian Bildad
who cheers him on his millennial quest with the hymn entitled
"There is a land of pure delight":

> Sweet fields beyond the swelling flood,
> Stand dressed in living green,
> So to the Jews old Canaan stood,
> While Jordan rolled between (p. 95).

The Canaan of the hymn corresponds to the Promised Land that
Christ will conquer for the spiritual Israel by crushing the head
of Leviathan.

Melville introduces a number of details to emphasize the parallel
between Ahab and Christ, and he takes pains to present his "ungodly, god-like" protagonist in a dramatic and imposing light. Ahab
bears a crucifixion in his face, he metaphorically wears the Crown
of Lombardy, supposed to contain the nails used in the Cross,
and he "lay like dead for three days and nights" after his first encounter with the white whale (p. 87). Impressing upon the "un-

13. *Winthrop's Journal: "History of New England,"* 2 vols. ed. James
Kendall Hosmer (New York: Barnes and Noble, 1966), 2: 347–48.

conscious understandings" of the crew his own vision of Moby
Dick as "the gliding great demon of the seas of life," he makes
his grievance as real to them as it is to himself (p. 162). He thinks
of himself as venturing forth on a mission to destroy "that intangible malignity which has been from the beginning" and which he
views as the cause of all bodily and spiritual suffering (p. 160).
The reader is encouraged to feel that he acts on behalf of all
mankind.

Melville fosters this impression, however, only in order to dramatize the gulf between the promise of America and its actual performance—to hold up the Republic embodied by Ahab as a counterfeit rather than a real Christ. For if Ahab is Christlike, he also
resembles the Satan of *Paradise Lost*.[14] In Milton's epic, the Arch-
fiend, who has suffered a mighty woe, is a virtual caricature or
parody of the Savior. Intent, like Ahab, on supernatural vengeance,
he scorns submission and inspires his followers with the hope of
regaining their lost estate. He too undertakes a perilous journey
to "seek/ Deliverance for us all," and he is hailed by the fallen
host as a god "equal to the Highest in Heaven" (2: 464–65, 479).
There are also similarities between Ahab and the Beast of Revelation, similarities which are not surprising in view of the American
obsession with the quest for the millennium. Even Ahab's apparently fatal injury, from which he revives after three days, can
be explained in terms of this identification, for it is stated of the
Beast that he "was wounded to death; and his deadly wound was
healed" (Rev. 13:3). Again, the Beast opens "his mouth in blas-
phemy against God, to blaspheme his name" (13:6), while Ahab
baptizes his harpoon not in the name of the Father, but in the
name of the Devil. What is more striking still, the Beast is reported
to do "great wonders, so that he maketh fire come down from
heaven on the earth in the sight of men/ And deceiveth them
that dwell on the earth by *the means of* those miracles." (13:13–14).

14. The most thorough treatment of Melville's knowledge of Milton is
Henry F. Pommer's *Milton and Melville* (Pittsburgh: University of Pittsburgh
Press, 1950). See in particular pp. 92–104. R. W. B. Lewis briefly discusses Ahab
as the Antichrist on page 208 of his essay "Days of Wrath and Laughter,"
which appears in his *Trials of the Word: Essays in American Literature and
the Humanistic Tradition* (New Haven: Yale University Press, 1965).

In the scene with the corposants, Ahab grounds the current and overawes "the enchanted crew" by hurling defiance at the lightning.

One can place these parallels in the most telling perspective by contrasting *Moby-Dick* with the first book of *The Faerie Queene*, where Spenser presents the story of Saint George and the dragon as an allegory of the imitation of Christ. The contrast is implicit in the novel, for Ishmael includes Saint George in his roster of illustrious whalemen, insisting that the dragon was "no other than the great Leviathan himself" (p. 305). As depicted by Spenser, St. George is the representative hero of the English people. Insofar as he conforms to the image of Christ, he achieves salvation, and through him the nation at large fulfills its destiny as the new Israel. This outcome is assured by his defeat of the monster in the ferocious three-day battle which clearly prefigures the Savior's ultimate conquest of Satan. In the case of *Moby-Dick*, where the result is exactly the opposite, Ahab is shown to resemble his enemy. He conforms to the image not of the Savior but rather of the thing that he hunts.[15]

If the redeemer nation, in the person of Ahab, accordingly imitates Satan, it is because Ahab himself fails to profit from the example of Adam—as it is found, once again, in *Paradise Lost*. The Adam of Milton's epic appeases God's anger by acknowledging his own complicity in the Fall. He repents and is spared the fate of Satan, who knows himself to be damned but blames only God for his misery. As for Ahab, he too is damned, and damned, as he expresses it, "most subtly and most malignantly! damned in the midst of Paradise" (p. 147). Charles Olson once remarked that "the conflict in Ahab's world is abrupt, more that between Satan and Jehovah, of the old dispensation than the new."[16] It is a world of hunter and hunted, bereft of forgiveness, where a wrathful Deity is chiefly known by his rod. What is important to realize, however,

15. The resemblance between Ahab and the whale has often been noted, recently by Richard Slotkin in his *Regeneration Through Violence: The Mythology of the American Frontier, 1600–1860* (Middletown, Conn.: Wesleyan University Press, 1973), p. 545.

16. Charles Olson, *Call Me Ishmael* (San Francisco: City Lights Books, 1947), p. 53.

is that it is a world of Ahab's own making. His quest is doomed
to disaster because its object is really himself: like an unrepentant
Adam, he "is very much his own Satan and his own vengeful
God."[17] In *Mardi* Melville cautioned his countrymen that "all evils
cannot be done away. For evil is the chronic malady of the universe; and checked in one place, breaks forth in another."[18] It is
well to remember this caveat when Ishmael states that "all evil,
to crazy Ahab, were visibly personified, and made practically assail-
able in Moby Dick" (p. 160). What Ahab is unable to see is that
the evil he externalizes in the whale also exists in himself. As his
likeness to the "white fiend" confirms, he is thoroughly implicated
in "that intangible malignity" he hopes to destroy. It is his blindness that ultimately damns him—unlike Oedipus, for instance, who
is humbled in his blindness and learns to see. Interestingly enough,
Ahab suffers a literal attack of blindness moments before his
death, crying out as Moby Dick bears down on the ship: "I grow
blind; hands! stretch out before me that I may yet grope my
way. Is't night?" (p. 467). The parallel to Oedipus appears to
have been quite deliberate on Melville's part. In 1849 he purchased an edition of Sophocles,[19] and he wrote into *Moby-Dick*
a chapter entitled "The Sphinx." It was Oedipus, of course, who
solved the riddle of the sphinx, the answer to which was man.
Moreover, he is lame like Ahab, and it turns out that the murderer
he seeks is himself.

But the world of Ahab does not exhaust the world of *Moby-Dick*.
Ishmael's narrative encompasses other worlds as well: he himself,
as his name indicates, is excluded from God's covenant with Israel.
His story can be read as a form of spiritual autobiography, with
the life of the individual recapitulating in miniature the drama
of paradise lost and regained. The novel opens, accordingly, with
a reference to the "thieves" in the garden, and it terminates in

17. The phrase is used by Lowry Nelson, Jr. in speaking of the monster in
Frankenstein. See "Night Thoughts on the Gothic Novel," *Yale Review* 52
(1963): 247.
18. Melville, *Mardi*, *Writings of Herman Melville*, Northwestern-Newberry
edition, 3: 529.
19. Merton M. Sealts, Jr., *Melville's Reading: A Check-List of Books Owned
and Borrowed* (Madison: University of Wisconsin Press, 1966), entry no. 147.

the unmistakable accents of Revelation. Accounting for his wish
to go whaling, Ishmael confides that the "portentous and mysterious monster roused all my curiosity" (p. 16). He is clearly a type
of postlapsarian man who voyages in search of the knowledge of
good and evil, which is also the knowledge of the self. He first
beholds Moby Dick, after all, in his innermost soul, "one grand
hooded phantom, like a snow hill in the air" (p. 16).

The initial stage of Ishmael's development consists of his "marriage" ashore to Queequeg. This opening section of the narrative
is reminiscent of the adventures of Tommo as recounted by Melville
in *Typee*. Like the hero of the earlier novel, who discovers paradise only to leave it, Ishmael feels at odds with the world and
estranged from his fellows. Forced to share a bed with Queequeg,
who treats him with warmth and kindness even though he is a
cannibal, his bitterness dissolves and he adopts the savage as his
bosom friend. But Queequeg is of little assistance when it comes
to the spiritual fears of the hunt: his acts of humanity, like his
cannibalism, are essentially unthinking, and Ishmael cannot regress
to his state of unconsciousness. For "whatever else the South Sea
Islander is," as D. H. Lawrence wrote in his essay on *Typee*, "he
is centuries and centuries behind us in the life-struggle, the con-
sciousness-struggle, the struggle of the soul into fulness."[20] Whereas
Queequeg dominates the earlier chapters, which almost all take
place on land, Ahab does not make his appearance in the book
until the *Pequod* is well under way. Speaking of Bulkington,
Ishmael states that "in landlessness alone resides the highest truth"
(p. 97), and he must undergo the test of the sea in order to complete his education in experience.

It is no small part of this education that he must come to terms
with Ahab and the "power of blackness" that Ahab represents—
that power which Melville admired in the stories of Hawthorne
and which his contemporaries seemed determined to ignore. As
it happens, Ishmael does at first try to discount the dark side
by suppressing his forebodings with respect to the voyage. "When
a man suspects any wrong," he says before the *Pequod* sets sail,

"it sometimes happens that if he be already involved in the matter, he insensibly strives to cover up his suspicions even from himself. And much this way it was with me" (p. 90). What Ishmael learns at sea, however, is that the old Adam cannot be denied. "Ahab's quenchless feud seemed mine," he confesses, adding that he listened with avidity to "the history of that murderous monster against whom I and all the others had taken our oaths of violence and revenge" (p. 155). This is the world of the old dispensation, and Ishmael, unlike Starbuck, who averts his eyes from the doubloon "lest Truth shake me falsely" (p. 360), unflinchingly faces the reality of evil. Seeing "naught in that brute but the deadliest ill," regarding Moby Dick as the symbol of all that appals and torments the soul of man, he abandons himself to the fiery quest (p. 163).

Ishmael differs from Ahab, however, in his understanding that the savagery of nature corresponds to the savagery of the self. Man's capacity for violence and butchery, he realizes, is fully the equal of that of his prey. He speaks, for example, of "the universal cannibalism of the sea" (p. 235), a cannibalism from which the whalemen are by no means exempt, and he characterizes the *Pequod*, manned by savages and freighted with a burning corpse, as "the material counterpart of her monomaniac commander's soul" (p. 354). He is a killer and savage himself, he says elsewhere, "owning no allegiance but to the King of Cannibals" (p. 232), and in the chapter called "Stubb's Supper," where the second mate dines on a whale-steak while the dead whale is devoured by hundreds of sharks, he spells out the fundamental equivalence between the sharkishness of nature and the voracity of man. Fleece, the black cook, speaking with Ishmael's (and Melville's) approval, draws the appropriate conclusion: do not disown complicity in evil, but rather "gobern dat wicked natur . . . for all angel is not'ing more dan de shark well goberned" (p. 251).[21]

Once made aware of his own involvement in a fallen world, Ishmael is reconciled to his fellow men. Whereas Ahab, in his blindness and pride, can only regret all "mortal inter-indebtedness"

21. For a more extensive analysis of Fleece's sermon see Robert Zoellner, *The Salt-Sea Mastodon: A Reading of Moby-Dick* (Berkeley: University of California Press, 1973), pp. 219–25.

as a curse, Ishmael abjures his vow of vengeance in favor of brotherly love. When he breaks free of the Captain's mode of perception, as he does in "A Squeeze of the Hand," his words deliberately echo the earlier passage in which Queequeg's kindness was said to have redeemed his "splintered heart and maddened hand" (p. 53). Squeezing the hands of his shipmates in a rapture of communion, he relates that he "forgot all about our horrible oath; in that inexpressible sperm, I washed my hands and my heart of it" (p. 348). Ishmael returns to the values associated with Queequeg, a process which culminates when he is saved from the wreck of the *Pequod* and finds himself, as he did on the first page of the book, "bringing up the rear" of a funeral. But he has not been unchanged by the power of blackness, for indeed his exposure to evil and suffering has made possible his knowledge of the self. In Christian terms, Ishmael integrates the new dispensation with the old, achieving a vision that is broad enough to accommodate both Queequeg's capacity for fellowship and Ahab's experience of woe.[22] In Melville's significant phrase, a phrase evocative of the middle way of American Calvinism, he emerges from the "vital centre" of the vortex that swallows up the *Pequod* (p. 470).

Ishmael's salvation has a political as well as religious dimension, since for Melville democracy is anchored in an acceptance of the fallible nature of man—is impossible, indeed, without a conviction of "that Calvinistic sense of Innate Depravity and Original Sin" of which he wrote in his review of the *Mosses*. Apropos of the "deeply thinking" Hawthorne, for whom truth is inseparable from the "blackness of darkness," Melville says that his fiction is informed by that democratic spirit which is America's boon to the world. The same spirit infuses Ishmael's apostrophe to "The Great God Absolute! The centre and circumference of all democracy! His omnipresence, our divine equality!" Ishmael mentions Bunyan, Cervantes, and Andrew Jackson as exemplifying the "high qualities" with which the God of democracy invests the common man, and he calls upon the "just Spirit of Equality" to vindicate his presentation of Ahab, a lowly whale hunter, as a subject commensurate

---

22. Cf. Daniel Hoffman, *Form and Fable in American Fiction* (New York: Oxford University Press, 1965), p. 277.

in dignity with royalty and kings (pp. 104–5, 130). But Ishmael's democratic creed is betrayed rather than realized by Ahab, who sets himself up as an actual emperor in the American Israel and who is variously described as a mogul, autocrat, czar, and sultan. This side of his character is closely related to his identification with the Beast of the Apocalypse. For in John's vision the Beast has the power to reign over the earth and to terrorize nations; and the number of the Beast "is the number of a man; and his number is Six hundred threescore *and* six" (Rev. 13:18)—the sum of the numerical values of the Hebrew letters for Nero Caesar. In *Mardi* Melville ascribed to the natives of Vivenza the conceit that their country was destined to establish a permanent and universal republic. In *Moby-Dick*, however, the American ship of state is commanded by a tyrant rather than a democrat.

And so it is fitting that Ahab, the would-be Messiah turned Caesar, spurns the plea for assistance by the *Rachel*. For the ship's namesake is the scriptural mother of Israel, a type of the true church whose marriage to Christ traditionally follows the final defeat of Leviathan. It is with considerable irony, therefore, that Melville describes the subsequent three-day chase in terms more appropriate to rape than to marriage. He compares Moby Dick, for example, to "the white bull Jupiter swimming away with ravished Europa clinging to his graceful horns; his lovely leering eyes sideways intent upon the maid" (p. 447). The quest that was to have inaugurated the apocalyptic union of heaven and earth comes to its end in a violent sexual assault. This climactic encounter gains in significance from Ishmael's characterization of Ahab as an "ungodly old man, chasing with curses a Job's whale round the world" (p. 162). It is Christ in his Second Coming who will fulfill the prophecy in Job 41 which Ishmael paraphrases with reference to an ulcerous sperm whale:

Is this the creature of whom it was once so triumphantly said —"Canst thou fill his skin with barbed irons? or his head with fish-spears? The sword of him that layeth at him cannot hold, the spear, the dart, nor the habergeon: he esteemeth iron as straw; the arrow cannot make him flee; darts are counted as stubble; he laugheth at the shaking of a spear!" (p. 300).

The relevance of this prophecy to Ahab, who has his own "pious" counselor named Bildad, is confirmed by the fact that the white whale he hunts is introduced in the forty-first chapter of the novel. But whereas Christ will triumph on the day of judgment by putting a hook in the nostrils of Satan, Ahab fails to slay Moby Dick. The last words he speaks before he is dragged to his death are "Thus, I give up the spear!" (p. 468).

Only Ishmael, the outcast son of Abraham, escapes with his life in the demonic apocalypse that engulfs the *Pequod*. Since the ship itself is said to resemble its prey, and since Ahab is accounted "a great lord of Leviathans" (p. 114), Ishmael's survival on the third day of the chase may be seen as a symbolic rebirth from the belly of the whale. In this respect he invites comparison to Jonah, and he may be regarded as a type of the Savior himself, a detail which imparts special meaning to his eventual rescue by the *Rachel*. For Melville's objective in *Moby-Dick* is nothing less than to rewrite the covenant that God was presumed to have made with the American people as the heirs of the biblical Hebrews. According to Genesis, Ishmael and his mother Hagar were banished to the wilderness, and they were pointedly left out of God's covenant with Israel. The twelfth chapter of Revelation deals with a woman and a male child who flee into the wilderness to avoid the dragon. They are interpreted in Reformed theology as Rachel and the promised seed. Melville's startling revision consists in the fact that Hagar and Ishmael, who according to orthodoxy exemplify the gentiles, are thus made into types of the spiritual Israel. We can scarcely miss the implication that the covenant forsaken by the nation at large survives in the person of Melville's fictional hero. Nor should it escape our attention that the "Epilogue" to the novel shows the influence of millennial prophecy, since for Ishmael at least paradise is figuratively regained. It is regained, that is, only in vision—regained because Ishmael realizes, as Ahab never does, that evil is intrinsic to the human condition and that destiny, as Melville suggested in *Mardi*, "is best served, by waiting events."[23] As he floats away from the wreck on Queequeg's coffin, whose hieroglyphic markings contain an apocalyptic "theory of

23. Melville, *Mardi*, *Writings of Herman Melville*, Northwestern-Newberry edition, 3: 530.

the heavens and the earth, and a mystical treatise on the art of attaining truth" (p. 399), Ishmael watches the "unharming sharks" glide by "as if with padlocks on their mouths; the savage sea-hawks sailed with sheathed beaks" (p. 470). It is a common theme in the Old Testament, as well as in the millennial writings of divines such as Edwards, that in the kingdom to come the beasts of prey will be transformed into peaceable creatures. By virtue of his redemption, in short, Ishmael figures as the saving remnant, a concept that the emigrant Puritans were wont to apply to themselves. There is this crucial difference, however: in *Moby-Dick* the dreaded judgment befalls America rather than England.

It befalls America, that is, because the redeemer nation has become indistinguishable from Babylon, the historical oppressor of the chosen people. There are innumerable hints to this effect, and they build inexorably as the *Pequod* plunges on to its doom. The biblical Ahab introduced the worship of Baal into Israel, and the scholarship of Melville's day equated the Tyrian Baal with the Babylonian Bel.[24] The Ahab of the novel is compared to King Belshazzar, and the fate of his ship is directly connected to the judgment on Babylon. It is said of Moby Dick, for example, that he is regularly sighted at a "set time and place," the Season-on-the-Line, much "as the sun, in its annual round, loiters for a predicted interval in any one sign of the Zodiac" (p. 173). The Line, of course, denotes the equator, and it may be inferred from the zodiac inscribed on the doubloon that the sign in question is Libra or the scales. Also pictured on the coin, which comes from Ecuador, the country named for the equator, are three summits or peaks which Ahab sees as himself and which suggest the three masts of the *Pequod*. Starbuck, who observes Ahab studying the coin, makes the portentous comment that "the old man seems to read Belshazzar's awful writing" (p. 360), an allusion to the prophecy in Daniel 5 foretelling the destruction of Babylon. Since the *Pequod* does in fact meet Moby Dick on the Line, as Ahab knew it would, and since Melville makes a point of quoting Daniel's warning verbatim in connection with the corposants, it seems clear that the scales of Libra signify the balances in which the Babylonian king-

---

24. See "Explanatory Notes" by Luther S. Mansfield and Howard P. Vincent in the Hendricks House edition of *Moby-Dick* (New York, 1952), pp. 637, 654.

dom was weighed and found wanting. Ahab's dying speech is a forceful reminder of the coin with its fateful inscription, for he refers to the masts of his foundering ship as "ye three unsurrendered spires of mine" (p. 468).

The fact that the *Pequod* sinks "to hell" under "the great shroud of the sea" suggests still another Scriptural authority for the judgment on Babylon (p. 469): the Book of Jeremiah. Ahab has flouted the God of democracy by instituting tyranny over the crew. He has callously rejected the appeal by the *Rachel*, whose biblical namesake is imagined by Jeremiah to weep for the children of Israel as they pass on their way toward Babylon. We are thus led to associate him not only with King Belshazzar but also with Nebuchadnezzar, who destroyed the Temple and carried off the Jews into captivity and exile. The ship he commands suffers the identical fate that Jeremiah prophesied for the conquerer of Israel: "The sea is come up upon Babylon: she is covered with the multitude of the waves thereof" (51:42).

But it is more than the Old Testament Babylon that concerns Melville in *Moby-Dick;* for there is a Babylon in the New Testament as well. It appears in Revelation, where it is the antithesis of the New Jerusalem, and it is ruled by the Beast or the Antichrist. The Beast, of course, is the dragon of Revelation 12, and he is in pursuit of the woman and child who figure for Melville as the *Rachel* and Ishmael. Not only, then, is the United States identified with the ancient empire that enslaved the Jews, but it is also linked to the mystical Babylon, the city that epitomizes wickedness in John's vision of the Apocalypse. Far from ushering in Christ's kingdom on earth, the redeemer nation, as symbolized by the *Pequod*, meets with the very disaster which is prophesied for Babylon by John:

> And a mighty angel took up a stone like a great millstone, and
> *cast* it into the sea, saying, Thus with violence shall that great
> city Babylon be thrown down, and shall be found no more at
> all (18:21).

It can hardly have escaped Melville's notice that the judgment on the mystical Babylon corresponds exactly to the fall which Jeremiah foresaw for the Babylon of old.

The foremost student of Melville's use of the Bible has argued persuasively that the conception of the prophet which underlies Father Mapple's sermon derives more from Jeremiah than Jonah.[25] Jeremiah was called by the Lord to prophesy against Israel, and he was vilified and imprisoned by his countrymen for daring to denounce their transgressions. In the words of the minister, he preached "the Truth to the face of Falsehood!" (p. 50). As such, as a "pilot-prophet, or speaker of true things," he inevitably suggests Melville's view of the artist as it appears in his essay on the *Mosses.* He suggests as well Melville's narrator Ishmael, who escapes "alone to tell" (p. 470) the story of the *Pequod* and whose vision of inner-worldly sainthood closely approximates Hawthorne's. Melville dedicated *Moby-Dick* to his fellow author, and rather like the narrator of "The Custom-House," his own narrator dons a veil by inviting us to call him Ishmael. For there can be no full "revelation" in "this world of lies," Father Mapple's sermon to the contrary notwithstanding. Ishmael quotes the minister as saying that woe is "to him who, as the great Pilot Paul has it, while preaching to others is himself a castaway" (p. 50). It is Ishmael himself who preaches the truth as a castaway, and who consequently knows the "wisdom that is woe" (p. 355). Certainly there is little reason to believe that his words will be taken to heart by his unheeding countrymen—a likelihood confirmed by the novel's concluding sentence, which again recalls Jeremiah: "It was the devious-cruising Rachel, that in her retracing search after her missing children, only found another orphan." Ishmael, as the solitary heir to the covenant, can only be an orphan in an America which has deserted its principles and turned a deaf ear to its speakers of truth.

Israel Potter

Another of Melville's figurative orphans is Israel Potter, an outcast from the nation that took such pride in claiming descent from the biblical Hebrews. The claim could not have been far from Melville's mind when in 1849 he chanced to obtain a copy of *The Life and Remarkable Adventures of Israel R. Potter.* "The Revolutionary narrative of the beggar"[26] which so arrested his notice was eventually to appear in fictionalized form as *Israel Potter: His Fifty Years of Exile* (1855). It is a book which puts to the test the promise of America and finds that promise empty for the aptly named hero. In Melville's retelling of Potter's career, the obscure and unremarked death of a common soldier becomes an analogue for the failure of the Republic itself.

The first chapter of the romance, called "The Birthplace of Israel," is wholly original.[27] Departing from his source, which tells us that Potter was born in Rhode Island, Melville makes him a native of Massachusetts, the literal birthplace of the American Republic, putative Israel of the author's own time. Here Melville pays tribute to the fortitude and endurance of the "original settlers" who wrested a livelihood from the rugged terrain of the Berkshires (p. 2).[28] A veritable race of Titans, he surmises, must once have occupied this ungrateful soil, so much did they accomplish with so little prospect of reward—a consideration, he adds, which affords some idea "of the temper of the men of the Revolutionary era" (p. 3). It is a detail of significance that the present-day visitor to the Berkshire mountains, home of the selfless patriot, Israel Potter, finds everywhere about him "an aspect of singular abandonment" and decay (p. 2).

Although Potter shares some of the traits of the Yankee of popu-

26. Jay Leyda, *The Melville Log: A Documentary Life of Herman Melville, 1819-1891*, 2 vols. (New York: Harcourt, Brace, 1951), 1: 350.

27. On Melville's revisions of his source see Roger P. McCutcheon, "The Technique of Melville's *Israel Potter*," *South Atlantic Quarterly* 27 (1928): 161-75. My reading of *Israel Potter* has been strongly influenced by Alexander Keyssar, *Melville's "Israel Potter": Reflections on the American Dream* (Cambridge: Harvard University Press, 1969). Also valuable are the interpretations by Harry B. Henderson III, *Versions of the Past: The Historical Imagination in American Fiction* (New York: Oxford University Press, 1974), pp. 138-47; and Charles N. Watson, Jr., "Melville's *Israel Potter*: Fathers and Sons," *Studies in the Novel* 7 (1975): 563-68.

28. Herman Melville, *His Fifty Years of Exile (Israel Potter)* (1855; New York: Sagamore Press, 1957). Page references are to this edition and are included in the text.

lar lore,[29] he actually represents the vital and independent potential of the native American. He is prudent, forbearing, and self-reliant, and his early adventures are more properly national than regional in character. After leaving home at the age of eighteen, he becomes by turns a hired laborer, surveyor, hunter, trapper, trader and sailor, finally earning enough to buy his own farm. He is the idealized backbone of the nation, a human symbol for America's natural resources, and with the outbreak of hostilities in 1775 he joins the patriot army at Bunker Hill, where he distinguishes himself for marksmanship and bravery. Shortly afterward, while serving aboard the brigantine *Washington*, he is captured and transported to England in chains.

Israel's wanderings began, according to Melville, when he threw off the yoke of his overbearing father and set out in search of "another home and other friends" (p. 8). For all his independence and ingenuity he often resembles a lost son. In England, he freely unbosoms himself to Sir John Millet, whose "patriarchal demeanor" moves him to tears of gratitude (p. 35). Thoroughgoing democrat that he is, however, Israel cannot bring himself to address the knight by his title, and he is too jealous of his rights as a freeman to submit without protest to the bullying overseer of the gardens of the Princess Amelia. When he later declines the king's offer of military preferment during the interview at Kew, Melville is quite explicit about spelling out the cost of his hero's refusal to budge from his principles. Under the patronage of the monarch, he writes, Israel might soon have advanced

> to no mean rank in the army of Britain. Nor in that case would we have had to follow him, as at last we shall, through long, long years of obscure and penurious wandering (p. 42).

Israel's disinterested patriotism is what stands between him and the dream of success as memorialized in America in the pages of Franklin's *Autobiography*. It is both appropriate and ironic,

29. As described by Constance Rourke, the Yankee folk figure is particularly adept at taking advantage of others for his own benefit. Potter, obviously, does not fall into this category. See *American Humor: A Study of the National Character* (New York: Harcourt, Brace, 1931).

therefore, that Melville wastes little time in ushering his exile into the presence of the venerable doctor himself.

Israel's quest is twofold: for a place in the brotherhood of man and for a just authority which renders respect to the individual regardless of station or class. Although he is personally treated with kindness by Millet and the king, there can be no room for him in an aristocratic society which by its very nature institutionalizes the oppression he suffered at the hands of his father. It is one of the manifold ironies of *Israel Potter* that the founders of a supposedly egalitarian republic turn out to be oppressors in their own right. This is clearly the case with regard to Franklin, whose homespun qualities are otherwise lacking in his English counterparts. Though a patriarch himself, he carries no rank, takes pride in his plainness, and is accustomed to dress in linsey-woolsey. His manner, writes Melville, is familiar and paternal, and he regularly addresses Israel, his fellow American, as "my good friend," even favoring him at one point with a confidential chat. But whereas Sir John Millet is described as a "true Abrahamic gentleman" (pp. 35–36), Franklin, the creator and personification of Father Abraham, is exposed as a consummate fraud.

Melville's Franklin is a tiresome moralizer, full of wisdom and years, who quotes Poor Richard almost verbatim and whose bible is *The Way to Wealth*. For "the grave man of utility" (p. 54), the Protestant ethic has become a substitute for Protestantism itself, and the inscrutable Deity of the Puritans has vanished altogether from a world in which "God helps them that help themselves." The commandments have vanished as well, and honesty— once enjoined for its own sake, as a moral imperative—is now prescribed as the best policy for correcting mistakes. Values have gone so completely awry that jokes are deemed equally unsuitable "at funerals, or during business transactions" (p. 58). When Israel lights up at the expectation of an early passage home, Franklin callously deflates his hopes by reciting a lesson in moderation and self-denial: "At the prospect of pleasure never be elated, but, without depression, respect the omens of ill" (p. 57). The complacency of his attitude, and its irrelevance to Israel's actual situation, are underscored in the later scene where the hero is denied access to France, recalls Franklin's words, and finds himself as incapable

MELVILLE 155

of complying "with the last section of the maxim, as before he
had with the first" (p. 117).

In commenting on Franklin's appearance, Melville writes that
he exhibits "nothing superfluous, nothing deficient." The description is revealing in light of Melville's subsequent remarks on nature's penchant for extremes—for overdoing or underdoing its creations, or still more frequently, going about its business in a
disorderly fashion (pp. 64–65). The point is that Franklin's ideology
fetters nature in general and stultifies human nature itself. Mounted
on his wall is a map

> of far countries in the New World, containing vast empty spaces
> in the middle, with the word DESERT diffusely printed there
> . . . which printed word, however, bore a vigorous pen-mark, in
> the Doctor's hand, drawn straight through it, as if in summary
> repeal of it (p. 52).

His chambers are cluttered with scientific charts and inventions,
and he is forever devising new schemes of improvement—a term
for which Melville supplied an admirable gloss in "I and My Chimney": "Improvement, which is a softer name for destruction."[30]
In much the same way, Franklin systematically endeavors to improve his "good friend" and compatriot Israel Potter. To Franklin,
indeed, Israel is less an individual than a pupil in want of instruction, whose desire for even the simplest of pleasures must be
sternly rebuked. The would-be benefactor reveals his true character as a disciplinarian, and effectively denies the hero the very independence for which the Revolution was fought. As Israel puts
it, "If he thinks me such a very sensible young man, why not let
me take care of myself?" (p. 74).

Franklin's passion for improvement is inseparably bound up
with the principle of delayed gratification which he invokes in
order to justify his treatment of Israel.[31] The desert can only be
"repealed" if men are taught to practice thrift and forego such
"luxuries" as pastry and wine. And Franklin, according to Melville,

30. Herman Melville, *The Complete Stories of Herman Melville*, ed. Jay
Leyda (New York: Random House, 1949), p. 406.
31. See Keyssar, *Melville's "Israel Potter,"* pp. 25-26, for a more extensive
discussion of this point.

is "the type and genius of his land" (p. 62): it is a telling detail that he orders Israel to remain in his room, "just as if you were my prisoner" (p. 59). The implication, to be developed inexorably as the tale proceeds, is that the promise of America, as represented by Israel Potter, is in bondage to Franklin's creed. Nor should we forget that Franklin is pointedly said by Melville to be "everything but a poet" (p. 62). His endless prohibitions and exclusive concern with the practical side of life are as stifling to art as they are to the human spirit.

In his discussion of Franklin, Melville draws a parallel between the cunning sage and the Hebrew patriarch Jacob. The parallel enriches his portrait of Israel Potter as an outcast and exile, for if Franklin is identified with Jacob, Israel can be compared to his twin brother Esau. Exactly like Potter, Esau is a "hunter, a man of the field," and he is similarly described as impulsive and trusting (Gen. 25:27). The sly Jacob twice takes advantage of his brother's simple good nature in order to cheat him of his birthright and blessing. He is rewarded for his duplicity with the assurance that his seed shall inherit the Promised Land, while Esau is cast out of the covenant and banished forever from the house of Abraham. In Melville's adaptation, Franklin usurps the inheritance that rightfully belongs to Israel Potter: Americans have made a mockery of the covenant. By transferring their allegiance from the Abraham of the Scriptures to the Abraham of *The Way to Wealth*, they have turned into outcasts—Esaus and Ishmaels—those who honor the Republic's most cherished ideals. His name notwithstanding, the Israel Potter of Melville's romance is an Esau in the American Israel.

It is no coincidence that Israel first meets John Paul Jones in Franklin's chambers. Franklin's moral relativism sanctions the unrestricted exercise of the individual will, and Jones is quick to seize upon Poor Richard's proverb "God helps them that help themselves" as a license for his own savage behavior. Captain Paul is another Revolutionary hero who mouths egalitarian slogans— "I'm a democratic sort of sea king," he tells Israel (p. 128)—while thinking only of himself. He demands "a separate, supreme command," wages war for reasons of personal revenge, and curses his misfortune at not having been born a Czar (pp. 80–81). George

III positively shines in comparison to this self-proclaimed Caesar of the sea. When Israel offers to share his bed with Jones—a gesture which is usually synonymous with brotherhood in Melville's work—the captain flatly refuses, preferring instead to muse upon future acts of barbarism and pausing occasionally to savor his reflection in the mirror. In the later scene where Israel is picked up by the *Ranger*, Jones temporarily unbends, confides his youthful ambitions, and cries out in a burst of enthusiasm, "Spring under me, good ship; on you I bound to my vengeance!" (p. 129). As his exclamation suggests, Jones exploits Israel for his own selfish purposes, a point which is made clear in chapter seventeen, where after a long account of the captain's exploits, Melville concludes with the following words:

> This cruise made loud fame for Paul, especially at the court of France, whose king sent Paul a sword and a medal. But poor Israel, who had also conquered a craft, and all unaided too—what had he? (p. 161).

Since "hunted Israel" is so often described in terms appropriate to a runaway slave, it is worth conjecturing that Melville intended a criticism of the Compromise of 1850 in his treatment of Franklin and Jones. Certainly there is reason to believe that he saw in their alliance an emblem of the collusion of Northern capitalist and Southern planter which led to the passage of the Fugitive Slave Act. Franklin, for example, is an obvious parody of the New Englander of sectional iconography. A Jack of all trades, he is prudent and crafty, and he guards his thoughts behind an impenetrable mask: "Having carefully weighed the world, Franklin could act any part in it. By nature turned to knowledge, his mind was often grave, but never serious" (p. 66). Israel is exactly right when he observes that the doctor is sly; and Franklin himself is unable to suppress an incredulous smile upon hearing Paul Jones commend him for "frankness" (p. 82). As for Jones, though a native of Scotland, he seems to have more in common with that "fiery and intractable race" which Melville found in the south of Vivenza than he does with his tight-fisted countrymen. He thinks of war in terms of the *code duello*—indeed, he is compared to a "fiery-hearted duellist" (p. 159)—and announces that he lives entirely for the sake of honor and glory. He looks, according to Melville, "like one who never had been, and never would be, a subordinate" (p. 78). His tawny complexion speaks of the tropical sun, and when he first shipped before the mast as a boy, his hammock-mate was a full-blooded Congo. Although he protests that the accusation is slanderous, he apparently once flogged a man to death for disobeying orders, and he revels in the idea of kidnapping kings and taking royalty captive: "the nobleman, Lord Selkirk, shall have a bodily price pinned on his tail-coat, like any slave up at auction in Charleston" (p. 131). It is quite in keeping with this overall portrait that during the courtly looting of the Selkirk mansion Jones conducts himself in a manner befitting the best Southern gentleman.

But the dominant metaphor for Jones, of course, is Indian, and it is his primitive blood-lust which brings out the worst in American character. It brings out the worst in Israel Potter, who is so enraptured with the captain's talk that he forgets "all about his previous desire to reach home" (p. 82). After brutally killing three British sailors, the hero confesses, "It was Captain Paul's voice that somehow put me up to this deed" (p. 126); and under Jones's tutelage, his patriotism turns into savagery. When Jones raids Whitehaven to avenge a long-standing grudge, Israel dashes alone and unarmed at the crowd on the shore, an action which Melville describes as insane. And it is Israel, not Jones, who first conceives the idea of renaming the *Duras* in honor of Franklin. We cannot overlook the fact that his uncritical service to Jones implicates the hero in the very system of values which frustrates his search for fraternity and contributes to his unheeded sufferings. Melville's account of the battle between the *Serapis* and the *Bon Homme Richard* furnishes an apt case in point. The battle itself is depicted as a clash between brothers: "It seemed more an intestine feud, than a fight between strangers. Or, rather, it was as if the Siamese twins, oblivious of their fraternal bond, should rage in unnatural fight" (p. 178). The combatants methodically tending their guns are likened to Lowell girls at work in the cotton factories, a simile which looks ahead to the brickyards of London, where we observe at first-hand the degrading effects of industrial production. Israel's part in the struggle is fully the equal of that played by Jones. When all seems lost, he saves the day by dropping a grenade down the hatchway of the enemy ship, with the result that twenty of the foe are killed and another forty severely wounded. It is Pearson of the *Serapis*, according to Melville, who does himself credit as an officer and man by hauling down his colors to preserve human life.

It cannot be emphasized too strongly that the butchery which characterizes such warfare, crowned as it is with success for the American cause, is justified by Poor Richard's saying that "God helps them that help themselves." The same saying can be used to justify the inhumane working conditions spawned by the rise of industrialism, as Melville suggests by his allusion to Lowell. It can be used to justify the most lawless individualism, whether martial or industrial, and it inevitably spells the death of Christian fellowship and republican ideals. It leads to the kind of world of which Israel gets a preview aboard the English ship after his separation from Jones—a world where class jealousy prevails and the spirit of brotherhood is appealed to in vain. Starting in the maintop and finally diving down among the waisters, the hero rehearses his eventual descent from an American freeholder to an English pauper. As his offers of intimacy are successively spurned, his wanderings become a parable of his plight as an outcast whose very endeavor to fraternize jeopardizes his safety by exposing him to the wrath of the crew. It is an ironic commentary on Poor Richard's gospel of self-reliance that Israel is forced to feign madness in order to escape detection and indeed to survive.

The full effects of the Protestant ethic on Israel Potter are manifested only after his arrival in London. Previously, Melville delineates alternative values or types of behavior against which he measures both Franklin and Jones. Captain Pearson's action to forestall further carnage is one such example; and another occurs on a Sunday when Jones hails a clergyman—whom he mistakes for an old woman because of the minister's robes—preaching to a congregation assembled on the shores of Fife. When the minister quotes his text—a verse from Psalms 58 which appeals to the Almighty for vengeance against the wicked—Jones chides him for lack of charity and answers back with Poor Richard's proverb. The minister denounces him as a "reprobate pirate," prophesying that a gale will harry his ships from the waters of Scotland. Jones, who is anything but charitable, and whose own creed equates predatory individualism with the blessings of heaven, replies with an oath to lay waste the harbor at Leith. The next morning, before the attack can begin, a squall comes up and disperses the fleet, an event which discredits the notion that God is on the side of those who live by Poor Richard's code (pp. 167–68).

The contrast between Scripture and Poor Richard suggested by Melville in the foregoing scene is reiterated in his presentation of Ethan Allen, the single most positive figure in the entire romance. There is no little significance in the fact that Allen and Israel are alike in so many respects. Both are blond, leonine in appearance, and gawked at and reviled by their English captors. Allen is introduced in the chapter entitled "Samson among the Philistines"; and Melville, in his sketch of Israel's birthplace, ascribed the power of Samson to the hardy race bred in the Berkshires. Both men took part in decisive and early engagements of the war, Israel at Bunker Hill and Allen at Ticonderoga. New Englanders by birth, each in his own way is representative of the authentic potential of the native American.

The interlude with Allen, like that with the Scottish minister, occurs on a Sunday, and the coincidence is not accidental. Having studied divinity in his youth, Allen proceeds to improve the occasion by delivering a text on the righteousness of God. It is a very different text from that expounded by Jones, for unlike Poor Richard, Allen can discourse with equal eloquence on theology and the rights of man. His speech is studded with quotations from Scripture, and when he is threatened with hanging as a rebel, he vows that "the great Jehovah and the Continental Congress shall avenge me; while I, for my part, shall show you, even on the tree, how a Christian gentleman can die." Admonished to look to his soul by a solicitous clergyman, he replies that mortals can know nothing with certainty of "the world of spirits" (p. 207). It is Christian treatment on earth he demands, not special favors from heaven, and he cordially expresses his thanks to the decent townspeople who intervene to protect him from the blows of a guardsman. His genuine gratitude for acts of kindness transcends nationality, and he pointedly disclaims any motives of personal hatred or glory.

Ethan Allen, Melville asserts, exhibits no trace of his New England origins, and his Western spirit is "the true American one." Whereas Franklin is sly, he is explicitly said to be frank, and whereas Jones is solitary and obsessed with himself, Allen is "companionable as a Pagan" (p. 212). But Ethan Allen, the ideal American, is seen only in chains, and there is an analogy to be drawn between his situation and that of Israel Potter. For Israel too is enchained and exploited—victimized by the values of Franklin and Jones. The analogy is strengthened by Melville's insistence that Allen is "essentially Western." By 1855, when Melville was putting the finishing touches on *Israel Potter*, the same coalition of Northern and Southern interests that enacted the Fugitive Slave Act had turned "Bleeding Kansas" into a battlefield. Further consequences of that coalition can be traced in *The Confidence-Man* (1857), Melville's most pessimistic work of fiction and the last to appear during his lifetime. Its action is set on a Mississippi river boat bound from St. Louis to New Orleans and agitated by "the dashing and all-fusing spirit of the West."

For Melville, then, the Western spirit is less an actuality than a potential, and Allen himself is but a brief detour on Israel's journey to Egypt and the City of Dis. A fugitive again, the hero hastens toward London, "the true desert" of modern man (p. 217). Melville's wording here invites comparison to his earlier description of Franklin's map of the New World, for the ideology disseminated by Poor Richard has repealed the desert only to reproduce it in a different form. Contrary to the widespread perfectionist views of his contemporaries, Melville questions whether history is progress, whether the changes which swept Europe and America in the nineteenth century had indeed bettered society and man. In his portrait of Franklin, he called attention to the doctor's conjurer's robe, his antique learning, and the "necromantic look" of his chambers (p. 52). He wrote of the Latin Quarter, where Franklin made his home, in similar terms, alluding to the "monastic and theurgic" air of its prison-like streets (p. 65). The same imagery carries over into his picture of London, a city of dismal and unrelieved blackness which Israel enters, significantly enough, on Guy Fawkes' Day. He approaches by way of London Bridge, which was built by a "cowled monk" and whose funereal arches once displayed "the withered heads and smoked quarters of traitors, stuck on pikes." Now besmoked and polluted by industrial waste, and teeming with "tormented humanity," the bridge, like the city itself, shows that oppression has persisted from the past into the present (pp. 226–28).

Chapters 23 and 24, together entitled "Israel in Egypt," yield important insights into Melville's social philosophy and go to the source of his quarrel with Poor Richard's ethic. They deal with Israel's experience in the London brickyards, and they show how his spirit is finally broken by a type of labor which robs individual men of their dignity by reducing them to little more than functional mechanisms. Devoid of pleasure or hope, the work begets in the worker an equally hopeless and despairing disposition. The Israel Potter who resigned his post with the Princess Amelia rather than endure the affronts of her overseer now toils indifferently in the dungeon-like pits, "lorded over by the taskmaster" (p. 221). The very ideology which extols self-reliance, Melville is suggesting, ends up by rendering self-reliance obsolete. It generates economic conditions which destroy the initiative it purports to prize, and it becomes oppressive by blinding its adherents—namely, Franklin's heirs—to the consequences of the conditions to which it gives rise. Self-reliance did indeed conduct "our forefathers to national freedom" (p. 10), as Melville himself is the first to admit; but it is only by altering material circumstances that self-reliance as a virtue can hope to survive. Melville drives home this point in his discussion of the bitter and uncaring mood produced in the brickmakers. If their recklessness be vice, he writes, it is "like that weed which but grows on barren ground; enrich the soil, and it disappears" (p. 221).

Melville does more, however, than call for economic changes in his analysis of the brickyards. He reiterates his faith in the value of human solidarity, and he envisages a society which is free from the inequities of class. Speaking metaphorically of bricks, he observes:

> Are not men built into communities just like bricks into the wall? Consider the great wall of China: ponder the great populace of Pekin. As man serves bricks, so God him, building him

up by billions into edifices of his purposes. Man attains not to
the nobility of a brick, unless taken in the aggregate (p. 222).

But it is precisely economic divisions which impair the nobility
of man in the mass, and Melville therefore goes on to expand his
critique of English society. Approaching his metaphor from a different tack, he considers the finished bricks in terms of their relative distance from the fire which bakes them. Whereas the bricks
nearest the flames are haggard and withered, "hardly fit for service," and the topmost layers are pale and languid, the middle bricks
are "sound, square and perfect . . . , bringing the highest prices"
on the market (pp. 223–24). In the England of *Israel Potter*, there
are mostly aristocrats and paupers, and even the farm hands whom
Israel passes on his first flight toward London are little more than
"human steers" (p. 23). Somewhere between the extremes of
wealth and poverty, in a community composed of Israel Potters,
Melville's earthly utopia is found. His preference is notably similar
in spirit to that of the original emigrants, and it recalls Robert
Cushman's lay sermon on "The Sin and Danger of Self-Love,"
with its caveat against "gentry and beggary." It is noteworthy
in this context that Melville, in adapting his source, suppressed
the information that Israel Potter was driven by want to beg.[32]
In the romance proper, it is reported "as a fact nationally characteristic" that though reduced to the sewers, "Israel, the American,
never sank below the mud, to actual beggary" (pp. 235–36).

The remainder of the book is devoted to Israel's hardships as
an exile in London and his eventual return to America. Although
Melville greatly condensed his source in treating this part of the
hero's career, he did include material on the human toll of an
economic system in which prosperity is contingent on the making
of war. Israel's fortunes take a turn for the better in 1793, with
the outbreak of the French war and the ensuing conscription of
London's superfluous hordes. His fortunes decline with the return
of peace, and they reach their lowest ebb after the defeat of Napoleon in 1817: "this second peace again drifting its discharged sol-

32. Israel R. Potter, *The Life and Remarkable Adventures of Israel R. Potter*
(1824; New York: Corinth Books, 1962), pp. 85–87. Potter, indeed, applied
for admittance to the parish almshouse.

diers on London, so that all kinds of labor were overstocked" (p. 235). The spirit of Franklin and Jones still imprisons the hero, and it is only the memory of the "Fortunate Isles of the Free" which keeps Israel Potter from plunging into total despair (p. 236). But when he does at last succeed in securing passage home, his expectations are cruelly dashed by the realities of American life. Disembarking in Boston on a Fourth of July, he narrowly escapes being run over by a "patriotic triumphal car" flying a banner in honor of the soldiers who served at Bunker Hill (p. 238). The nation which builds monuments to commemorate its wars, which takes for its paradigm Franklin's *Autobiography* and for its motto Paul Jones's oath that "I will mount, not sink" (p. 80), is too intent upon self-glorification to notice the actual heroes who suffered on its behalf.

It comes as no surprise, therefore, that Israel's pilgrimage to his Berkshire homestead only increases his sense of being a stranger in the land. Journeying to the mountains in the company of his son, he discovers that the very dwelling in which he was born has vanished from the face of the earth. The last words he utters in the book are spoken in response to the boy, who asks his grief-stricken father why he stares transfixed at the ground:

"Father!" Here . . . *my* father would sit, and here, my mother, and here I, little infant, would totter between, even as now, once again, on the very same spot, but in the unroofed air, I do. The ends meet. Plough away, friend (p. 241).

The hero's quest for an American father—and by implication, a just society—terminates in failure. The ends do indeed meet in *Israel Potter*, as indicated by Melville's ironic dedication "To His Highness the Bunker Hill Monument." For the Revolution was fought not to perpetuate royalty, but rather to replace it with a republic committed to the equality of man. America, by forsaking its principles, has become indistinguishable from its English sire. Melville had feared as much as early as *Mardi*, in a passage which bears repeating in light of his present concerns. Addressing those "sovereign kings," his boastful countrymen, he had written regarding Vivenza: "The maxims once trampled underfoot, are now printed on his front; and he who hated oppressors, is become an oppressor himself."[33]

The United States emulating Britain is an ironic reminder of Melville's famous celebration of American destiny in *White-Jacket*. What the biblical references ultimately mean is that the redeemer nation, escaped from the house of bondage, has belied its promise by following after the ways of the Egyptians. It has squandered its express dispensation and abandoned its mission as "the Israel of our time." The results for Israel Potter can be traced through the resurrection motifs which figure so prominently throughout the romance. To cite but a single example: when Potter conceals himself in the chimney at Brentford, he is assured by Squire Woodcock that his "resurrection will soon be at hand" (p. 94). As this example suggests, the motifs conform to a general pattern; from the Squire to America itself, the would-be deliverer fails to materialize. There is nothing in *Israel Potter* to support Melville's previous hope that the Messiah had come in the American people. There is only the purposeless exile of "our Wandering Jew" (p. 235) and his crucifixion as "the bescarred bearer of a cross" (p. 239) in the service of his indifferent countrymen. But Israel Potter is more than just an individual man: he is also a symbol and repository of the collective destiny of "the peculiar, chosen people." It is not by chance, after all, that he comes home to die as an octogenarian. For between the battle of Bunker Hill and the book's publication in 1855, exactly eighty years had elapsed, and when Israel Potter passes away, the dream of a national Israel perishes with him.

"Benito Cereno"

"Benito Cereno" is set in 1799, at the threshold of a new century —the century, as Melville put it in his review of the *Mosses*, when the United States was "rapidly preparing for . . . political suprem-

33. Melville, *Mardi*, *Writings of Herman Melville*, Northwestern-Newberry edition, 3: 526.

acy among the nations" of the world.[34] The year 1799 also found
le genre noir flourishing in both England and America: *Caleb Williams*, for example, had been published in 1794, *Wieland* in 1798,
and Godwin's *St. Leon: A Tale of the Sixteenth Century* in 1799
itself.[35] The Gothic (and thus Calvinist) associations evoked by
the date of the narrative are reinforced by the disclosure that the
ship of Amasa Delano—a native, like the fictional Israel Potter,
of Massachusetts, the destination of the 1630 migration and the
fountainhead of American liberty—is anchored off the coast of
Chile, in the harbor of Santa Maria. The world of "Benito Cereno"
is dense with ecclesiastical motifs; and as the name of the harbor
confirms, the tale follows the conventional Gothic pattern of displacing the action to a Catholic setting. The usual array of iniquitous monasteries and moldering catacombs is present as well, here
compressed into Melville's description of the strange ship uncertainly maneuvering into the bay. The stranger proves to resemble
"a white-washed monastery," its bulwarks teeming with dark
figures who look like friars and monks pacing ruined cloisters (p.
257).[36] References to the Pyrenees, to "superseded Acapulco treasure-ships" and "superannuated Italian palaces" heighten the impression of Old World decadence and decline. But the most striking
disclosure of all, perhaps, pertains to the American captain himself,
whose "singularly undistrustful good nature," according to Melville, precludes any "imputation of malign evil in man." Amasa
Delano, that is to say, is far too "benevolent" and enlightened
to entertain the notion of original sin, the cardinal tenet of the
faith of his forebears (p. 256).

Upon closer inspection, of course, the curious vessel reveals its
true character as a Spanish merchantman transporting a cargo
of Negro slaves. The "principal relic of faded grandeur" which
catches the eye of the American captain as he nears the ship is

34. Melville, *Moby-Dick*, Norton Critical Edition, p. 546. The actual date of
the events in which Amasa Delano took part was 1805.

35. Of the works mentioned Melville had at least read *Caleb Williams*
(Sealts, *Melville's Reading*, entry no. 255). He also knew Beckford's *Vathek*,
Mary Shelley's *Frankenstein*, and Walpole's *The Castle of Otranto* (Ibid.,
entries nos. 54, 467, 544).

36. Melville, *Complete Stories of Herman Melville*, Leyda edition. Page
references for "Benito Cereno" are to this edition and are included in the text.

its elaborate sternpiece, carved with the arms of Castile and Leon
and medallioned about by heraldic devices

> uppermost and central of which was a dark satyr in a mask,
> holding his foot on the prostrate neck of a writhing figure, like-
> wise masked (pp. 258–59).

This mysterious emblem is crucial to an understanding of "Benito
Cereno." On the most obvious level, it suggests the lordship of
master over slave. We know from *Mardi* and *Redburn* that Melville personally detested slavery and regarded its corollary, the
degradation of the Negro, as a violation of "the principle that
stands at the head of our Declaration of Independence." It is quite
significant, as we shall see, that the overseer Nulli (Calhoun), when
pressed to answer if his serfs are human, replies that the souls
have been bred out of them, "as the instinct of scent is killed
in pointers."[37]

In view of the tale's religious overtones, it is also possible that
the figure of the satyr and victim is meant to symbolize the relationship of Old Testament God to unregenerate sinner. Chattel
slavery can be seen, after all, as the physical correlative for the
spiritual condition of fallen man under the legal covenant, oppressed and persecuted by a tyrannical Deity. As if in support
of this truth, the text invariably refers to the Spaniard and his
black as "master and man," not master and slave. It is well known,
moreover, that Melville, in reworking his principal source for "Benito Cereno," assigned a far more prominent role to Babo than he
plays in Captain Amasa Delano's *Narrative of Voyages and Travels* (1817). As Melville's revisions make clear, his treatment of Babo
was decisively influenced by his reading of Shakespeare's *Othello*.
After his capture, for example, the Negro refuses to utter a single
word, and after *his* capture Iago declares to Othello, "From this
time forth I never will speak word" (V, ii, 305). Most important
of all, Babo is black and Iago is white, confirming that for Melville
human evil is independent of race.

---

37. Melville, *Redburn*, *Writings of Herman Melville*, Northwestern-Newberry edition, 4: 202; idem, *Mardi*, *Writings of Herman Melville*, Northwestern-Newberry edition, 3: 532.

If Babo, accordingly, is associated with man in his fallen estate, his putative owner, Benito Cereno, is frequently said to possess the attributes of divinity. Enfeebled though he is, he appears to hold absolute dictatorship over both slaves and crew. As captain of the *San Dominick*, he is invested with a power "beyond which, while at sea, there was no earthly appeal." He condescends to "no personal mandate" but delegates all orders to his presumably faithful body-servant, maintaining throughout an air of reserve and aloofness which prompts Delano to surmise that "the Spaniard, perhaps, thought it was with captains as with gods" (p. 265).

It is important to emphasize, however, that Cereno is described not simply in terms of divinity, but with specific reference to the Hebraic God and the Catholic Church. Observing the oakum-pickers and hatchet polishers hard at work, Delano says to Cereno, "I see you keep some, at least, of your host employed" (p. 274). In the prophetic books, Jehovah is commonly portrayed as the Lord of hosts, and Cereno, of course, is Delano's "host"—the word is Melville's—while the American is on board the *San Dominick*. We are further given to understand that Cereno is not immune to fits of wrath ill-suited to his beleaguered circumstances but altogether appropriate to the vengeful Deity of the Old Testament. He has had the giant Atufal placed in collar and chains, constrained by irrevocable decree to appear before him at two-hour intervals for the purpose of beseeching his pardon. Atufal has given the captain "peculiar cause of offense": he is a much fallen figure indeed, having been—like Adam in the Garden or Satan before his rebellion—a "king in his own land" (p. 277). It is after witnessing a repetition of this charade that Delano protests to the Spaniard that "you are a bitter hard master" (p. 320). Elsewhere he is troubled by fears for his life and suspects that Cereno's debility is "but the silky paw to his fangs" (p. 280).

It goes without saying that Delano's anxieties are misapplied, and that the real threat to his safety comes from the Negroes instead of the Spaniard. His perceptions are nevertheless true if invariably reversed. For if Cereno is not the "master," he is then the "man," and we are still left with the fact of enslavement, a condition whose theological equivalent was associated by Calvinists with the Roman Church. Delano himself invites this association when he ponders the very word Spaniard and detects a "Guy-Fawkish twang to it" (p. 300). Fawkes, a recusant, was involved in the Gunpowder Plot of 1605, a conspiracy to blow up James I and Parliament in order to restore England to Catholic rule. The reference is enriched by the numerous parallels between Cereno and the titular head of the Church of Rome. From the perspective of Calvinism, the Catholic faith, by slighting the depths of innate depravity and the corresponding need for Christ, simply perpetuates the bondage of the legal covenant. It comes as no surprise, therefore, to discover that the Spanish captain himself is regularly likened to an abbot or monk, making him the high pontiff of the ship's priesthood, and that suspended from his neck there hangs the key to Atufal's padlock (p. 278)—an apparent allusion to Matthew 16:19, where Jesus gives Peter the keys to the kingdom of heaven, empowering the Church to bind and loose. In much the same vein is the exchange which takes place between Delano and Cereno concerning the oakum-pickers. When the American inquires, "have you appointed them shepherds to your flock of black sheep," the Spaniard portentously rejoins, "What posts they fill, I appointed them" (p. 274).

It has been demonstrated, furthermore, that Melville drew heavily upon William Stirling's *The Cloister Life of the Emperor Charles the Fifth* as a source for "Benito Cereno," and that the Spanish captain's cuddy is filled with objects related to either monasticism or the Inquisition.[38] His table, for example, holds a "thumbed missal," and over it, attached to the bulkhead, is a crucifix. Cutlasses and old rigging lie "like a heap of poor friars' girdles," while his washstand, as Melville describes it, resembles a font. The

38. The discovery was first made by H. Bruce Franklin, *The Wake of the Gods: Melville's Mythology* (Stanford: Stanford University Press, 1963), pp. 136–52. Although I am indebted to Franklin's essay, I feel that his excessive reliance on Stirling is misleading and ultimately more of a hindrance than help to understanding the story. My own interpretation more closely resembles those of Joyce Adler, "Melville's *Benito Cereno*: Slavery and Violence in the Americas," *Science and Society* 38 (1974): 19–48; Edward Grejda, *The Common Continent of Men: Racial Equality in the Writings of Herman Melville* (Port Washington, N.Y.: Kennikat Press, 1974), pp. 135–49; and Carolyn L. Karcher, "Melville and Racial Prejudice: A Re-evaluation," *Southern Review* 12 (1976): 287–310.

references to the Inquisition are even more to the point, suggesting as they do the spiritual bondage enforced by the Roman Church. The captain's settees are as "uncomfortable to look at as inquisitors' racks," and the armchair in which he is shaved seems "some grotesque engine of torment" (p. 305).

It is predictable, in view of these recurrent Gothic motifs, that Amasa Delano—rather like Arthur Dimmesdale—finds himself lost in a maze of confusion. Indeed, the imagery of mazes and knots is pervasive throughout, and comes to a head in the well-known scene where Delano approaches an aged seaman toiling over a coil of hemp and asks him why he is knotting the rope. "For some one else to undo," is the muttered reply. Tossing the knot toward Delano, the Spaniard then whispers the urgent entreaty, "Undo it, cut it, quick," using the first English words heard on the ship. But the dumbfounded captain, according to Melville, stands utterly speechless, "knot in hand, and knot in head," and hastens to dispel the misgivings aroused by the sailor's mysterious action and speech (p. 296).

This entire incident is resonant with meaning, and we cannot do it full justice by interpreting it solely in terms of the accepted usage of the phrase "Gordian knot" as an intricate puzzle to be solved at a single stroke. A knot, after all, is an appropriate symbol of servitude, and it is doubly so in a story replete with references to shackles and chains and veiled allusions to the bondage of fallen man to Old Testament legalism. The sailor's prayerful request, suggestively spoken in English, can thus be seen as a plea for release from both spiritual and physical enslavement. It can be construed as an appeal for the coming of Christ, and regarded as Melville's adjurement to his countrymen to fulfill their mission as the "political Messiah," the homeland of freedom and social justice whose living ideals put to shame "the Chinese Legitimists of Europe."[39] But if the sailor's words convey a measure of hope, they also convey an unspoken fear, and they accordingly take us to the core of "Benito Cereno" by raising the question of the part that Amasa Delano, as representative American, is destined to play.

39. Melville, *White-Jacket, Writings of Herman Melville*, Northwestern-Newberry edition, 5: 150.

Before evaluating that part, however, and in order to place it in the proper perspective, it is helpful to glance briefly at the Greek fable from which the term "Gordian knot" derives. The fable tells us that Gordius, upon being chosen king of Phrygia, contrived a knot so ingenious that no one could untie it. Whereupon Alexander the Great, informed that whoever undid the knot would reign over the whole East, proceeded to cut it in twain with his sword. The fable thus seems to suggest that by "solving" the mystery of the *San Dominick*, Delano—and by inference America —will fall heir to the mantle of the Macedonian tyrant who conquered and scourged the continent of Asia. It is significant that Cereno's late friend, the original owner of most of the slaves, is named Alexandro Aranda. But the fable also suggests a more metaphorical reading, a reading that deals with the promise of deliverance. It brings to mind the lamb-like stranger who appears in the first chapter of *The Confidence-Man*, holds up a slate with the legend "Charity thinketh no evil," from I Corinthians 13:5, and is identified with "a mysterious impostor, supposed to have recently arrived from the East." For Christ also came with a sword, and he too was said to rule over the East.

And there are, as it happens, several hints to the effect that Captain Delano, if he is not exactly identified with Christ, is nevertheless endowed with traits which are common to the New Testament rather than the Old. He is swift to offer assistance to a brother ship in distress, and goes to inordinate lengths to exercise "charity" in judging Cereno, loath as he is to think ill of others (p. 264). Melville repeatedly describes him as "the good captain," credits him with numerous acts of kindness and forbearance, and writes that his natural instinct is to drown "criticism in compassion" (p. 271). He further makes a point of calling Delano the "guest." In the parable of the marriage of the king's son, which is peculiar to the Gospel of Matthew, Christ is associated with the "wedding guest." The American himself, just prior to taking his leave of the *San Dominick*, suspects that Cereno is plotting against him, and compares their situation to that of Judas and Christ: "was the Spaniard less hardened than the Jew, who refrained not from supping at the board of him whom the same night he meant to betray?" (p. 323).

If Delano is occasionally linked to Christ, however, he is notably lacking in the one belief which according to Calvinist divines sets the true catholic church apart from the false one. He is thoroughly convinced of his own innocence and of the goodness of human nature in general. He has heard, it is true, "of fiends in human form," but has never been inclined to credit such things; and now when they recur "as stories" to trouble his peace of mind, he hastens to dismiss them as the fictions they are (p. 285). His thinking, as befits a good American, has been shaped by "certain general notions" which construe happiness as the infallible reward of virtue, and interpret pain and suffering as stemming from vice (p. 290). Whenever he is visited by forebodings of foul play, he strives, "by ignoring the symptoms, to get rid of the malady" (p. 297) —a mannerism which is best understood in light of Melville's observation in *Mardi* regarding the universal malady of evil. Blind to the wickedness of others, Delano is equally incapable of fathoming the evil in himself, and the idea of a vengeful God, which hinges on belief in original sin, lies completely beyond his ken:

> I to be murdered here at the ends of the earth, on board a haunted pirate-ship by a horrible Spaniard? Too nonsensical to think of! Who would murder Amasa Delano? His conscience is clean. There is some one above (pp. 297-98).

Delano's ignorance of innate depravity, as indicated by the passage quoted above, is one of a number of shortcomings attributed to him by Melville that are more properly associated with Catholicism and the Old World than with Calvinism and the principles professed in the Declaration of Independence. Like Alexandro Aranda, who refrained from fettering his slaves because he believed "that they were all tractable" (p. 335), the American is wont to look upon black men as affectionate dogs. "In fact," writes Melville, "like most men of a good blithe heart, Captain Delano took to negroes, not philanthropically, but genially, just as other men to Newfoundland dogs." Watching Cereno shaved in his cuddy, Delano feels "all his old weakness" for Negroes returning, and he exchanges a playful remark with Babo concerning the bright colors of the Spanish flag, with its heraldry of the castle and lion (pp. 307-9). At one point, impressed by Babo's prompt execution of his duties, he even offers to purchase the slave for fifty doubloons, declaring to Cereno, "I should like to have your man here, myself" (pp. 288–89). Here as elsewhere Melville has Delano say "man" rather than slave. His view of the Negro is as unrealistic as his view of mankind; and it is altogether to the point that the whaleboat attached to his vessel is called the *Rover*, and that the American thinks of it also "as a Newfoundland dog" (p. 297). As we know from Melville's other writings, "rover" is a term he uses often when speaking of man, specifically in reference to the social outcast and solitary wanderer who figures so prominently in *le genre noir* and whose archetype, of course, is Lucifer himself. The cumulative effect of such details is to drive home Delano's obtuseness with regard to the Fall.

We are now in a position to clarify Melville's central concern in "Benito Cereno." What principally interests him is the issue of American destiny: will his countrymen heed the example of Spain and Alexander or Christ; will they, too, embrace Old Testament legalism, or put into practice the precept of brotherly love and truly become the new chosen people? Melville enriches the theme of succession with carefully selected borrowings from history and the Gospels. The ship's motto, "*Sequid vuestro jefe*" (Follow your leader), is an obvious echo of Christ's message: "Follow me." The message has a vital historical relevance as well: for the New World, of course, was discovered by Columbus under the imperial aegis of Spain. And it was discovered, as Melville well knew, as a result of the wealth and power which accrued to the Spanish throne when the kingdoms of Castile and Leon were united by the marriage of Ferdinand and Isabella—a detail which heightens the irony of the shaving scene in the cuddy. Taken together, Christ's summons and the flag of Spain pose the question at the heart of the story: whose lead will America follow as it enters upon the nineteenth century?

Melville's answer is that the United States has betrayed its calling as the savior of nations by following after the ways of the Spaniards. That betrayal is spelled out in both the story proper and the legal deposition which ostensibly "clears up" the mystery of the *San Dominick*. We learn, for example, that exactly three days after his murder by the blacks, the body of Alexandro Aranda reappears "at

sunrise" and appropriately replaces "the image of *Christ*opher
Colon, the discoverer of the New World," as the figurehead of
the ship (italics added). A palpably ironic resurrection, Aranda's
chilling fate suggests that America has sold out its ideals by continuing to tolerate slavery, and that the New World has become as
spiritually dead as the Old.[40] Gesturing at the slaveholder's skele-
ton, Babo demands that the Spaniards "keep faith with the
blacks," warning that otherwise "you shall in spirit, as now in
body, follow your leader" (p. 339). His words take on an ominous
meaning—a meaning which bears directly on the America of Melville's day—when read in conjunction with the account of the
assault on the *San Dominick*. The American mate, upon boarding
the slave ship, repeats the cry "Follow your leader," and takes
the lead in ruthlessly slaughtering the blacks, who "fain would
have had respite" but fall steadily before the sealing-spears and
cutlasses of the "unflagging" whites (pp. 331–32). Being virtually
unarmed, they fail to kill a single boarder, while losing nearly
a score of their own. There can be little doubt from Melville's
description that the sailors hold human life cheaper than material
gain. "The more to encourage" them, he says, they are told that
Cereno has written off his vessel as lost, and that a fair portion
of its spoils will accordingly be theirs if they succeed in subduing
the blacks, an inducement to which they respond "with a shout"
(p. 330). Their outcry confirms that the American republic, in its
hunger for riches, has failed to "keep faith" with the Negro by
following the leadership of Aranda and Spain.

The clearest piece of evidence that America has taken over from
Spain as the slaveholder of the modern world emerges from Melville's graphic depiction of the scene in which Don Benito and
Babo leap from the *San Dominick* into the swiftly departing
whaleboat. Still at a loss to account for the behavior of the Spaniard and his servant, Captain Delano clutches the fainting Cereno
and urges his men to row for their lives, "while his right foot,
on the other side, ground the prostrate negro" (p. 327). The vi-
gnette is an exact replica of the image of the satyr "holding his

40. Compare Harry Levin's remark in *The Power of Blackness: Hawthorne,
Poe, Melville* (New York: Alfred A. Knopf, 1958), pp. 189–90: "The implication, for the new world, is a change of course: from discovery to corruption."

foot on the prostrate neck of a writing figure" which adorns the
stern-piece of the *San Dominick*. To strengthen the parallel, Melville adds that Babo, though trampled underfoot, is seen "snak-
ishly writhing up from the boat's bottom" with dagger in hand. The
scene dramatically emphasizes that America has perpetuated the
tyranny of Europe by subjugating the black.

This episode also provides additional insight into Melville's attitude toward America's messianic pretensions. For the heraldry of
the satyr and victim has a scriptural precedent which ultimately
derives from the prophecy in Genesis that the seed of Adam shall
bruise the serpent's head. Its immediate source is the thirteenth
verse of the ninety-first Psalm: "Thou shalt tread upon the lion
and adder: the young lion and the dragon shalt thou trample under
feet." Interpreted typologically, the verse foretells the triumph of
Christ over the demonic host; the image of the Savior with his
feet planted on the neck of Satan occupies an important place
in the iconography of American millennialism.[41] Melville's version
of the icon exposes the religious and political bankruptcy of a nation which professes Christian and democratic ideals while enslaving a sixth of its population. The masks are stripped away from
the heraldic figures, and the "flash of revelation" is the reader's
as well as Delano's (p. 328). It is not Christ with his feet on the
dragon but rather a white man treading on a black that expresses
for Melville the truth about contemporary America.

It is a stroke of brilliance on Melville's part that roughly one-
fifth of "Benito Cereno" consists of official legal documents pur-
porting to "shed light" (p. 333) on the narrative proper.[42] The effect

41. An early use—or abuse, rather—of this motif can be found in Edward
Johnson's account of the war with the Pequots: "March on with a cheerful
Christian courage in the strength of the Lord and the power of his might, [you]
who will forthwith inclose your enemies in your hands, make their multitudes
fall under your warlike weapons, and your feet shall soon be set on their
proud necks" (*Johnson's Wonder-Working Providence*, ed. J. Franklin Jameson
[New York: Barnes and Noble, 1959], p. 166).
42. On the "truth" of the legal extracts see Allen Guttmann, "The Enduring
Innocence of Captain Amasa Delano," *Boston University Studies in English* 5
(1961): 35-45; Dryden, *Melville's Thematics of Form*, pp. 199-209; and Kingsley
Widmer, *The Ways of Nihilism: A Study of Melville's Short Novels* (Los
Angeles: California State Colleges, 1970), pp. 59-90. All three critics agree that
the law proves a misleading guide to the meaning of the tale.

of the documents is twofold: to undercut the legalistic mentality which mistakes them for truth, and to reiterate Melville's indictment of his countrymen. His purpose in comparing Babo to a snake, for example, is emphatically not to espouse a Manicheanism based on race.[43] It is not "the negro" who is a corrupting influence but rather the institution of slavery, a point confirmed by the brutal and lawless behavior of the Spanish sailors after retaking the *San Dominick:*

> Besides the negroes killed in the action, some were killed after the capture and re-anchoring at night, when shackled to the ring-bolts on deck; . . . these deaths were committed by the sailors, ere they could be prevented (p. 349).

The wanton slaughter inflicted by the Spaniards duplicates the murderous cruelty of the Negroes, and even includes the detail, which Melville incorporated into his account of the overpowering of Babo, that one of their number, having secreted a dagger at the time of the uprising, is arrested in the act of stabbing a black. Since the sailors themselves were enslaved by the Negroes, and could not "act otherwise" than their masters decreed (p. 386), the obvious moral is that slavery begets hatred in the slave regardless of race. It is Captain Delano, the enlightened, liberal American, who intervenes to put a stop to the violence against the bound captives. Yet it is also the captain, acting on his own initiative and against the frantic pleas of Benito Cereno, who authorizes the pursuit which restores them to bondage.

Delano's decision to give chase and recapture the fugitives is a measure of the legalism which he holds in common with the Spanish tribunal. A comparable legalism had become the hallmark of American politics by 1855, the year when "Benito Cereno" was first published in serial form. It was Captain Delano's heirs, statesmen of the order of Daniel Webster and Stephen A. Douglas, who lent their support and prestige to the Compromise of 1850, with its provision for the recovery of runaway slaves, and who sponsored the Kansas-Nebraska Act of 1854, which repealed the Missouri

43. Widmer, for example, claims that "Melville's art in *Benito Cereno* testifies to our enslaving Manicheanism" (*Ways of Nihilism*, p. 75).

Compromise and effectively sanctioned the spread of slavery north of latitude 36°30′. It was Captain Delano's heirs who sacrificed the Declaration of Independence to a legalistic justification of what Melville, in *Mardi*, called "a blot foul as the crater-pool of hell."[44] Delano himself echoes Melville's sentiments when he muses that "this slavery breeds ugly passions in man" (p. 312). But there is nothing to indicate that the "good captain" raises objections to the hideous punishment meted out by the court in the name of the law. The deposition speaks truer than the royal judges know when it declares "Amasa Delano incapable of sounding such wickedness" (p. 347). For Babo's malice and cunning are nowhere more evident than in the example he makes of Aranda's remains as a warning to the Spaniards of the fate that awaits them if they dare to challenge his will. Ironically following their leader, the tribunal retaliates by ordering Babo's head severed from his body and impaled on a pole as a gruesome deterrent to acts of rebellion.

The brief sequel to the official documents underscores the Calvinist implications of the legalism upheld by the court and tacitly endorsed by Delano. The conventional reading of the final section dwells on the contrast between the optimistic outlook of the genial American and the darkened but somehow "deeper" vision of the Spaniard. Melville's point, however, is that the differences are outweighed by a crucial area of resemblance. Each of the two captains in his own way bears witness to the medieval double standard, with its divided emphasis on good works and ascetic withdrawal, and each glosses over the reality of innate corruption. Renouncing the world over which there now falls the shadow of "the negro," Cereno retires to the monastery on Mount Agonia to meet his untimely end. But his perception of evil, which otherwise sets him apart from the American, does not extend to himself. With Babo's plot still fresh in his mind, he sadly remarks to Delano that "your last act was to clutch for a monster, not only an innocent man, but the most pitiable of all men" (p. 351). The Spaniard's words ring hollow indeed in light of the numerous parallels between him and the black. Both have been slaves and captains aboard the *San*

44. Melville, *Mardi*, *Writings of Herman Melville*, Northwestern-Newberry edition, 3: 534.

Dominick, and they are roughly the same age. Upon first meeting Cereno, Delano judges him to be "about twenty-nine or thirty" (p. 280), and according to the deposition, "he is twenty-nine years of age" (p. 349). The extracts describe Babo as "a small negro of Senegal . . . aged about thirty" (p. 335). The master and servant, in short, have far more in common than Don Benito would like to believe, and his adamant refusal, following his rescue, to acknowledge Babo's existence is the proof of his failure to confront his own fallen nature:

> During the passage, Don Benito did not visit him. Nor then, nor at any time after, would he look at him. Before the tribunal he refused. When pressed by the judges he fainted. On the testimony of the sailors alone rested the legal identity of Babo (pp. 352–53).

Captain Delano is wide of the mark when he attempts to rally the Spaniard by telling him that he is saved. Divested of his omnipotence—his scabbard empty of its silver-mounted sword, "apparent symbol of despotic command" (p. 352)—he is more properly the object of divine wrath, damned by his denial of original sin. The three months which intervene between the trial and his death are a reminder of the three days during which Aranda's body disappeared into the ship's hold, and the bier on which he is borne to his grave is an obvious substitute for the "hearse-like" *San Dominick* (p. 259). Stared at by Babo's unseeing eyes, which he shrank from meeting in life, Don Benito Cereno does indeed follow his leader to everlasting perdition.

As for Delano, he, too, we are told, has been saved, and saved, as he puts it, "against my knowledge and will" (p. 351). Melville's irony here, in implicitly falling back on the Calvinist doctrine of irresistible grace—the doctrine that the individual, by virtue of his total depravity, is wholly passive in the work of redemption —is underlined by the American captain's unshakeable faith in his goodness of heart. The man who takes such pride in the "kindly offices" he discharges for a stranger, who believes that an "ever-watchful Providence" blesses his praiseworthy works (p. 324), ascribes his salvation to his "good-nature, compassion, and charity" (p. 351). We can hardly miss Melville's implication, however, that Captain Delano, like his "good friend" the Spaniard, is in no ultimate sense really saved. As his remarks on the "human-like healing" power of the trade winds suggest, he remains as reluctant as ever to impute "malign evil" to either nature or man (p. 352). It seems rather probable that he will eventually follow his historical leader, Benito Cereno, to hell.

Melville made numerous other changes in the legal extracts that he adapted from the *Voyages and Travels*, and his revisions add greatly to the likelihood that he intended "Benito Cereno" to be read as a judgment, not only on Amasa Delano, but on America as well. The changes which particularly concern us here include the following: Melville altered the site of the trial from Concepción in Chile to Lima, Peru, and he further transferred the place of execution to Lima from the nearby Chilean port of Talcahuano. According to the original documents, the trial began in the last week of February, 1805, with the sentences handed down on the second of March; Melville tells us only that "the criminal cause commenced the twenty-fourth of the month of September" (p. 334). In the *Voyages and Travels*, the chief mate is named Don Joaquin Aramboalaza; mistakenly shot by the Americans, he is reported to be recovering from his wounds. In "Benito Cereno," he is given the more elaborate title of "the young Don Joaquin, Marques de Aramboalaza," is discovered to have on his person a jewel meant as a votive offering "to attest his gratitude, when he should have landed in Peru, his last destination, for the safe conclusion of his entire voyage from Spain," and is instantly killed by the gunfire of the boarders (p. 348).

The most obvious effect of the changes summarized above is to focus attention on the city of Lima at the expense of Concepción. Melville's reason for departing from the original narrative here is readily grasped if we remember "The Town-Ho's Story" from *Moby-Dick*, where Lima is identified as an emblem of Babylon or hell. While holding forth at an inn in the city, which is characterized by the "whiteness of her woe" and thus resembles the "white-washed" hull of the *San Dominick*, Ishmael refers to the "Venetianly" corruption of the Great Lakes and is congratulated by one of his auditors on the tact of his metaphor. "Oh! do not bow and look surprised," cries the Limeese, speaking on

behalf of the entire company, "you know the proverb all along
this coast—'Corrupt as Lima.' "[45]

It is with Lima's corruption in mind that we can begin to appreciate the significance of Melville's revisions with regard to Don
Joaquin. In the New Testament, Joseph, the husband of Mary,
is described as a descendant of Joachim or Jehoiachin. Steeped
in the Bible, Melville was certain to have known that Jehoiachin,
son of Jehoiakim, was the last king of Israel before the Babylonian
captivity. According to Jeremiah, the sire incurred God's wrath
by building "his house by unrighteousness, and his chambers by
wrong; *that* useth his neighbour's service without wages, and giv-
eth him not for his work" (22:13). The prophet goes on to pronounce God's sentence on Jehoiakim for countenancing slavery,
admonishing the tyrant that unless he mend his ways, the Lord
"will punish him and his seed and his servants for their iniquity"
(36:31). Jeremiah twice expressly threatens the unheeding king
with improper burial, declaring that "his dead body shall be cast
out in the day to the heat, and in the night to the cold" (22:19,
36:30). Although nothing further is heard of this particular threat
—which may nevertheless have furnished the inspiration for Aranda's
interment—the prophet's warning is otherwise strictly fulfilled. In
II Kings 24:8–15, we learn that the young Johoiachin, ascending to
the throne at the age of eighteen, "did *that which* was evil in the
sight of the LORD, according to all that his father had done." After
a brief reign of three months, he is deposed by the armies of Nebuchadnezzar, whose successful seige of Jerusalem seals Israel's doom.
Jehoiachin is taken prisoner and carried off to Babylon with an
enormous booty, consisting of the wealth of the palace and "all the
treasures of the house of the LORD."

It seems likely from the foregoing chronicle that Melville composed "Benito Cereno" with the last days of Israel directly in mind.
The Biblical parallels clarify such matters as Don Joaquin's youth,
his elevation to royal rank, and his possession of the jewel. It could
scarcely have escaped Melville's notice, moreover, that Aramboalaza,
the actual surname of Cereno's chief mate, bears a pronounced

---

45. Melville, *Moby-Dick*, Norton Critical Edition, pp. 168, 214. The patron
saint of the Cathedral of Lima, appropriately enough, is Saint Dominic.

likeness to "arambelosa," the Spanish adjective for tattered or covered in rags. This detail agrees nicely with the forced deportation of King Jehoiachin, and it figures as well in Melville's account of the young Spanish nobleman, whose refined features form a singular contrast to his ragged frock "of coarse woolen, much spotted with tar" (p. 283). Don Joaquin's journey from Spain to the New World, which ironically parallels that of Columbus, is best understood in terms of the Babylonian exile; for it is a journey which ends in enslavement and death, and its final destination is the present-day hell. What the biblical analogues are accordingly meant to suggest is that the American Israel has committed anew the sins of its predecessor and repeated the kingdom's downfall. The dream of a just and righteous society has been shattered by the reality of slavery. America, in succeeding to the Spanish throne and the throne of Jehoiakim the elder, has sold itself into Babylonian captivity. It has abdicated its calling as the "political Messiah" by restoring the bondage of Old Testament legalism and spurning the injunction of brotherly love. Like the backsliding Israelites, who provoked Jeremiah to his outbursts of wrath, its people "have forsaken the covenant of the LORD their God, and worshipped other gods, and served them" (22:9). And presumably they, like the Israelites and the Spaniards, will come to grief smartly for their transgressions.

It is altogether appropriate that in revising his source for "Benito Cereno" Melville availed himself of his extensive knowledge of the books of the prophets. The tale, after all, is his own jeremiad, sounding the alarm over national declension and calling upon his compatriots to reform and avert the vengeance of God. If it thereby takes its place in the tradition of American Puritanism, it also belongs in the rank of the native romances which effectively translated the sermon into art. The "stories" of "fiends in human form" which return to haunt Captain Delano eventually turn out to be true; and it is less the legal extracts which hold the key to the *San Dominick* than it is Melville's fictitious additions. As mentioned before, "Benito Cereno" resembles *The Scarlet Letter* in its Gothic confusion, and it evinces a kindred concern with the spiritual fate of its characters. But it holds out no comparable hope of redemption for either the individual or the nation at large,

and ends with Amasa Delano as confused and benighted as he
is at the start. It is the ultimate failure of the exemplary American
to "follow me"—to answer the summons of Christ—that accounts
for Melville's decision to alter the date of the criminal proceedings.
We are told that the tribunal takes Cereno's deposition on September twenty-fourth, and that the Spaniard expires "three months
after being dismissed by the court" (p. 353). He dies, that is
to say, on approximately the twenty-fifth of December, the date
of the Savior's birth—a circumstance that further illuminates
why Melville changed the site of the trial from Concepción to
Lima. It is noteworthy that Melville leaves us with a death, not
a birth, on this date of such moment in the history of the West.
For the underlying theme of the tale as a whole is that the Redeemer has not come in the American people, and historical time
must accordingly be reckoned as if there had been no advent of
Christ.[46]

Billy Budd

The Gothic elements which figure importantly in "Benito
Cereno" are also prominent in Billy Budd, and Melville invites
us to read his last work of fiction as a theological drama charged
with more real mystery than any Ann Radcliffe could ever devise.
As in his earlier tale, the setting and date of the narrative have
a crucial bearing on Melville's thematic concerns. The truly mysterious occurrences which form the subject of Billy Budd unfold
against a background of revolutionary questioning with respect
to the nature of society and man. It is 1797, England and France
are at war, and the uprising at Nore, only recently suppressed,
is fresh in the minds of the officers and crew of the imperial fleet.
The background and foreground meet in the connection between
the upheavals of the 1790s and the tragic events which transpire
aboard the Bellipotent. For the issues which confront Captain Vere

---

46. Although the Spaniard dies and the American survives, Melville makes a
point of choosing Benito Cereno rather than Amasa Delano as his title character. His choice may have been dictated by the fact that the two characters
have names whose initials are A. D. and B. C.

are finally inseparable from those which endanger the survival
of England itself.

Melville's account of Billy's impressment supplies a good introduction to a number of the issues at stake. The account might
be read as a parable in which Billy, as individual man, is forced
to surrender his natural rights upon entering a fallen world ruled
by war. But the opening of the tale is surely meant to caution
us against too simplistic a reading. The *Rights-of-Man* is owned
by a staunch admirer of Thomas Paine and named in honor of
the French Declaration of the Rights of Man; but it can scarcely be
said to vindicate the Enlightenment theory that human nature
is neutral or innocent in its original state. We are told that Captain
Graveling of the *Rights* is a prudent and respectable man, a lover
of "peace and quiet" who takes his responsibilities as a shipmaster
to heart; and yet we have it from his own lips that before Billy's
arrival his "forecastle was a rat-pit of quarrels." Nor was it by
means of example alone that Billy composed the strife which de-
prived the good captain of the comfort of his pipe. If "a virtue
went out of him, sugaring the sour ones," it took an act of physical
violence to bring Red Whiskers into line. And without Billy's presence, the captain declares, the brotherly love now found on the
Rights is certain to degenerate into the anarchy which formerly
prevailed. As Lieutenant Ratcliffe correctly points out, Billy is
a fighting peacemaker whose strong right arm might fairly be likened to the cannons protruding from the portholes of the *Bellipotent*. What Melville thus seems to suggest—in direct opposition
to the doctrines invoked on behalf of the French Revolution—is
that human nature is tainted by evil: even aboard the *Rights-of-
Man* social disorder can only be checked by a display of superior
force (pp. 45–48).[47]

47. All citations are from Herman Melville's *Billy Budd, Sailor* (*An Inside
Narrative*), ed. Harrison Hayford and Merton M. Sealts, Jr. (Chicago: University of Chicago Press, 1962). Page references are included in the text. My
reading of *Billy Budd* is indebted to the following studies: Richard Harter
Fogle's "Billy Budd: The Order of the Fall," *Nineteenth-Century Fiction* 15
(1960): 189–205; Joel Porte's *The Romance in America: Studies in Cooper,
Poe, Hawthorne, Melville, and James* (Middletown, Conn.: Wesleyan University Press, 1969), pp. 184–92; and Milton R. Stern's *The Fine Hammered
Steel of Herman Melville* (Urbana: University of Illinois Press, 1957), pp. 206–

This is not to deny, of course, that Billy's liberties are curtailed
as a result of his removal to the *Bellipotent*, or to gloss over the
severity of martial discipline on a man-of-war. A merchantman
and a battleship offer important contrasts, and the contrasts are
accentuated by Melville's portrayal of Billy himself. A foundling
whose origins are shrouded in mystery, Billy is likened to a number
of classical gods; stationed aloft in the foretop, he surveys from
an aerial vantage the mundane life of the decks. Certainly as Melville describes him he is ill equipped to deal with the complex
realities of a world at war. Billy, who has not yet "been proffered
the questionable apple of knowledge," and who is incapable of
either committing or fathoming deliberate malice, is little more
than a "sort of upright barbarian, much such perhaps as Adam
presumably might have been ere the urbane Serpent wriggled himself into his company" (p. 52). Of a piece with this characterization,
and of particular interest here, is Billy's reaction to the rigors
of martial law. The erstwhile peacemaker of the *Rights* is
thoroughly horrified by his first exposure to a public scourging
—the punishment meted out to an afterguardsman for dereliction
of duty—and he resolves on the spot that never through negli-
gence will he make himself liable to even so much as verbal re-
proach. But Billy's resolution to live up to the letter of the law
is more appropriate to the Garden of Eden than a city of Cain
afloat—and not simply because he finds himself in a realm where
prompt execution of orders is no safeguard against sinister designs
on the part of others. For Billy, being fallen, is potentially prone
to lawless action himself.

We have already seen that Billy is not free of violent instincts,
and Melville goes on to make clear that for all his primitive recti-
tude he is a postlapsarian creature who has not escaped the mark
of the Serpent. In corroboration of the doctrine of the Fall—"a
doctrine now popularly ignored"—Melville cites Billy's tendency
to stutter while under stress, comparing his vocal defect to Georgiana's blemish in Hawthorne's tale "The Birthmark." The comparison takes us back to Melville's piece on the *Mosses*, the collec-

39. A problem in interpreting the story is that it was left unfinished at Melville's
death. On this point see Mary Everett Burton Fussell, *"Billy Budd:* Melville's
Happy Ending," *Studies in Romanticism* 15 (1976): 43–57.

tion in which the story appears, and it recalls his remarks on his
fellow romancer's "Calvinistic sense of Innate Depravity and Original Sin."⁴⁸ Nor should we forget that Georgiana's flaw takes the
form of a crimson hand. Melville pointedly notes that Billy's im-
pediment is Satan's way of reminding us that "I too have a hand
here," and when the foretopman is later confronted with Claggart's
false accusation, the only reply he can muster in his overwrought
state is a fatal blow from his fist (pp. 52–53).

Whereas Billy impulsively violates the law, Claggart, the satanic
master-at-arms, embodies a legalism which is thoroughly corrupt.
He is also, again in contrast to Billy, the very type of civilized
and citified man, a virtuoso of indirection whose proper sphere
is the underground side of the ship. He is rumored to have volun-
teered for the navy in order to escape prosecution for some unknown offense, and is even suspected by the bluejackets of having
been drafted directly from jail. As the maritime chief of police,
with a host of underlings at his command, he now uses the law
to mask and advance his own diabolical ends. He is often associated
with conspiracy and fraud—Melville remarks, for example, on
his resemblance to Titus Oates, the renegade cleric who fabricated
the story of the popish plot—and his manner reminds Captain
Vere of a bandsman who perjured himself in a capital case. Though
seeming to possess "a mind peculiarly subject to the law of reason,"
he is in fact a depraved individual whom Melville pronounces a
madman at heart (p. 76). Even his conscience is powerless to
swerve him from the pursuit of his aims. "Being but the lawyer
to his will," it whitens his motives and justifies his persecution
of Billy as "retributive righteousness" by systematically inflating
trifles into calculated affronts (p. 80).

Although Melville undeniably presents Claggart and Billy as
opposites, he makes it clear that the foretopman's innocence—
which is rather an innocence of evil intent than a radical purity
—renders him singularly vulnerable to his victimizer's wiles. Bor-
rowing from Milton and *le genre noir*,⁴⁹ Melville creates a Calvinist

48. Randall Stewart discusses *Billy Budd* with reference to Hawthorne's story
in *American Literature and Christian Doctrine* (Baton Rouge: Louisiana State
University Press, 1958), pp. 98–102.
49. The influence of Milton on *Billy Budd* has been discussed by many critics.

drama which amounts in effect to a reenactment of the primal transgression. Although the law broken by Billy is the Mutiny Act, a statute framed by man, it is fully as remorseless in its penalty as the edict imposed on Adam and Eve. And much like Adam in the Garden, Billy plays an unwitting partner to the demonic chief of police in bringing about his own initiation into sin and death. As Melville remarks repeatedly, Billy's innocence is little more than "blank ignorance" (p. 86)—indeed it is his "blinder" (p. 87)—and it contributes to his eventual undoing by playing into Claggart's hands. "Such innocence as man is capable of," the old Dansker wisely reflects, does not "always sharpen the faculties or enlighten the will" in moral emergencies (p. 70). When the master-at-arms tries to implicate Billy in a bogus conspiracy, the foretopman recoils in disgust from an overture which "he instinctively knew must involve evil of some sort" but is loath to comprehend. Speculations on this subject are "so disturbingly alien to him" that he does "his best to smother them," it never entering his mind that it is his responsibility as a loyal seaman to report the attempted bribe to his immediate superiors (pp. 84–85). Shrinking from knowledge of the malign, and derelict in duty as well, Billy leaves himself open to Claggart's allegation of a capital crime. Whereupon "guilt and innocence personified in Claggart and Budd in effect changed places" as a result of the foretopman's blow and in light of the military code under which the case is to be tried (p. 130).

With this dramatic reversal—an apparent nod in the direction of *Caleb Williams*—Melville reminds us of the state of "Things as They Are" in the world of *Billy Budd*.[50] Claggart's temptation of Billy, leading as it does to an act of insubordination which threatens chaos aboard the ship, affords unmistakable parallels to contemporary political events. The chief of police and the Handsome Sailor are often depicted in terms which relate them respectively to the menace from abroad and the danger of mutiny at home.

See, for example, Norman Holmes Pearson, "*Billy Budd:* 'The King's Yarn,'" *American Quarterly* 3 (1951): 99–114; and Robert L. Perry, "Billy Budd: Melville's *Paradise Lost*," *Midwest Quarterly* 10 (1969): 173–85.

50. See Roland A. Duerksen, "*Caleb Williams, Political Justice* and *Billy Budd*," *American Literature* 38 (1966): 373–76.

Billy, for example, is associated with the ancient Britons, being purely Saxon in appearance and presumably free "of any Norman or other admixture" (p. 51). "The bonfire in his heart" (p. 77), while it surely betokens his essential good nature, also suggests that he is all too inclined to be carried away by the force of emotion, and it eventually issues in a punch like "the flame from a discharged cannon at night" (p. 99). Billy's sudden outburst demands comparison to the uprising at Nore, which is likened by Melville to an "irruption of contagious fever in a frame constitutionally sound" (p. 55). Melville further describes the Great Mutiny as a combustion ignited by "live cinders blown across the Channel from France" (p. 54), and Claggart has a slight accent indicating that he is foreign rather than English by birth. Flashing forth from his eyes is a red light like "a spark from an anvil in a dusk smithy" (p. 88)—a spark which sets off an explosion in Billy not unlike the insurrection at Nore. Although he is linked to "the enemy's red meteor of unbridled and unbounded revolt" (p. 54), what Claggart represents in reality is the danger of despotism. His iron control of his subordinates demands a degree of subservience almost "inconsistent with entire moral volition" (p. 67). And whereas Billy's lawlessness is sporadic and swiftly repented —much like that of the mutineers who subsequently rallied to the royal standard at Trafalgar and the Nile—Claggart's abuse of the law foments disorder, undermines legitimate authority, and effectively paves the way for oppression. It is for this reason that Melville mentions him in the same breath as Napoleon, the "portentous upstart from the revolutionary chaos" who exploited the disturbances in France to establish a military dictatorship with himself at its head (p. 66).

To turn to Captain Vere at this point is to emphasize that his involvement in the tragic episode of the *Bellipotent* is also defined and determined by "Things as They Are." For Vere's cause is identical to Britain's, and Britain, as "the sole free conservative" power of the Old World, is dedicated to the preservation of the principles symbolized by the union and cross of its flag: "founded law and freedom defined" (p. 54). These are political terms, but in the context of the romance they are religious as well, and their full implications can scarcely be ignored in a story which owes so much to the Scriptures. Though a member of the lower aristocracy, Vere disinterestedly opposes the revolutionary "torrent" of novel opinions emanating from France, not because the theories in question are inimical to privilege, but rather because they seem to him "at war with the peace of the world and the true welfare of mankind" (p. 63). And so Vere too is a fighting peacemaker, who fights on behalf of truths both secular and spiritual and wages war to put an end to warfare itself.

Vere's character and principles commit him to a middle way which is jeopardized by Billy and Claggart alike. Known to his peers as "Starry Vere" because of his occasional "dreaminess of mood" (p. 61), he also possesses a knowledge of men and a mastery of practical affairs. His seat of command on the quarter-deck is located figuratively midway between Billy's position in the foretop and the master-at-arms' subterranean realm. A foe—like England itself—of legalism and license, always mindful of the welfare of his crew but tolerating no infractions of discipline, Vere finds himself faced with an extraordinary clash of contraries in which a false witness is "struck dead by an angel of God" and yet according to the Articles of War "the angel must hang" (p. 101). In the ensuing crisis he is forced to confront and accept—with important modifications—the parts of himself which correspond to Billy and Claggart.

Vere's forthrightness and candor are stressed from the first, and Melville informs us that he is repelled and then angered by Claggart's circuitous air. Obviously a man of strong emotions, he is all but overwhelmed by the scene in his stateroom whose outcome is the master-at-arms's violent death. His extreme agitation, as shown by his impassioned exclamations, prompts the surgeon to suspect that the captain is temporarily insane. But much like Melville himself, who steals into literary bypaths and resorts time and again to indirection in telling his tale, Vere—though given by nature to rapid decisions—is persuaded by circumstances to adopt a policy in which circumspection "not less than promptitude was necessary." Here, writes Melville, referring to the captain's desire for concealment, "he may or may not have erred." When Melville goes on to detect some lurking resemblance between Vere and Peter the Barbarian, he appears to suggest that the captain is guilty of an act of oppression worthy of Claggart. As Melville hastens to add, however, Vere "was no lover of authority for mere authority's sake," and his decision is dictated by the exigencies of war. Billy's crime—which amounts, after all, to the killing of a military superior—follows hard on the heels of the recent insurrections, and Vere, as a loyal commander, is simply not authorized to judge it on the "primitive basis" of deliberate intent (pp. 103–4). For a true naval officer, according to Melville,

> is in one particular like a true monk. Not with more of self-abnegation will the latter keep his vows of monastic obedience than the former his vows of allegiance to martial duty (p. 104).

Vere is a monk in the world, and as such he is bound by the oath of his office to implement a code which admits of no mercy —but a code whose harsh provisions are necessary to beat back the threat posed by France.

The deliberations which follow Billy's testimony take place in the stateroom whose opposing compartments contain the imprisoned foretopman and the corpse of the master-at-arms—figuratively in the presence of sin and death, which came into being with the original breach of God's law. With "the one now temporarily a jail and the other a dead-house" (p. 105), the compartments serve to reiterate that human nature, like nature itself, is thoroughly implicated in the Fall. (Claggart's depravity, Melville is careful to state, is a "depravity according to nature" [p. 75].)[51] It is this consideration which proves decisive with Captain Vere, and finally wins over the members of the court, who are swayed by the argument that the "people," meaning the sailors, will misconstrue leniency as an invitation to license. Though "the last Assizes . . . shall acquit" (p. 111), Vere lives and acts not in heaven but a world at war, and his martial responsibilities include averting a recurrence of the outbreak at Nore.

Vere's devotion to duty and military law requires the suppression of his "primitive instincts strong as the wind and the sea"

---

51. F. O. Matthiessen notes that Melville was reading extensively in Schopenhauer at the time he composed *Billy Budd*, and that he scored this sentence in his copy of *Studies in Pessimism*: "Accordingly, the sole thing that reconciles me to the Old Testament is the story of the Fall" (*American Renaissance: Art and Expression in the Age of Emerson and Whitman* [New York: Oxford University Press, 1941], p. 502).

(p. 109). That instincts so rooted in the heart can be a source
of elemental chaos or worse, is confirmed by an anecdote which
Melville claims to have heard from his anonymous scholar:

> In a matter of some importance I have seen a girl wind an old
> lawyer about her little finger. Nor was it the dotage of senile
> love. Nothing of the sort. But he knew law better than he knew
> the girl's heart (p. 75).

But if the heart, for Melville, jeopardizes the law, it can also
express a compassion and love which partake of the divine, and
Vere now yields to his "primitive instincts" by seeking out Billy
to communicate the edict of the court. Casting a veil over the
details of the interview, Melville nevertheless conjectures that the
captain may frankly have confessed his part in bringing about
the sentence of death. Certainly, Melville asserts, it would have
been characteristic of Vere to have withheld nothing from Billy.
He may even have shed the austere disciplinarian and clasped the
condemned youth to his heart. In effect Vere acknowledges the
Billy within him by "letting himself melt back into what remains
primeval in our formalized humanity." This is the captain's moment of freedom, and it is a moment, to judge from Melville's
description, which resonates with religious significance. "There is
no telling the sacrament," he writes, when two such spirits as Billy
and Vere embrace. "There is privacy at the time, inviolable to
the survivor; and holy oblivion, the sequel to each diviner magna-
nimity, providentially covers all at last" (pp. 114–15).

The interview in the stateroom underlines the depth of Vere's
tragedy, a tragedy which consists in precisely the fact that he
must sacrifice Billy to forms which owe their severity to the realities of war. Emerging from his private talk with the foretopman,
he wears a look "expressive of the agony of the strong" (p. 115).
What is important to remember, however, is that Vere fights to
hasten the advent of a world at peace where the Mutiny Act is
unnecessary and the spirit of charity can temper the law. He abides
by horologicals because he knows that warfare spells the death
of chronometricals, an axiom to which Melville gives his assent
when he observes of the *Athée* (the *Atheist*) that its name is the
fittest ever bestowed on a battleship. Melville develops this idea
in his discussion of the man-of-war's chaplain, whose presence

aboard the *Bellipotent* is "as incongruous as a musket would be on the altar at Christmas." The musket, emblematic of Mars, usurps the place of Christ, but the chaplain, whose manner speaks of "the genuine Gospel," is a reminder that England—as opposed to the "infidel" power from abroad—is at war to ensure the restoration of peace: to *defend*, not despoil, the altar. It is entirely appropriate, therefore, that when Billy delivers his final benediction, Captain Vere stands "rigidly erect as a musket in the ship-armorer's rack" (pp. 122–24). He becomes the likeness of the weapon he uses to safeguard the union of freedom and law essential to the welfare of man.

In Billy's case, spontaneous impulses violate the law, and for Claggart the law means only legalism. Vere upholds the Articles of War not for the sake of mere expediency but rather because he looks to the ultimate good. In the sense that he shuns the extremes without denying their existence, he truly deserves to be seen as a saint in the world. He is compared by Melville himself to a Calvinist clergyman during the scene where he publicly announces the finding of the court. With "considerations both practical and moral" governing his actions (p. 114), Vere's middle way is neither personal prudence nor the utilitarianism exemplified in America by Benjamin Franklin. In this regard, he is not unlike Admiral Nelson, whom Melville defends against the "Benthamites of war" for having challenged death at Trafalgar, pointing out that few naval officers have been "so painstakingly circumspect" in preparation "as this same reckless declarer of his person in fight" (pp. 56–58). Vere similarly exercises tactical judgment when he must, and he too is willing to give his life on behalf of a cause in which "priestly" motives have their share. His heroism is evident from Melville's account of the engagement with the *Athée*. He is shot while exposing his person in the act of issuing the order to board, and mortally wounded he drops to the deck. Expiring shortly thereafter, his death, like Nelson's, is crowned with victory, for the *Bellipotent* defeats and takes captive the enemy craft. His dying words are a forceful reminder that his final objective is not martial discipline nor even the conquest of France. The words are "Billy Budd, Billy Budd," and they are uttered, so Melville insists, in accents that betray no remorse (p. 129).

Returning to Billy, we have yet to consider the most startling reversal of all: his exclamation "God bless Captain Vere!" just before he is hanged (p. 123). It seems strange indeed that "Baby" Budd, whom the chaplain endeavors in vain to impress with the idea of death, who "to all appearance" cannot entertain "the thought of salvation and a Savior" (p. 121), should pronounce such a blessing—a blessing which even more surprisingly is echoed by the crew of the ship, thereby contributing to the maintenance of the very martial discipline to which Billy is martyred. And yet Melville has carefully prepared for this turn of events in which the Handsome Sailor once again performs the office of a peace-maker. We know that the tension of Billy's agony did not survive "the something healing in the closeted interview with Captain Vere." There is reason to believe, however, that his "virgin experience of the diabolical incarnate and effective in some men" may not have been without its effect on his understanding of the need for law (p. 119). For form and the law are systematically associated with music in *Billy Budd*, and music in turn is associated with Billy and Vere.

The most obvious instance of this association is the statement attributed to Captain Vere:

"With mankind," he would say, "forms, measured forms, are every-thing; and that is the import couched in the story of Orpheus with his lyre spellbinding the wild denizens of the wood." And this he once applied to the disruption of forms going on across the Channel and the consequences thereof (p. 128).

It is vital to emphasize in connection with this passage that Vere's "measured forms," contrasted as they are to the collapse of order sweeping the Continent, are inseparable from England's ideals of "founded law and freedom defined." The corollary to chaos is the formalism or tyranny imposed by Napoleon, and Vere is neither a formalist nor tyrant. Surely it is safe to infer from his extensive reading that he is fully aware that the wild shouts of the bac-chantes drowned out the sound of Orpheus's lyre, with the result that they tore him apart in a frenzy. But this is exactly the point: forms, as embodied in music, are essential to keep the demonic at bay. And the demonic exists in both nature and man, a truth repudiated by the proselytizing manifestoes of the French Directory but upheld by Vere and presumably grasped in some manner by Billy. We notice, for example, that when Billy blesses the captain, his words are "delivered in the clear melody of a singing bird on the point of launching from the twig" (p. 123). And certainly Melville expects us to recall that though Billy "could not read . . . he could sing, and like the illiterate nightingale he was sometimes the composer of his own song" (p. 52). No doubt he expects us to remember as well that in his account of the foretopman's impressment, he recorded of Billy that he "made no demur," explaining that "any demur would have been as idle as the protest of a gold-finch popped into a cage" (p. 45). Most important of all, perhaps, we should not forget that Lieutenant Ratcliffe explicitly likened his "King's bargain" to the classical deity Apollo (p. 48). The god of music and poetry, of song and the lyre, Apollo was the patron and father of Orpheus himself.

When Billy sings out his blessing, in short, he effectively lends his support to the doctrine of the Fall by putting his music at the service of order and law. When license prevails, as it did briefly at Nore, the event, according to Melville, "converted into irony" the patriotic strains of Didbin, "as a song-writer no mean auxiliary to the British government at that European conjuncture" (pp. 55). When the law is corrupted into legalism, as it is by the master-at-arms, Melville indicates as much by comparing Claggart's demeanor to that of a perjurous *bandsman*. Appropriately, music is the means whereby the ship's multitude is pacified and dissolved after sullenly revoking its echoing of the foretopman's blessing. As Billy's remains slide into the sea, the band, Melville writes, "played a sacred air . . . the drum beat the retreat; and toned by music . . . the men in their wonted orderly manner dispersed to the places allotted them when not at the guns" (p. 128).

But Billy's death is not the finale of *Billy Budd*. The tightly controlled narrative of the Handsome Sailor's career, which "properly" terminates the story, yields to the "three brief chapters" which constitute the sequel.

> The symmetry of form attainable in pure fiction cannot so readily be achieved in a narrative essentially having less to do with fable than with fact. Truth uncompromisingly told will always have its ragged edges; hence the conclusion of such a narration is apt to be less finished than an architectural finial (p. 128).

In a fashion analogous to Captain Vere, who melts back "into what remains primeval in our formalized humanity," Melville refuses to confine himself to a rigid fictional mold. But again like Vere, he makes a point of reasserting order as well as freedom by ending his tale with music, a ballad composed in memory of Billy by a fellow foretopman of the *Bellipotent* who is gifted "with an artless *poetic* temperament" (p. 131). His own art accordingly replicates the very union of liberty and law, spontaneity and form, which constitutes his central theme.

It is quite true, of course, that "Melville is not Jonathan Edwards," as Charles Olson once remarked, and equally true that "we are reading a nineteenth-century, not a seventeenth-century, writer."[52] When Melville insists, however, on "Truth uncompromisingly told," we cannot ignore the fact that the surname of his protagonist literally means "truth," and that he originally considered mentioning a specific divine when he compared Captain Vere to a Calvinist clergyman: Edwards himself. For Vere's truth, like that of Edwards, is the truth of the middle way, and it inevitably takes us back to the seventeenth-century context in which Calvinism flourished. It takes us back as well to Melville's essay on Hawthorne, where he paid tribute to the older romancer's mastery of the "great Art of Telling the Truth," surmising that the metaphysical depth which he found in the *Mosses* derived from Hawthorne's Puritan origins.[53] What matters is not that Hawthorne's conception of art "influenced" Melville—although it surely did—but rather that their writings evince a similar habit of thought, shaped by a common religious heritage. It is quite to the point that Melville protests time and again against the obsolescence of a lexicon based on Holy Writ. And it is even more to the point that Captain Vere, who embodies the vision of inner-worldly sainthood treasured by Hawthorne and Melville alike, is killed by a ship whose name is the *Athée*.

52. Olson, *Call Me Ishmael*, p. 83; the second quotation is from Warner Berthoff, *The Example of Melville* (Princeton: Princeton University Press, 1962), p. 187.
53. One might also recall here Hawthorne's moral from *The Scarlet Letter:* "Be true!"

VI

Henry James

The Golden Bowl

Many of the ideas which we have traced in
the work of Hawthorne and Melville are present as well in the
writings of Henry James. They are vital, in fact, to an understanding of *The Golden Bowl*. A fruitful approach to James's last
complete novel is by way of his study of Hawthorne. For the strain
of Puritanism which he detected in Hawthorne's fiction, divested
of its dogma but still operative as a source of imaginative power
—"the old Puritan sense of sin, of penalties to be paid, of the
darkness and wickedness of life"—surely this strain also makes
itself felt in the pages of *The Golden Bowl*. It makes itself felt
most insistently, perhaps, in James's refusal to mitigate the reality
of evil and suffering, and it impregnates the entire novel with "a
haunting care for moral problems." It also suggests how deeply
James was involved, like Hawthorne before him, with the Calvinist
drama of the Fall and redemption, the drama of paradise lost and
regained. He spoke of the Civil War, for example, in precisely these
terms, as marking a watershed in American history, and his remarks
illuminate *The Golden Bowl*. The war "introduced into the national
consciousness," he wrote in the book on Hawthorne, a sense

> of the world being a more complicated place than it had hitherto
> seemed, the future more treacherous, success more difficult . . .
> The good American, in days to come, will be a more critical

person than his complacent and confident grandfather. He has eaten of the tree of knowledge.[1]

And so has Maggie Verver. The heroine of *The Golden Bowl* eats of the tree of knowledge and grows, as it were, from an antebellum to a postwar consciousness. She grows, like the nation itself, from childhood to maturity, innocence to experience; and if she finds the world more complicated than she imagined, her growth is nonetheless crowned with success.

In *The Golden Bowl*, much as in *The Scarlet Letter*, the Fall results from an act of adultery. The place of the tree of knowledge is taken by the bowl itself. Maggie must drain the bowl in order to shed her childlike innocence, which James associates with Roman Catholicism. The association has roots in the Protestant tradition from which he sprang: it figures prominently, for example, in his brother William's *Varieties of Religious Experience,* a book that he read while composing his novel.[2] According to William, the "once-born" soul tends to be Catholic rather than Protestant because the Roman Church lacks the profound sense of evil that distinguishes the Reformed tradition. Henry develops a similar idea in *The Golden Bowl,* and in his view of Catholicism he comes strikingly close to the strictures of the Puritans, who condemned both the immorality of the laity and the "fugitive and cloister'd virtue" of the monks. For it is not only Maggie whom he associates with the Roman Church: throughout book one he uses imagery and allusions drawn from Catholicism to characterize both the innocent and unworldly Ververs, on the one hand, and their adulterous spouses on the other. He thus indicates the profound distance which separates all the major protagonists from the "twice-born" soul whom William describes in *The Varieties of Religious Experience* as awakened to the consciousness of sin.

We are told, for instance, that Maggie and Charlotte attended convent school together in Paris; and James makes a point of

1. Henry James, *Hawthorne* (1879; London: Macmillan and Co., 1887), pp. 101, 183, 144.

2. See F. O. Matthiessen, *The James Family: Including Selections from the Writings of Henry James, Senior, William, Henry, and Alice James* (New York: Alfred A. Knopf, 1947), pp. 338–40.

connecting both Adam and Amerigo to the Pope, the Prince by ancestry, and Adam by virtue of his patronage and wealth. Maggie and her father are presented as living in almost monastic seclusion. Their estate at Fawns, where Adam makes his first appearance in the novel, is actually said to be "out of the world" (1: 211).[3] To the other characters, Maggie in particular seems an ethereal being, a kind of Catholic saint whose standard of goodness, according to Charlotte, is unattainable "without prayer and fasting" (1: 102). The Prince remarks of his wife that "the Blessed Virgin and all the Saints . . . have her in their keeping" (1: 52); and even Adam concurs in the general observation that Maggie resembles a nun, an observation to which "she had replied that she was delighted to hear it and would certainly try to" (1: 188). Adam's own marriage to Charlotte only intensifies his and his daughter's withdrawal. "They had brought her in," so Charlotte muses, "to do the 'worldly' for them, and she had done it with such genius that they had themselves in consequence renounced it even more than they had originally intended." At Eaton Square, where they seek refuge in each other's company, they are once again said to be virtually out of the world (1: 319–21).

The impression of otherworldliness produced by the Ververs is such that they appear to the Prince to go about "in a state of childlike innocence, the state of our primitive parents before the Fall." His words may serve as an index of their isolation from the actual and fallen circumstances of the nineteenth century, and he naturally resents them "as a man of the world" (1: 335). It is Charlotte, not Maggie, who adopts the air of royalty in book one, and who embarks with Amerigo on the social circuit from which the Ververs withdraw. But worldliness without morality, James suggests, is just as foreign to the Protestant ideal as

---

3. Henry James, *The Golden Bowl* (New York: Charles Scribner's Sons, 1909). Quotations are from this edition (volumes 23 and 24 of the New York edition); page references are cited in the text. Studies of *The Golden Bowl* which I have found especially useful include Frederick I. Carpenter's "'The American Myth': Paradise (To Be) Regained," *PMLA* 74 (1959): 599–606; Laurence B. Holland's *The Expense of Vision: Essays on the Craft of Henry James* (Princeton: Princeton University Press, 1964), pp. 331–407; and Dorothea Krook's *The Ordeal of Consciousness in Henry James* (New York: Cambridge University Press, 1962), pp. 232–324.

renunciation of the world. Charlotte, for example, thinks of her social office in the language of Catholic devotion, calling her duties "the absolute little gods of my worship, the holy images set up on the wall" (1: 318). The paradoxical kinship between the Ververs and their mates is made all but explicit in the scene where the Prince and Charlotte embrace at Portland Place. The lovers vow to trust each other as "we trust the saints in glory," and they murmur the words "it's sacred" as they seal their pledge with a passionate kiss (1: 312).

The full significance of such language becomes apparent only in book two, where Maggie figuratively enters the world to save her marriage. For it is only then that James ceases to associate his heroine with Roman Catholicism. Indeed, he is emphatic in reminding the reader that Maggie has weathered her ordeal without the assistance of Father Mitchell. Once again, illuminating parallels can be drawn between *The Golden Bowl* and *The Varieties of Religious Experience*. Discussing the transformation of the once-born soul who encounters evil and surmounts disillusionment, William explains that

> the process is one of redemption, not of mere reversion to natural health, and the sufferer, when saved, is saved by what seems to him a second birth, a deeper kind of conscious being than he could enjoy before.

He is referring to what the Puritans called conversion, and he goes on to mention such representative examples as Bunyan and David Brainerd. He cites, too, the "vastations" experienced by himself and his father, vastations strikingly similar to Maggie's illumination on the terrace at Fawns, when she is overwhelmed by "the horror of finding evil seated, all at its ease, where she had dreamed only of good" (2: 237). Finally, William differentiates between the Catholic saint, who renounces the world for the sake of purity, and the inner-worldly sainthood of the converted Protestant, who translates his awakening into action and endeavors to bring about change for the better. Saints of this character, he writes, must be willing to acquire a "worldly temper" in order to be efficacious: "Christ himself was fierce upon occasion."[4]

4. William James, *The Varieties of Religious Experience: A Study in Human*

The Golden Bowl is the story of Maggie's transformation into just such a saint, an *imitator Christi* who implicates herself in the world with a view toward changing it. Much of her characterization, prior to the adultery, turns precisely on her failure to measure up to this role. It cannot be accidental, after all, that one of the first details we learn about Maggie is that she was first attracted to Amerigo because of his illustrious ancestor and namesake. To live in the world is to live in history or time, and Maggie, who enumerates her husband's appeal in terms of his family's "archives, annals, infamies," boldly avows that she is unafraid of history (1: 10). Yet she is completely ignorant of Amerigo's personal past—the doings, not of his ancestors, but of his particular self—and she disclaims any desire for knowledge when her father questions her about the identity of Charlotte's former lover. She refuses involvement in the history of the people who directly affect her, as opposed to the history of events that occurred long ago. She and Adam are repeatedly likened to children, moreover, and the comparison encourages the inference that they are somehow exempt from the passage of time.

Amerigo for very different reasons is almost as intent as his wife upon disowning the past. In rejecting the golden bowl as exquisite but cracked, as an omen of danger for his happiness and safety, he figuratively rejects his relations with Charlotte, and he welcomes his marriage to Maggie as an opportunity "for some new history that should, so far as possible, contradict, and even if need be flatly dishonor, the old" (1: 16). When he goes on to reflect that the charm of his situation lies "in its being wholly a fresh start" (1: 95), he sounds like a Transcendentalist. He is also, however, as he realizes himself, "somehow full of his race" (1: 16), and his determination to break with the past inevitably weakens in the face of Maggie's neglect. With time heavy on his hands, he takes to brooding as "his main recreation" (1: 294), and the world he is forced to inhabit strongly recalls the world of *Haw-thorne*, the antebellum America where "introspection—thanks to

<hr>

Nature (New York: Longmans, Green, and Co., 1902), pp. 157, 375-76. The fullest treatment of the intellectual affinities between Henry and William James is Richard A. Hocks, *Henry James and Pragmatistic Thought: A Study in the Relationship between the Philosophy of William James and the Literary Art of Henry James* (Chapel Hill: University of North Carolina Press, 1974).

the want of other entertainment—played almost the part of a
social resource."[5] Charlotte, who takes the initiative in rekindling
their romance, represents the power still exerted by his personal
history. Her unexpected appearance at Portland Place is said to
revive "the sense of the past" in which they were lovers (1: 297-98).
The fact that she has come from a visit to the British Museum,
which houses the records of the Prince's race, suggests that her
interest in history is firmly tied to the present. James's point is
that history in general is inseparable from individual history. One
gets the impression, indeed, that Charlotte is thoroughly conversant, as Maggie is not, with the personal relevance of time. On
the day of the adultery, she not only contrives the pretext of tour-
ing the historic cathedral at Gloucester, she also anticipates the
Prince by looking up the schedule of the appropriate train: "A local
one—11:22; with several stops, but doing it a good deal, I forget
how much, within the hour. So that we've time. Only . . . we must
employ our time" (1: 362).

What Charlotte becomes, in short, is Amerigo's consort or guide.
This is a second area in which Maggie disappoints her husband
and one that bears directly on her failure to enter the world. It
is an area, too, in which he explicitly asks for help, for he thinks
of his marriage as a kind of adventure at sea.[6] He has embarked,
as he says to Fanny, on a "great voyage," and he freely admits
that he "can't sail alone; my ship must be one of a pair, must
have, in the waste of waters, a—what do you call it?—a consort"
(1: 26). The pervasive imagery of travel, the metaphor of seafaring,
and the many allusions to *The Narrative of Arthur Gordon Pym*
—all these suggest that life in the Jamesian world takes the form
of a journey or voyage, much as it did for the Puritans. It is not
Maggie, however, but Charlotte who is described as a fearless and
experienced traveler, and who tests with Amerigo the waters of
intimacy. Their kiss at Portland Place is metaphorically represented
as a passage out to sea, and Maggie herself, after the Prince's

5. Henry James, *Hawthorne*, p. 85.
6. Joel Porte has called attention to the importance of the metaphor of
oceanic exploration in *The Romance in America: Studies in Cooper, Poe,
Hawthorne, Melville, and James* (Middletown, Conn.: Wesleyan University
Press, 1969), pp. 215-19.

return from Matcham, reflects that "he had stood there before her as if restored from some far country, some long voyage, some combination of dangers or fatigues" (2: 21).

As a voyager, however, Amerigo has a defective moral vision. Here, too, in his treatment of the theme of vision, James is part of an American tradition, a tradition which dates back to Jonathan Edwards. According to Edwards, the ability to perceive rightly so as to act accordingly was what distinguished the Protestant saint. In *The Golden Bowl* we read that although Amerigo's taste is unimpeachable, he lacks what he calls the "moral sense" of Americans, and morality is identified with the capacity for vision. Feeling "his own boat move upon some such mystery" as the "great white curtain" beheld by Arthur Gordon Pym (1: 22), wishing above all safely to navigate his marriage, he urgently appeals to Fanny for assistance: "I can do pretty well anything I *see*. But I've got to see it first. . . . Therefore it is that I want, that I shall always want, your eyes" (1: 30). If here as elsewhere he turns to Fanny to "see him through"—and the phrase recurs like a refrain through-out the book—it is because Maggie can hardly be said to see at all. She refuses to see just as she refuses to know or to live; "her little lucidities," as Fanny says, are "really so divinely blind" (1: 396). Once again, Charlotte capitalizes on Maggie's failure, and it is only appropriate that when she and Prince commit adultery, they fabri-cate the story of sightseeing at Gloucester.

With the adultery itself, we come to the turning point in the evolution of Maggie's character. Her transformation, which gathers together the central motifs of the book, demands to be understood in terms of the Christian overtones which now make themselves heard with increasing emphasis.[7] The infidelity is surely meant to remind us of the Fall of Man. Fanny correctly predicts that it will have the effect of opening Maggie's sense "to what's called Evil—with a very big E: for the first time in her life. To the discovery of it, to the knowledge of it, to the crude experience

---

7. See Frederick C. Crews, *The Tragedy of Manners: Moral Drama in the Later Novels of Henry James* (New Haven: Yale University Press, 1957), pp. 105-9, for a sensitive discussion of "the wealth of Christian overtones that James has suggested."

of it" (1: 385). These echoes are further developed in connection with the symbol of the bowl. The Prince compares the adultery to "a great gold cup that [he and Charlotte] must somehow drain together" (1: 359); and later, in the scene with the antiquarian, the bowl confirms for Maggie her suspicions of their affair. It seems clear, then, that the bowl is linked to the primordial sin, to the tree of knowledge—an identification made by James in his earlier work, most notably in *Roderick Hudson*. Here it is relevant to recall William James's view of conversion as the new birth of the soul that survives the discovery of evil. For the adultery occurs, after all, during the "Easter revels" at Matcham, and Maggie's growth of awareness is described as a virtual resurrection. As Fanny puts it, her friend "has begun to live." She will eventually "triumph" by securing the Prince and redeeming her marriage (1: 383)—she will enter the world, so to speak, for the sake of love.

Maggie is thus identified with Christ because she conforms to the Savior in the manner of a Protestant saint. There is even reason to believe that she recognizes her own complicity in sin, an inference encouraged by the question she puts to Fanny after purchasing the golden bowl: "Then it's a good deal my fault—if everything really began so well?" (2: 172).[8] Certainly she shows herself willing to make use of worldly means, including deception and intrigue, to accomplish a moral end. Even so seemingly minor an act as her awaiting the Prince at Portland Place reflects this resolve; for "the 'world,'" as he had stated himself, "included Portland Place without including to anything like the same extent Eaton Square" (1: 320). Her waiting at home is also said to acquire "an historic value" because it marks an unprecedented break with custom (2: 16). It is the first indication of Maggie's determination to participate in history.

For history or time begins with the Fall, and one meaning of the golden bowl is that the loss of paradise—the beginning of time—is reenacted in the life of every individual. Significantly,

8. The question of whether Maggie recognizes any responsibility for the Prince's infidelity is much debated. A convincing (to my mind) argument that she does see her guilt is made by Oscar Cargill, *The Novels of Henry James* (New York: Macmillan Co., 1961), pp. 405–11.

when Maggie purchases the bowl, she places it on her mantle in the spot formerly occupied by a Louis XVI clock, as if it were itself a timepiece. It is significant, too, that she makes the purchase on the very same day that she visits the British Museum to renew her acquaintance with the annals of Amerigo's family. The implication, now grasped by Maggie herself, is that racial and personal history flow in a single continuum of time. To pursue her discoveries "at the altar of the past" (2: 149), in Fanny's apt phrase, is accordingly to sound her husband's particular history as well as the history of his race. This she proceeds to do by opening "a chapter of history into which she could but a week before not have dipped without a mortal chill" (2: 221). And if in book one she seemed an eternal child impervious to time, in book two she turns time to her advantage. She wordlessly appeals to Fanny to help her "gain time—time as against any idea of her father's . . . [time to] take care of the Prince; and it's beautiful and wonderful, really pathetic and exquisite, to see what she feels that time may do for her" (2: 131–32). Engaged as she is in "a *high* fight," Maggie elsewhere reflects, she feels herself "learning, almost from minute to minute, to be a mistress of shades" (2: 141–43).

As this last image suggests, Maggie's attempt to win back her husband is portrayed as a struggle or battle. Again and again she is said to be metaphorically wayfaring and warfaring—the very imagery used by the Puritans to dramatize the career of the saint in the world. Whereas previously she had regarded herself as "a small creeping thing" who lived "in terror" (1: 181), she is now said to have shouldered arms and "taken the field" (2: 35).[9] And whereas in book one she had seldom gone out except to visit her father, in book two she is compared to "a settler or a trader in a new country" (2: 323). Her awakening unfolds like a journey of discovery, and is rendered in terms of the novel's pervasive seagoing metaphors. The Maggie who had clung to the shore and "not got wet," now takes to the sea and ventures into "submarine depths" (2: 7, 43). Confronting the Prince with the golden bowl, and sensing his confusion, she realizes that "she had her feet,

9. Such imagery, of course, was a conspicuous feature of the naturalist fiction popular around the turn of the century; it is used by Stephen Crane, for example, to express his sense of the struggle for existence.

somewhere, through it all—it was her companion, absolutely, who was at sea. And she kept her feet; she pressed them to what was beneath her" (2: 203). She is ready, as never before, to play the part of the consort Amerigo had said he needed to guide him in his exploration of Americans.

In order to do this, she has to dare to see, and the verbs "to know" and "to see" are used almost interchangeably in connection with Maggie's awakening. As Fanny explains to the Colonel, "It isn't a question of belief or of proof . . . it's inevitably, with her, a question of natural perception, of insurmountable feeling. She irresistibly *knows* that there's something between them" (2: 131). No longer content to go about "with bandaged eyes" (2: 182), and not "too stupid to have arrived at knowledge" (2: 216), Maggie imagines saying to her husband: "Only *see*, see that *I* see, and make up your mind, on this new basis, at your convenience" (2: 184). What she wants above all is somehow to impart her moral vision to the Prince. And it is here that James introduces the figure of the labyrinth—the figure used by Spenser, Milton, and Hawthorne—to express the spiritual bafflement of his protagonists. Maggie, who assumes the role of Ariadne, places herself in the labyrinth with Amerigo precisely in order that "she might securely guide him out of it" (2: 187). By now it is evident that she has taken her rightful place beside her husband, the place she had abdicated to Charlotte, while Charlotte as a result of this reversal finds herself in the position of the abandoned "Ariadne roaming the lone sea-strand" (2: 307).

And so Maggie earns her title as the Princess, which is also the title of book two, by combining the morality of the fair lady with the worldliness and daring of her dark counterpart. That the Prince himself grows to the state of awareness characterized by William James as twice-born is confirmed by his recognition that "Everything's terrible, *cara*—in the heart of man" (2: 349). It is confirmed, too, by his admission, on the eve of Charlotte's departure with Mr. Verver, that "taste, in him, as a touchstone, was all at sea" (2: 345). What Maggie has created in the Prince is an entirely new mode of perception. And we are accordingly not surprised when he confesses to his wife, "I see nothing but *you*" (2: 369), for we recall that James has associated the moral sense with vision. The last water image to appear in the book dissolves any doubt that Maggie has replaced Charlotte both morally and sexually in her husband's estimation: " 'Wait!' It was the word of his own distress and entreaty, the word for both of them, all they had left, their plank now on the great sea" (2: 352–53).

A very different fate lies in store for Charlotte and Adam. Nothing about their relationship indicates moral growth, and their marriage itself seems a savage parody of the union of Maggie and the Prince. In the Greek fable alluded to by James, Ariadne helps Theseus to escape from the labyrinth by giving him a ball of string. Adam, in contrast, is pictured as leading Charlotte about with the aid of "a long silken halter looped round her beautiful neck" (2: 287). The most telling irony of all, perhaps, is that Charlotte, who had coveted the role of Amerigo's guide, is reduced to doing the *cicerone* in her husband's gallery at Fawns. Here she puts to good use her perfect taste, for what she and Adam have in common is their aesthetic discrimination. In her blindness and pride, Charlotte remains to the last a creature of taste alone, utterly bereft of the moral sense which Maggie fosters in the Prince. It makes for a fitting conclusion that she is banished to America like another of James's female villains who "does the worldly": Madame Merle. At the novel's end, she prepares to embark for American City, which James describes as a virtual Babylon, a hollow city on a hill:

> It was positively civilization condensed, concrete, consummate, set down by his hands as a house on a rock—a house from whose open doors and windows, open to grateful thirsty millions, the higher, the highest knowledge would shine out to bless the land (1: 145).

It has been James's point all along that "taste" in itself is emphatically *not* the highest knowledge; Adam's sterile aestheticism makes him an appropriate consort for Charlotte, with whom he will "ship" to American City. Comparing his mission to that of Cortez—and the comparison is an apt one, for Cortez rifled his own "Golden Isles" by conquering Mexico—Adam had ruefully surmised that "no companion of Cortez had presumably been a real lady" (1: 142–43). Although in Charlotte he has found the

tasteful companion he wished for, the wife who can share his "peak
in Darien," their union only deepens one's sense of his project
as a soulless vision of modern America.

When Amerigo first learned of Charlotte's engagement to Adam,
he telegraphed his former mistress: "We must lead our lives as
we *see* them" (1: 290, italics added). They have come to see their
lives very differently indeed. And if Amerigo accordingly seems
saved, Charlotte, surely, is damned. Whereas Maggie conforms to
Christ, and Amerigo follows her lead, Charlotte suggests an analogy
to Judas, an analogy supported by her treacherous kiss on the
terrace at Fawns. There are also several hints to the effect that
she is identified with another sinister figure in Christian thought,
namely the whore of Babylon. She has been thoroughly tainted
by the corruption of London society, that "great grey Babylon"
of which James spoke in his critical prefaces.[10] Her affair with
the Prince took place in Rome. Her manner is queenly (she is
reported to "throne" in the final scene), and she is always proud
and acknowledges no sorrow. She is associated, moreover, with
money and fornication. On her first appearance in the book, the
Prince compares her to a purse filled with coins; and when she
later arranges the adultery, her words ring in his ear like a "chink
of . . . gold" (1: 345). The golden cup of the whore comes to mind
in this connection, and it is not surprising that moments before
her departure Charlotte is said to be "great for the world that
was before her" (2: 365). The phrase, which is unmistakably Miltonic, and which implies that her banishment is a form of expulsion
from Eden, confirms that she is associated with the fallen Eve,
Satan's accomplice; her husband, as it happens, bears the name
of Adam. Such echoes, in the work of another author, might be
construed to reflect an apocalyptic or millennial vision. In James,
however, their import is ultimately tragic. They speak of the in-
eradicable existence of spiritual evil.

Maggie and the Prince, it is true, succeed in restoring the bowl
"as it was to have been" (2: 216), and thus in achieving a kind of
paradise regained. Yet theirs is a private and chastened happiness

10. From the preface to *The Princess Casamassima* in Henry James, *The Art
of the Novel: Critical Prefaces by Henry James*, ed. R. P. Blackmur (1934;
New York: Charles Scribner's Sons, 1962), p. 59.

when they are last seen together in the company of Charlotte
and Adam. For salvation can only be personal in a fallen world.
The scene at Portland Place which is said to "crystallize" to "the
right quiet luster" and whose "harmony was not less sustained
for being superficial," in reminding us of the bowl, reminds us
as well of the impossibility of universal redemption (2: 358). It calls
to our attention the fact that Henry, Jr. could never accept his
father's theological system, which he considered invalidated by
an "optimism fed so little by any sense of things as they were
or are." He could never share his father's faith in the imminent
millennium, never believe "in the virtue of his consequent and
ultimate synthesis."[11] He believed instead that man was condemned to endure the trauma of history, and he vehemently rejected, as Melville had done a decade earlier in *Billy Budd*, the facile
optimism of his contemporaries. The conclusions of his novels have
often been condemned, in the notable phrase of an otherwise sympathetic critic, for their "manifest ambiguity."[12] Better manifest
ambiguity, James might reply, than Manifest Destiny. His theory
of fiction and his "eschatology" reveal a common contempt for
the conventional "happy ending" which ignores or minimizes sin
and sorrow—the ending characterized by a "distribution at the
last of prizes, pensions, husbands, wives, babies, millions, appended
paragraphs, and cheerful remarks." The quotation appears in his
own essay, "The Art of Fiction," where he also flatly stated that
"the novel is history."[13]

In accepting history, then—in performing her devotions at "the
altar of the past"—Maggie accepts the burden of secular sainthood,
and she learns to live in the world without being of it. In this
regard, she asks comparison to James himself, who called the
artistic process "the religion of doing" in his preface to *The Golden*

11. Henry James, *Notes of a Son and Brother* (1914), in *Henry James: Autobiography*, ed. Frederick W. Dupee (New York: Criterion Books, 1956), pp.
370, 373.

12. William Troy, "The Altar of Henry James," in *The Question of Henry
James*, ed. Frederick W. Dupee (New York: Henry Holt and Co., 1945), p. 269.

13. Reprinted in Matthiessen, *James Family*, pp. 355-56. My discussion of the
ending of *Golden Bowl* is indebted to Frank Kermode, *The Sense of an Ending: Studies in the Theory of Fiction* (New York: Oxford University Press,
1967).

Bowl (1: xxiv). Surely it is not without meaning that he so often likens his heroine to an artist, actress or dancer, even comparing her on one occasion to the author of a drama. (Adam, in contrast, is pointedly said *not* to resemble "the author of the play": "he might be at the best the financial 'backer,' watching his interests from the wing, but in rather confessed ignorance of the mysteries of the mimicry" [1: 170].) What Maggie masters is "the spiritual and the aesthetic vision," the unified vision extolled by James in his preface (1: xxiii). Or we might describe her by saying that she occupies—to borrow a phrase used by James in an early essay on George Eliot—"a certain middle field where morals and aesthetics move in concert."[14] This was his own ideal for the art of fiction, his translation into literature of the calculus of Calvinism, his imaginative correlative for the middle way.

14. Henry James, "The Novels of George Eliot," in idem, *Views and Reviews*, ed. Le Roy Phillips (Boston: Ball Publishing Co., 1908), p. 37.

Afterword

In August of 1904, having completed *The Golden Bowl*, Henry James sailed for America after a twenty-year absence from his native land. One result of his trip was *The American Scene* (1907), a book in which he recorded his impressions of "our vast crude democracy of trade." The United States, according to James, resembled nothing so much "as a huge Rappacini-garden, rank with every variety of the poison-plant of the money-passion." The representative American, he felt, had the face of a businessman and proclaimed by his relentless pursuit of gain "the main American formula": "to make so much money that you won't . . . mind anything." The bourgeois, the commercial, the middling—everywhere about him James beheld a "jealous cultivation of the common mean": even the "citronic" South, he discovered to his chagrin, had been thoroughly "Protestantized." Far from being an Anglo-Saxon supremacist, James feared that America would "monotonize" its immigrants, whose quarters he scoured in a search for some "unconverted residuum" of the alien. With its corrosive materialism, its merciless exploitation of man and nature, America was a monument to "the triumph of the superficial and the apotheosis of the raw."[1]

1. Henry James, *The American Scene*, ed. Leon Edel (1907; Bloomington: Indiana University Press, 1968), pp. 67, 57, 64, 237, 442, 313, 124, 465. The suggestion that James "drifted dangerously close to a doctrine of racism" is made by F. O. Matthiessen in *Henry James: The Major Phase* (New York: Oxford University Press, 1944), p. 110.

Also in August of 1904, Max Weber sailed for America to deliver a paper before the St. Louis Congress of Arts and Science. Within a year he had completed his seminal study of *The Protestant Ethic and the Spirit of Capitalism.* Weber argued that Calvinism, especially as it developed in England and America, created the psychological conditions necessary for the emergence of capitalist civilization. Calvinist theology, in his view, sanctioned and indeed encouraged the rational pursuit of riches by interpreting success in one's calling as the outward sign of invisible grace. As Weber occasionally seemed to realize himself, however, he was not describing Calvinism proper so much as the debased currency that passed for Calvinism in the era of its decline. It was in the maxims of Benjamin Franklin that he found the supreme expression of the acquisitive mentality fostered by ascetic Protestantism. Fresh from his trip to America, Weber was moved to suggest that "the pursuit of wealth, stripped of its religious and ethical meaning" —the ethos he identified with Franklin—had reached its zenith in the United States. Assessing the prospects that faced such a society, he quoted from Nietzsche to characterize the soulless culture of the future: "Specialists without spirit, sensualists without heart; this nullity imagines that it has attained a level of civilization never before achieved."[2]

To Henry James, this bleak prophecy had already been fulfilled: Franklin's way to wealth had hardened into Weber's "iron cage." The sameness he deplored in his rediscovered country was not a literal sameness of appearance, and it was certainly not social and economic equality. On the contrary, James was appalled by the inequities of American life, and he took note of both the squalor of the slums and the garish "monuments of pecuniary power" which had transformed the Newport of his youth into "a witless dream" of the rich.[3] What filled him with despair was the uniformity in manners and belief spawned by the American cult of money and success. In his *Hawthorne*, published in 1879, James had written that as a result of the Civil War the American had eaten of the tree of knowledge. Twenty-five years later, he saw that the growth of industrialism and commercialism accelerated by the war had

2. Max Weber, *The Protestant Ethic and the Spirit of Capitalism,* trans. Talcott Parsons (1930; New York: Charles Scribner's Sons, 1958), p. 182.
3. James, *American Scene,* pp. 212, 224.

despoiled the garden itself. "The Eden of the present world," in
Hawthorne's phrase, had degenerated by the turn of the century
into a materialistic Rappaccini's garden.

The despoilment, in fact, had begun long before, and one cause
of the malady, as Weber surmised, was the spread of Franklin's
ideas. The creed that "God helps them that help themselves," as
disseminated by Franklin and others like him, thwarted rather
than realized the promise of a just and relatively classless society.
By placing all responsibility for success or failure on the individual,
Franklin's ideology misrepresented social and economic realities,
inhibited feelings of Christian brotherhood, and widened the split
between America's potential good and its actual privations. It
exacted its heaviest toll upon those who dwelt in the "poverty
and obscurity" to which Franklin himself claimed to have been
bred. The belief that achievement is possible for all, and that
opportunity in America is equal, served only to legitimate injustice
and worsen the suffering of the oppressed. It was Melville, in a
story published in 1854, who best calculated the human cost of
Poor Richard's code:

> The native American poor never lose their delicacy or pride;
> hence, though unreduced to the physical degradation of the Euro-
> pean pauper, they yet suffer more in mind than the poor of any
> other people in the world. Those peculiar social sensibilities
> nourished by our own peculiar political principles, while they
> enhance the true dignity of a prosperous American, do but minister
> to the added wretchedness of the unfortunate; first, by prohibit-
> ing their acceptance of what little random relief charity may
> offer; and second, by furnishing them with the keenest apprecia-
> tion of the smarting distinction between their ideal of universal
> equality and their grindstone experience of the practical misery
> and infamy of poverty—a misery and infamy which is, ever has
> been, and ever will be, precisely the same in India, England, and
> America.[4]

Not in India, not in England, but in America, in John Winthrop's
"good land," a dissenting tradition developed in the realm of letters.
Almost without exception our greatest writers of fiction, from the

4. From Herman Melville, "Poor Man's Pudding and Rich Man's Crumbs,"
in idem, *The Complete Stories of Herman Melville*, ed. Jay Leyda (New
York: Random House, 1949), p. 176.

birth of the Republic to the end of the nineteenth century, have been of Reformed ancestry or upbringing. They have stood in relation to their dominant culture much as the emigrant Puritans stood in relation to Stuart England. Sharing the ideals of that culture but loathing its cant and compromises, they have revived the spirit of nonseparating Congregationalism and assimilated into their art the middle way of inner-worldly sainthood. Few of them were religious in any conventional sense. More often they were indifferent or hostile to institutional Christianity because they felt that religion in America lent sanction to the American way of life. They saw, as too many of their contemporaries failed to see, that there is a difference between the divinity of Divinity and the divinity of the American republic. They saw, too, that national millennialism and the worship of progress gave rise to an ideological conformity which rendered dissent as difficult as it was dangerous. As the heirs to a radical movement within English Protestantism, they did not abandon the principle that God's will was to be done on earth so far as human nature allowed. What they refused to accept was the equation of America with the mandate of heaven.

For Hawthorne and James, both of whom rejected the notion that America was God's agent in the work of historical redemption, salvation was personal rather than national. With a greater sense of disillusionment because he had believed more deeply, Melville reached the same conclusion. He went outside the covenant to find his American heroes among such pariahs as Ishmael and Esau. In *Billy Budd*, his heroes were not even American, and he pointedly dedicated his last book to Jack Chase, "Englishman."

In at least this one crucial respect, in their denial of American exceptionalism, the romancers parted company with colonial Puritans like Winthrop, Cotton, and Mather. But there was one Puritan whose position ironically resembled their own: John Milton. Swept up by the millennial fervor of the Civil War, Milton had briefly shared his countrymen's faith in England's role as world redeemer. His apocalyptic expectations were crushed, however, by the failure of the Puritan experiment to build a society founded on justice and righteousness. In *The Ready and Easy Way*, published in the year of the Restoration, he implored the English people not to forsake "*The Good Old Cause*" for the idols of king and trade.

When the English chose for themselves "a Captain back for *Egypt*," Milton adopted the view that the holy community was composed of believers of different countries. It was in *Paradise Lost* that he bid a last farewell to the dream which had launched the Civil War as well as the Great Migration. He had the Angel Michael explain to Adam that Eden would be washed away in the Flood in order to teach mankind

> that God attributes to place
> No sanctity, if none be thither brought
> By men who there frequent, or therein dwell (11: 836–38).[5]

This was the bitter lesson also taught by the American romancers.

5. The standard work on Milton's eschatology is Michael Fixler's *Milton and the Kingdoms of God* (Evanston, Ill.: Northwestern University Press, 1964).

Index

Church of England. *See* Anglican Church

Cloister Life of the Emperor Charles the Fifth, The (Stirling), 169

Colacurcio, Michael J., 47n., 79n.

Coleridge, Samuel Taylor, 6n., 130n.

Communion. *See* Lord's Supper

Companion for Communicants, A (Mather), 41-42, 43

Confession: in Puritanism, 20; and Stoddardism, 36; and witchcraft, 37-40; Hawthorne's use of, in "The Custom-House," 70-79; in *The Scarlet Letter*, 79, 92, 97-100, 103, 107, 108-11, 112-13; in *The House of the Seven Gables*, 116. *See also* Conversion, Lord's Supper, Puritanism

Confessions, The (Augustine), 56

Confidence-Man, The (Melville), 10, 161, 171

Conscience with the Power and Cases thereof (Ames), 24

Conversion: in Puritanism, 20-21; and Halfway Covenant, 31-33, 35-36; and Stoddardism, 36; and witchcraft, 37-40; and Jonathan Edwards, 40-41; and Cotton Mather, 41-46; and Benjamin Franklin, 52-54; and Hawthorne, 212; and "The Custom-House" narrative, 70-79; and Hawthorne's conception of the romance in "The Custom-House," 79, 80-85; in *The Scarlet Letter*, 87-89, 92-94, 94-95, 97-100, 100, 104-11, 111-13; in *The House of the Seven Gables*, 123-27; and Melville, 212; in *Moby-Dick*, 141-43, 145-46; in "Benito Cereno," 177-79; and Henry James, Jr., 212; in *The Golden Bowl*, 196, 197-99, 201-4, 205-8; and William James, 196, 198, 202, 204. *See also* Confession; Lord's Supper; Puritanism

Coolidge, John S., 15n.

Cooper, James Fenimore, 81; *The Leather-Stocking Tales*, 6

Cotton, John, 3, 11-12, 15-17, 18-19, 21, 24-25, 31, 45, 212; *The Way of Life*, 15

Covenant of grace: in Puritanism, 11, 31; and confession, 40; in *The Scarlet Letter*, 93, 111

Covenant of works (legal covenant): in Puritanism, 11, 31; in *The Scarlet*

Letter 91, 93, 94, 96-97, 98, 111; in *The House of the Seven Gables*, 120; in "Benito Cereno," 168, 169

Crane, Stephen, 203n.

Crews, Frederick C., 72n., 105n., 106n., 111n., 201n.

Cromwell, Oliver, 66, 68

Cushman, Robert, 25-26, 29, 59, 163

"Custom-House, The" (Hawthorne), 70-79, 79-86, 91, 96, 105-6, 115, 119, 128, 151

Davidson, Edward H., 105n.

Dawson, Edward, 87n.

Delano, Amasa, *Narrative of Voyages and Travels*, 167, 179

Demos, John, 39n., 40

Denham, Thomas, 53-55

Dissertation on Liberty and Necessity, Pleasure and Pain, A (Franklin), 52

Drake, Frederick C., 40n.

Dryden, Edgar A., 131n., 175n.

Dunn, Richard S., 12n.

Duyckinck, Evert, 117n.

Dwight, Timothy, 136; *Travels in New England*, 131-34

"Earth's Holocaust" (Hawthorne), 122-23

Eakin, Paul John, 70n.

Edwards, Jonathan, 3, 40, 56, 57, 58, 108, 127, 132, 133, 149, 194, 201; *Life and Diary of David Brainerd*, 4; *Religious Affections*, 3

Eisinger, Chester E., 65n.

Eliot, George, 208

Eliot, John, 45

Elliott, Emery, 38n.

Emerson, Ralph Waldo, 83, 122, 130n.; *Nature*, 104

Enthusiasm, 3, 4

Faerie Queene (Spenser), 142

Feidelson, Charles, 70n.

Fiction. *See* Romance

Fiedler, Leslie A., 2n.

Fisher, Marvin, 131n.

Fixler, Michael, 213n.

Fletcher, Angus, 92n.

Fogle, Richard Harter, 65n., 183n.

Foster, Stephen, 23n., 27n., 32n.

Franklin, Abiah, 48

Franklin, Benjamin, ix; and ideology, 8-10, 35, 47-48, 62-64, 210-11; rejection of father's religious beliefs, 47-